AF433564

MARCUS CALDWELL

Battles of the Ages: American Civil War 1862

Copyright © 2023 by Marcus Caldwell

All rights reserved. No part of this publication may be reproduced, stored or transmitted in any form or by any means, electronic, mechanical, photocopying, recording, scanning, or otherwise without written permission from the publisher. It is illegal to copy this book, post it to a website, or distribute it by any other means without permission.

First edition

Contents

Introduction

As the first light of 1862 illuminated the American skies, the nation was entrenched in an unparalleled internal strife: the American Civil War. This tumultuous period, which had begun less than a year earlier, was poised to enter a phase of unprecedented intensity and transformation. The battles of 1862, remarkable in their ferocity and impact, would come to represent the very essence of this epic struggle.

The critical nature of 1862 in the context of the Civil War cannot be overstated. It was a time defined by pivotal battles, strategic shifts, and evolving leadership, each leaving an indelible mark on both the Union and the Confederacy.

As the year unfolded, the Union was still grappling with the aftermath of the Confederacy's early victories in 1861. President Abraham Lincoln, confronted with a nation divided, was under immense pressure to act decisively. Meanwhile, Confederate leaders like Jefferson Davis and General Robert E. Lee sought to leverage their early successes to garner international recognition and support.

The year bore witness to several of the most memorable battles in American military history. Iconic conflicts such as Shiloh, Antietam, and Fredericksburg resonated with the sounds of combat and anguish, securing their place in American collective memory. Each battle, with its distinct challenges and consequences, contributed uniquely to the narrative of the war.

The Battle of Shiloh in April was a stark reminder of the war's harsh realities. It dispelled any remaining notions of a brief conflict, with its staggering casualties and intense combat. This battle set a precedent for the escalating severity of the war.

Of particular note was the Battle of Antietam, fought on September 17. Holding the grim title of the bloodiest single day in American military history, its ramifications were far-reaching. It prompted President Lincoln to issue the preliminary Emancipation Proclamation, altering the war's moral and political trajectory and affecting international perceptions of the conflict.

The Battle of Fredericksburg in December highlighted the tactical prowess of the Confederates and the challenges facing the Union in achieving a decisive victory. Its outcome intensified the urgency felt in the North and laid the groundwork for future military and political strategies.

In addition to these land battles, 1862 was marked by significant naval developments. The clash between the ironclads USS Monitor and CSS Virginia in March signaled a new era in naval warfare. These naval engagements played a vital role in the Union's strategy to blockade the Confederacy.

The year also saw significant shifts in leadership and strategy. Union leaders like Ulysses S. Grant and William Tecumseh Sherman began to rise in prominence, their aggressive and innovative military tactics shaping the later stages of the war.

In the Confederate ranks, figures such as Robert E. Lee and Stonewall Jackson became symbols of Southern defiance and military acumen. Their leadership in key battles solidified their status as legendary commanders.

Politically, the events of 1862 laid the foundation for substantial changes in policy and public opinion. The Emancipation Proclamation, while initially limited in scope, marked a pivotal shift in the war's objectives, transforming it from a battle to preserve the Union to a fight against slavery.

As the year came to a close, the American Civil War had evolved from a regional dispute into a comprehensive conflict that would fundamentally reshape the nation. The battles of 1862 laid the groundwork for the ensuing struggles and triumphs, marking a crucial turning point in American history.

Battle of Mill Springs

In the pivotal year of 1861, amidst the burgeoning American Civil War, the strategically crucial border state of Kentucky declared its neutrality, seeking to be a non-combatant in the escalating conflict between the Union and the Confederacy. However, this stance of neutrality was short-lived and dramatically altered the course of the war in the Western Theater.

The first breach of Kentucky's neutrality came on September 3, when Confederate forces under Brigadier General Gideon J. Pillow, following orders from Major General Leonidas Polk, aggressively occupied the city of Columbus. This bold move was quickly countered just two days later by Union Brigadier General Ulysses S. Grant, who strategically seized Paducah. This tit-for-tat military action marked the end of Kentucky's neutrality, with both the Union and Confederate forces disregarding the state's declared neutral status. Consequently, Kentucky's position as a buffer zone, which could have been advantageous in defending Tennessee for the Confederacy, was effectively nullified.

By the early months of 1862, the Confederate military presence in the region was under the command of General Albert Sidney Johnston, who had a daunting task. His command extended from Arkansas all the way to the Cumberland Gap, covering a vast and thinly spread defensive line. His left flank was anchored in Columbus by Polk with a force of 12,000 men. The central part of his line was fortified by two critical forts, Henry and Donelson, under Brigadier General Lloyd Tilghman, commanding 4,000 men. These forts were key as they protected the vital Tennessee and Cumberland rivers. On his right flank, in Kentucky, Brigadier General Simon Bolivar Buckner led 4,000 troops in Bowling Green. Additionally, about 4,000 men were stationed in the Military District of East Tennessee under Major General George B. Crittenden, tasked with guarding the Cumberland Gap, a strategic pass and crucial entry point into the pro-Unionist East Tennessee.

Brigadier General Felix Zollicoffer, commanding Crittenden's 1st Brigade, was tasked with a crucial role in guarding the strategic Cumberland Gap. However, in a bold move in November 1861, Zollicoffer advanced his forces westward into Kentucky, aiming to fortify the Confederate presence near Somerset and establish a closer link with the Confederate stronghold in Bowling Green.

Zollicoffer's strategic position at Mill Springs presented a striking contrast in geography. The southern bank of the Cumberland River, a bluff, offered a formidable defensive stance, while the northern bank was markedly less advantageous, being low and flat. In a decision fraught with risk, Zollicoffer chose to position the bulk of his troops on the northern bank, perilously close to Union forces. His assumption that this position was more defensible would prove to be a critical miscalculation. Despite urgent orders from both Crittenden and Albert Sidney Johnston to relocate to the more secure southern bank, Zollicoffer faced a daunting obstacle: the lack of sufficient boats to swiftly cross the unfordable river. He feared that an attempted crossing might leave his brigade vulnerable to Union attack, trapped mid-river.

Meanwhile, Union Brigadier General George H. Thomas was on the move with a clear directive: to drive the Confederates back across the Cumberland River and disrupt Crittenden's army. Thomas embarked from Lebanon, navigating through rain-drenched landscapes. On January 17, he arrived at Logan's Crossroads, pausing there to await the arrival of Brigadier General Albin F. Schoepf's troops from Somerset. This was a calculated pause, allowing his forces to consolidate for a stronger offensive.

In the Confederate camp, Crittenden, who had remained at his headquarters in Knoxville until early January, hastened to Mill Springs upon realizing the precarious position of his inexperienced subordinate, Zollicoffer. Crittenden quickly formulated a plan to pre-emptively strike the Union force before it could amass a greater strength against him. The Union army was split, with Thomas and three brigades at Logan's Crossroads and Schoepf's brigade at Somerset, the two factions separated by the swollen Fishing Creek. This natural barrier could potentially delay the Union forces from uniting.

Seizing the moment, Crittenden ordered Zollicoffer to launch an assault on the Union camp at Logan's Crossroads at dawn on January 19. This decision set the stage for a critical engagement, with the elements of surprise and geography playing pivotal roles in the unfolding battle.

As the fateful night progressed, the Confederate troops embarked on a treacherous march towards Logan's Crossroads. Hindered by relentless rain and treacherous mud, the conditions were abysmal. The soldiers, many equipped with outdated, Napoleonic-era flintlock muskets, trudged through the mire, their spirits dampened and their weaponry compromised by the wet weather. The inclement conditions and the slow pace eroded the critical element of surprise that they had hoped to leverage in their attack.

Yet, despite these adversities, the Confederate forces, with undiminished resolve, launched a determined assault at dawn, led valiantly by Brigadier General Felix Zollicoffer. The initial phase of the battle saw a surge of momentum for the Confederates. The 15th Mississippi Infantry and the 20th Tennessee, with remarkable fervor, managed to push back Union forces including the 4th Kentucky Infantry under Colonel Speed S. Fry, the 2nd Minnesota, the 10th Indiana, and some Union cavalry. This early success, however, was about to be overshadowed by a tragic and chaotic turn of events.

In the midst of battle, the dense woods, clouded with gunsmoke and the dim light of dawn, became a scene of utter confusion. Zollicoffer, distinctly visible in a white raincoat, made a fatal mistake in the chaos. He approached the Union 4th Kentucky Infantry, mistaking them for his own men who he believed were firing on each other. In this tragic misstep, Zollicoffer was shot and killed, reportedly by Colonel Fry himself. The sudden loss of their leader plunged the center of the Confederate line into disarray, causing them to momentarily fall back in confusion.

Meanwhile, Confederate General Crittenden, amidst the turmoil, valiantly rallied his troops, calling for a general advance by both Zollicoffer's brigade and that of Brigadier General William H. Carroll. But the tide of battle was turning.

Union Brigadier General George H. Thomas, sensing the moment, arrived on the field with tactical acumen. He commanded the 9th Ohio to advance, while the 2nd Minnesota maintained a relentless volley of fire. Colonel Robert L. McCook, leading Thomas's 3rd Brigade, described the intensity of the close-quarters combat, noting that Union and Confederate soldiers were so near that they "were poking their guns through the same fence."

The crucial moment came when the 9th Ohio outflanked the Confederate left, decisively tipping the balance. The Confederate lines, already shaken by the loss of Zollicoffer and the ferocity of the Union onslaught, crumbled into a chaotic retreat toward Mill Springs. Crittenden, rumored to be intoxicated during the battle, was unable to stem the tide of defeat. In their frenzied escape, the Confederates abandoned valuable resources: twelve artillery pieces, 150 wagons, over 1,000 horses and mules, and tragically, their dead and wounded. Their retreat continued relentlessly all the way to Chestnut Mound, Tennessee, about 50 miles east of Nashville, marking a significant Union victory and a momentous shift in the war's trajectory in this region.

The aftermath revealed a relatively modest toll in terms of battlefield casualties, yet the repercussions extended far beyond the immediate losses. For the Union, the cost was 39 lives lost and 207 soldiers wounded. The Confederates suffered more heavily, with 125 killed and an additional 404 wounded or missing. However, the impact of the battle was not limited to these numbers; it had far-reaching consequences on the careers and strategies of those involved.

For Confederate General George B. Crittenden, the Battle of Mill Springs was a turning point, but for all the wrong reasons. In the wake of the defeat, Crittenden faced serious allegations, including accusations of drunkenness and even treason. These charges led to the dissolution of his army, and he was subsequently reassigned as a corps commander under General Simon Bolivar Buckner at Bowling Green. However, this role was short-lived. Within just two months, Crittenden was again relieved of his command and arrested following another episode of alleged drunkenness.

In October 1862, after undergoing a court of inquiry ordered by General Braxton Bragg, Crittenden's military career effectively ended. He resigned his generalship and, in a diminished capacity, served without rank on the staff of Brigadier General John S. Williams and other officers in western Virginia for the remainder of the war. This marked a significant decline from his earlier position of influence.

Strategically, the Battle of Mill Springs, coupled with the Battle of Middle Creek on January 10, had a profound effect on the Confederate defensive strategy in Kentucky. These engagements effectively shattered the main Confederate defensive line in eastern Kentucky. Although Confederate efforts in the state would see a temporary resurgence in the summer with General Braxton Bragg and Major General Kirby Smith's Kentucky Campaign, culminating in the Battle of Perryville, the tide had turned. Bragg's subsequent retreat after Perryville underscored the shifting momentum.

Of the two Union victories in Kentucky in January 1862, Mill Springs was the more significant. These victories enabled the United States forces to carry the war into Middle Tennessee by February, marking a crucial phase in the conflict.

Battle of Fort Henry

Initially, Kentucky sought to remain an oasis of neutrality in the escalating conflict, a stance that was soon to be dramatically upended. The first breach of this delicate neutrality occurred on September 3, 1861, marking a significant turning point in the war's early stages. On this day, Confederate Brigadier General Gideon J. Pillow, acting under the directives of Major General Leonidas Polk, audaciously occupied Columbus, Kentucky. This riverside town, perched on commanding 180-foot high bluffs along the Mississippi River, was not only a symbol of strategic might but also a vital transportation nexus. It was the terminus of the Memphis & Ohio railroad, which linked directly to the critical Charleston & Memphis railroad further south.

The Confederates' occupation of Columbus was more than a mere military maneuver; it was a statement of intent and power. They fortified the town with an imposing arsenal of 140 large guns, underwater mines, and an extraordinary mile-long chain stretched across the Mississippi, effectively severing Northern commerce routes to the South. This formidable stronghold, garrisoned by 17,000 Confederate troops, transformed Columbus into a linchpin of Southern defense and a significant impediment to Union ambitions.

Yet, this Confederate thrust was met with an equally decisive Union response. Just two days later, Union Brigadier General Ulysses S. Grant, in an early display of the bold leadership that would define his military career, captured

Paducah, Kentucky. This strategic move was not merely a retaliation but a shrewd acquisition of a major transportation hub, rich with rail and port facilities at the Tennessee River's mouth. Grant's action signaled the end of Kentucky's neutrality and shifted the war's balance, eroding the Confederate advantage.

As 1862 dawned, the Confederate forces, under General Albert Sidney Johnston, faced the daunting challenge of defending an extensive territory stretching from Arkansas to the Cumberland Gap. Johnston's forces, though vast in their spread, were thinly stretched across this wide defensive front. His left flank, commanded by Polk with 12,000 men, held Columbus. The right flank, under Brigadier General Simon Bolivar Buckner and his 4,000 troops, fortified Bowling Green, Kentucky. The central anchor of Johnston's line was the twin forts, Henry and Donelson, each manned by 4,000 soldiers under Brigadier General Lloyd Tilghman's command. These forts were not mere military installations; they were the guardians of the vital Tennessee and Cumberland Rivers. If these waterways fell to Union forces, they would open direct invasion routes into the heartlands of western and eastern Tennessee, threatening critical supply lines, including the Memphis & SC Railroad.

In the early stages of 1862, the Union's military strategy in the Western Theater was marred by a lack of cohesive leadership and coordination among its separate departments. This disarray was evident in the distinct approaches of the three major departments: the Department of Kansas led by Major General David Hunter, the Department of Missouri under the command of Major General Henry W. Halleck, and the Department of the Ohio, directed by Brigadier General Don Carlos Buell. Each department, operating independently, struggled to formulate a unified strategy for the region, leading to disjointed and inefficient military operations.

By January 1862, the consequences of this fragmented command structure became increasingly apparent. Buell, facing political pressures to secure pro-Union eastern Tennessee, advanced tentatively towards Nashville. Meanwhile, in Halleck's jurisdiction, General Ulysses S. Grant initiated movements along the Tennessee River, intended as a diversion to cover Buell's slow advance, which ultimately stalled. Both Halleck and Buell, along with other Western generals, were feeling the heat from President Abraham Lincoln, who urged for a coordinated offensive to coincide with Washington's birthday on February 22.

Despite his usual caution, Halleck was swayed by Grant's bold proposal to target Fort Henry, seeing an opportunity to bolster his reputation and gain an edge over his rival, Buell. Additionally, both Halleck and Grant were concerned by rumors of Confederate General P.G.T. Beauregard's impending arrival with a significant force. On January 30, 1862, Halleck gave Grant the green light to seize Fort Henry.

Grant, ever decisive, departed Cairo, Illinois, on February 2. His formidable force, numbering between 15,000 and 17,000 men and organized into two divisions led by Brigadier Generals John A. McClernand and Charles F. Smith, converged on the Tennessee River by February 4 and 5. This invasion force was bolstered by the Western Gunboat Flotilla, commanded by United States Navy Flag Officer Andrew Hull Foote, featuring four ironclad gunboats and three timberclad gunboats. Due to limited transport capabilities early in the war, multiple trips were needed to deliver all troops for the operation.

On the Confederate side, General Albert Sidney Johnston faced pressure from the Confederate government to defend key strategic points, including the Cumberland & Tennessee rivers and vital railroads. Johnston consolidated his forces further south, anticipating Buell's advance at the Cumberland Gap. However, his subordinate, Beauregard, vehemently disagreed with Johnston's defensive stance, advocating for a more aggressive approach or, at the least, stronger fortifications along the rivers. Johnston, however, remained firm in his strategy, leaving only a modest force to defend Fort Donelson. Fort Henry, deemed vulnerable due to poor positioning and susceptibility to flooding, was manned by a token force of 3,000-4,000 men, deemed sufficient for repelling naval attacks while a new, more strategically positioned fort was being constructed upriver.

Fort Henry, named after Tennessee Senator Gustavus Adolphus Henry Sr., was a notable five-sided, open-bastioned earthen fortification that spanned 10 acres. It was strategically positioned on the eastern bank of the Tennessee River, near Kirkman's Old Landing. Its location was carefully chosen, approximately one mile above Panther Creek and six miles below the confluence of the Big Sandy River and Standing Rock Creek.

The genesis of Fort Henry can be traced back to May 1861, when Isham G. Harris, the Governor of Tennessee, entrusted Daniel S. Donelson, a state attorney turned brigadier general, with the task of constructing defensive structures along the rivers of Middle Tennessee. Donelson initially identified promising sites for these fortifications, but they lay within Kentucky's borders, which was then a neutral state. To maintain this neutrality, Donelson moved upstream, within Tennessee's border, and chose the site for what would become Fort Donelson on the Cumberland River.

With Fort Donelson's construction underway, Donelson ventured further, about 12 miles west to the Tennessee River, to select the location for Fort Henry. His strategic reasoning for this site was that it allowed a single garrison to travel between Fort Henry and Fort Donelson, efficiently defending both locations, as he did not anticipate simultaneous attacks on them.

However, Fort Henry's location contrasted sharply with Fort Donelson's. Unlike its counterpart on the Cumberland River, Fort Henry was situated on low-lying, swampy terrain, overshadowed by hills across the river. This geographical disadvantage led to frequent flooding of the fort, particularly during high tides or heavy rains, often submerging over half of the fort, including most of its armory. Despite this flaw, the fort did have the advantage of an unobstructed field of fire extending 2 miles downriver.

The site selection for Fort Henry faced significant opposition. Donelson's surveying team, which included civil engineer Adna Anderson and Major William F. Foster from the 1st Tennessee Infantry, strongly objected to the chosen location due to its vulnerability. They appealed to Colonel Bushrod Johnson of the Tennessee Corps of Engineers, seeking to overturn this decision. Surprisingly, despite the apparent drawbacks of the site, Colonel Johnson inexplicably gave his approval.

The primary design objective of Fort Henry was to control river traffic, rather than to endure the kind of large-scale infantry assaults that would become commonplace in the Civil War. Construction of the fort began in mid-June 1861, employing labor from the 10th Tennessee Infantry and enslaved individuals. The fort's first cannon roared to life with a test fire on July 12, 1861. However, after this initial burst of activity, the remainder of the year saw a slowdown in development, primarily because forts along the Mississippi River were prioritized for manpower and artillery resources. This prioritization led to the neglect of Forts Henry and Donelson, especially by General Polk, who focused his efforts on fortifying Columbus, Kentucky.

As 1861 drew to a close, additional reinforcements arrived at Fort Henry. These included men from the 27th Alabama Infantry and around 500 enslaved workers tasked with constructing a smaller fortification across the river on Stewart's Hill. Within artillery range of Fort Henry, this new structure was christened Fort Heiman. By January 1862, Brigadier General Lloyd Tilghman had taken command of both Forts Henry and Donelson, overseeing a combined force of approximately 4,900 men. At Fort Henry, the garrison numbered between 3,000 and 3,400 men, divided into two brigades under Colonels Adolphus Heiman and Joseph Drake, and were primarily equipped with outdated flintlock rifles from the War of 1812.

By the time of its battle, Fort Henry was armed with seventeen cannons.

Eleven of these were positioned to control river traffic, while the remaining six were oriented for land-based defense, including 18-pounder smoothbores. The fort's artillery also featured two heavy guns: a 10-inch Columbiad and a 24-pounder rifled cannon, supplemented by several 32-pounder smoothbores. Additionally, there were two 42-pounder guns, but they were rendered ineffective due to a lack of suitable ammunition. Under normal river conditions, the fort's walls stood an imposing 20 feet high and were 20 feet thick at the base, narrowing to nearly 10 feet at the parapet. However, in February 1862, heavy rains caused the Tennessee River to swell, submerging much of the fort, including its powder magazine.

The Confederate forces at Fort Henry also employed a novel defensive tactic, anchoring several underwater torpedoes (akin to modern naval mines) in the main shipping channel. These were designed to detonate upon contact with passing vessels. However, this strategy was undermined by the high river levels and leaks in the torpedoes' metal casings, rendering them ineffective.

On February 4 and 5, Grant strategically landed his divisions at two separate locations near Fort Henry. McClernand's division was positioned three miles north of the fort on the east bank of the Tennessee River. Their task was to block any potential retreat by the fort's garrison. Meanwhile, C.F. Smith's division was tasked with capturing Fort Heiman, located on the Kentucky side of the river, and to use its artillery against Fort Henry. However, heavy rains on the night of February 5 hampered the Union troops' advance towards the forts, shifting the focus of the battle to naval operations before the infantry could engage.

Brigadier General Lloyd Tilghman, aware of the fort's precarious situation, recognized that Fort Henry's fall was imminent. With only nine guns remaining functional above the waterline, he made a tactical decision. Leaving behind enough artillery in the fort to challenge the Union gunboats, he ordered the bulk of his force, led by Colonel Adolphus Heiman, to retreat along an overland route to Fort Donelson, located 12 miles away. Fort Heiman was abandoned on February 4, and the next afternoon, fire from Union gunboats caused four Confederate casualties at the Fort Henry garrison.

By the evening of February 5, Tilghman had relocated to the steamer Dunbar, positioned 1.5 miles upstream from Fort Henry. From there, he communicated the dire situation to General Johnston before returning to the fort just before dawn on February 6.

On the morning of February 6, Flag Officer Andrew Hull Foote's Union gunboat fleet, comprising seven vessels, arrived at Fort Henry. By 12:30 p.m., they had taken up positions and commenced a long-range bombardment from approximately 1,700 yards away. After Tilghman refused an initial surrender demand, the Union fleet intensified its attack. This marked the first combat use of the Union's newly designed ironclads. Foote arranged his four ironclad gunboats in a line abreast, with the three timberclads under the command of Seth Ledyard Phelps providing supporting fire from a distance. The high river levels and the low positioning of Fort Henry's guns meant the Union fleet largely evaded catastrophic damage. However, the Confederate fire did manage to repeatedly strike the ironclads, especially the USS Essex, which sustained severe damage. A 32-pound shot from Fort Henry breached the USS Essex, hitting its middle boiler and releasing scalding steam throughout the vessel. This incident resulted in 32 casualties among the crew, including the commander, William D. Porter, and rendered the ship inoperable for the rest of the campaign.

Following 75 minutes of intense bombardment, Brigadier General Lloyd Tilghman, realizing the untenable situation at Fort Henry, capitulated to Flag Officer Andrew Hull Foote's fleet, which had advanced to within 400 yards for a more effective assault. Tilghman had previously promised his men an hour's resistance to buy time for their retreat. With the fort's armament reduced to a single operational cannon and ammunition dwindling due to the submerged powder magazine, he saw no alternative but to surrender. Consequently, he ordered the lowering of the Confederate flag and the raising of a white sheet, signaling their capitulation. The Union gunboats ceased fire upon sighting the white flag. The extent of the fort's inundation was such that Tilghman had to be collected from the fort's sally port by boat for the formal surrender aboard the USS Cincinnati. The garrison's remnants, comprising 12 officers and 82 men, were taken prisoner, with estimated casualties of 15 killed and 20 wounded. The evacuating Confederate forces abandoned all artillery and equipment.

Meanwhile, General Ulysses S. Grant and his infantry arrived at Fort Henry around 3 p.m. on February 6, only to find the fort already surrendered. McClernand's division reached shortly thereafter. Smith's division, on the other hand, had advanced to the deserted Fort Heiman. Had Grant delayed his approach by two days, he would have found the battle over before it began. By February 8, Fort Henry was completely submerged.

The fall of Fort Henry opened the Tennessee River to Union naval and transport activities as far south as the Alabama border. Immediately following the surrender, Foote dispatched Lieutenant Phelps with the three timberclad gunboats—Tyler, Conestoga, and Lexington—on an upriver mission to destroy Confederate military installations and supplies. The damaged ironclads were deemed unsuitable for this task, which required speed and maneuverability. Phelps' raid extended to Muscle Shoals, near Florence, Alabama, marking the navigable limit of the river. They disrupted Confederate supply lines, destroyed a key bridge of the Memphis and Ohio Railroad, and seized several Confederate vessels, including an ironclad under construction. The citizens of Florence successfully petitioned Phelps to spare their town and its railroad bridge, as they held no strategic military value.

Phelps' raid was deemed a resounding success, revealing the Confederacy's vulnerability in that region and the possibility of a Union advance deep into Confederate territory. The mission also uncovered strong Union sympathies in Tennessee, Mississippi, and Alabama, with several pro-Union Southerners assisting Phelps. The Union gunboats returned to Fort Henry on February 12.

With the subsequent fall of Fort Donelson to Grant's forces on February 16, the Tennessee and Cumberland Rivers became crucial Union waterways for troop and material movement. The capture of these forts and rivers effectively outflanked the Confederate forces at Columbus, prompting their withdrawal from both the city and western Kentucky, affirming Grant's strategic foresight.

Battle of Roanoke Island

The enchanting sounds of Northeastern North Carolina are vast expanses of brackish-to-salt water, nestled between the mainland and the alluring Outer Banks. These are not mere bodies of water; they are the lifeblood of the region, divided conceptually into distinct, interconnected realms. The largest, Pamlico Sound, lies like a serene giant behind Hatteras Island, while to its north, Albemarle Sound stretches its arms towards Virginia's southern border. Between them, Roanoke Island and Croatan Sound form a narrow, vital linkage, with Roanoke Sound gracefully skirting the island's eastern edge.

These waters have cradled civilization, with cities like New Bern, Beaufort, Edenton, and Elizabeth City blossoming on their shores. They have seen rivers weave into their embrace, bringing life to a third of the state. In the Civil War's early days, these sounds were Confederate lifelines, enabling trade and communication even under the threat of blockade. Canals like the Albemarle and Chesapeake, and the Dismal Swamp Canal, were strategic arteries, connecting to Norfolk, Virginia, and beyond.

But it was Roanoke Island, a jewel amidst these waters, that held the key to control. A bastion for the Union would mean a stronghold unassailable except by sea, turning every mainland shore into a potential front. For the Confederates, defending this island was a daunting task – a choice between yielding without resistance or spreading their forces perilously thin. This narrative isn't just about waters and lands; it's about the strategic dance of war, the ebb and flow of power, and the eternal embrace of nature and history.

In late August 1861, the 3rd Georgia Infantry, initially bound for Hatteras Inlet, found themselves rerouted to Roanoke Island as the Federal fleet advanced. This move marked the beginning of a haphazard defense, characterized by minimal efforts to dislodge Union forces from Hatteras.

It wasn't until October that General Hill, tasked with fortifying North Carolina's coastal defenses, began erecting earthworks on Roanoke Island. However, his reassignment to Virginia left the project incomplete. The defense zone was subsequently divided, with Generals Branch and Wise overseeing the southern and northern parts, respectively. Notably, Wise was left without the Pamlico Sound and its cities under his command.

Wise, previously leading the Wise Legion, arrived without his troops, left with a patchwork force including two Virginia regiments and three North Carolina units. These men, often ill-equipped and inadequately armed, faced harsh conditions that left many sick and unable to fight.

Desperate for resources, Wise echoed Hill's earlier pleas for reinforcements and artillery. However, the reinforcements were meager, leading to the creation of modest fortifications like Forts Huger, Blanchard, and Bartow, alongside improvised defenses like Fort Forrest. Yet, crucially, the island's southern half, the anticipated direction of attack, remained undefended.

In an innovative move, Wise used pile drivers to obstruct the sound between Forts Huger and Forrest, although this barrier was incomplete when the Union attacked.

The Confederate Navy's Mosquito Fleet, under Flag Officer Lynch, contributed to the defense with its limited firepower. Wise, critical of the fleet's effectiveness, lamented the diversion of resources and manpower from essential tasks to these ineffectual gunboats.

Soon after the Union's triumph on Hatteras Island, General Burnside championed the concept of a Coast Division, an innovative unit comprising fishermen, dockworkers, and other maritime experts from the Northeast. His rationale was straightforward: these men, already adept at sea, could be swiftly trained for amphibious warfare. Enjoying a close rapport with General-in-Chief George B. McClellan, Burnside's proposal received serious consideration. Originally envisaged for operations in Chesapeake Bay, the plan evolved under McClellan and the War Department into a full-fledged assault on North Carolina's coast, starting with Roanoke Island. Part of the rationale for this shift was a belief, albeit erroneous, that North Carolina harbored suppressed Unionist sentiments ready to surface upon liberation.

This vision took shape as the Burnside Expedition. Burnside, moving ahead with recruitment, structured the Coast Division into three brigades, each led by his West Point comrades—Brigadier Generals John G. Foster, Jesse L. Reno, and John G. Parke. By early January, a formidable force of nearly 13,000 men stood ready.

The Union Navy was set to provide the primary firepower, but Burnside insisted on Army-controlled gunboats, leading to inevitable inter-service friction. The Navy, skilled in maritime acquisitions, snapped up suitable vessels, leaving the Army with a less reliable fleet. Despite these challenges, the expedition mustered 20 Navy gunboats and nine from the Coast Division, complemented by makeshift floating batteries armed with boat howitzers.

As Burnside's agents scrambled to acquire gunboats, they also secured various transports. Troops and vessels converged in Annapolis, embarking on January 5, 1862. Their journey began on January 9, heading towards Fort Monroe at Chesapeake Bay's mouth. There, they joined naval forces, and on January 11, set sail for Cape Hatteras, the mission's true destination known only to Burnside and his closest aides until then.

The journey to Hatteras Inlet proved to be an ordeal for many Union soldiers, arguably more challenging than the ensuing battle. Known for its treacherous weather, Cape Hatteras lived up to its reputation, plunging the troops into a maelstrom of seasickness and turbulent seas. In a display of solidarity, General Burnside left his comfortable quarters on the George Peabody to join his men aboard the Picket, a vessel he deemed the least seaworthy. This gesture of shared hardship endeared him to his troops, even as he privately questioned his decision during the height of the storm. Fortunately, the Picket weathered the tempest, safely delivering Burnside to his destination.

Not all vessels were as lucky. The City of New York, carrying vital ordnance and supplies, the Pocahontas with its cargo of horses, and the Army gunboat Zouave succumbed to the harsh conditions. While all passengers were rescued, a tragic incident claimed the lives of two officers from the 9th New Jersey Infantry.

Navigating through Hatteras Inlet into Pamlico Sound proved laborious. The anticipated depth of eight feet was misleadingly shallow at six feet, complicating the passage for some Union Army ships. Several vessels had to be lightened and kedged in, while others, too deep for even this approach, offloaded their cargo onto Hatteras Island. The Bark John Trucks, burdened with the bulk of the 53rd New York Regiment, failed to make the passage and returned to Annapolis, leaving only a detachment to participate in the Battle of Roanoke Island. It was not until February 4 that the Union fleet regrouped and readied in Pamlico Sound.

Meanwhile, Confederate response was surprisingly lackluster. No reinforcements reached the island or other potential targets in the region. The number of Confederate infantry on Roanoke Island stagnated at around 1,400, with an additional 800 in reserve at Nag's Head. A significant setback occurred on February 1 when General Wise fell ill with a severe lung condition, confining him to bed and effectively passing command to Colonel H. M. Shaw of the

8th North Carolina Infantry. Wise, despite his illness, continued to issue orders from his sickbed until after the battle had concluded.

On the morning of February 5th, after assembling in the sound, the Union fleet set sail. By evening, they had reached the southern end of Roanoke Island, anchoring there as rain and strong winds delayed further movement. The next day's notable event was Admiral Goldsborough transferring his flag from the USS Philadelphia to the Southfield.

On February 7th, with improved weather, the Navy gunboats assumed their positions. Their initial task was to shell Ashby Harbor, the planned landing site, to ascertain the presence of Confederate batteries. Finding none, they advanced up Croatan Sound, splitting their focus between Fort Bartow at Pork Point and the Confederate Mosquito Fleet.

At noon, the bombardment commenced, swiftly exposing the weaknesses in the Confederate defenses. Fort Bartow could only bring four guns to bear against the Union gunboats, while Forts Huger and Blanchard were rendered ineffective. Fort Forrest's utility was completely nullified when the CSS Curlew, damaged and seeking to avoid sinking, beached herself, inadvertently blocking the fort's guns.

Despite the ferocity of the battle, losses were surprisingly light on both sides. Several Union ships sustained hits but no critical damage. The Confederate fleet, barring the Curlew, also held up but was forced to withdraw due to ammunition shortages.

Meanwhile, the Union Army transports and gunboats reached Ashby Harbor. At 3 PM, Burnside commanded the landings to commence. By 4 PM, troops were reaching the shore. A Confederate force of 200 men under Colonel John V. Jordan (31st North Carolina) was positioned to resist the landing but was quickly scattered by gunfire from the gunboats, offering no return fire.

By midnight, nearly 10,000 Union soldiers had landed without further opposition. Accompanying them were six launches armed with boat howitzers, led by the young midshipman, Benjamin H. Porter. The Union forces made a short inland push before setting up camp for the night, poised for the next phase of the battle.

On the morning of February 8th, the Union forces, led by the 25th Massachusetts of the First Brigade, began their northward march along the island's sole road. Accompanied by Midshipman Porter's howitzers, their progress was soon impeded by a Confederate redoubt manned by approximately 400 soldiers. Additional Confederate forces, numbering around a thousand, were stationed about 250 yards behind the front lines. Colonel Shaw, commanding the Confederates, faced constraints in deploying his troops due to the narrow battlefield flanked by swamps, believed to be impassable.

For two hours, the Union's First Brigade and Confederate defenders exchanged fire amidst dense smoke. The 10th Connecticut Regiment relieved the 25th Massachusetts, which had endured the battle without severe losses, but they too were unable to make significant headway. The situation changed with the arrival of the Second Brigade under Brigadier General Jesse L. Reno. Reno ordered an attempt to penetrate the swamp on the Union's left flank, while Brigadier General John G. Foster directed two of his reserve regiments to probe the right flank.

Simultaneously, Brigadier General John G. Parke's Third Brigade arrived and joined the effort. The two flanking maneuvers, though uncoordinated, converged from the swamps at roughly the same time. Reno's 21st Massachusetts, 51st New York, and 9th New Jersey Regiments launched an attack, soon joined by the 23rd Massachusetts from the First Brigade. This multi-directional assault overwhelmed the Confederate line.

With no secondary defenses and lacking artillery support, Colonel Shaw faced an untenable situation and chose to surrender to General Foster. The surrender included not only Shaw's 1,400 direct command but also the forces manning the nearby forts. Two additional Confederate regiments, the 2nd North Carolina and 46th Virginia, arrived too late for battle but in time to be included in the surrender. In total, about 2,500 Confederate soldiers were captured.

The battle, while decisive, resulted in relatively modest casualties by Civil War standards. Union forces suffered 37 fatalities, 214 wounded, and 13 missing. Confederate losses included 23 killed, 58 wounded, and 62 missing.

Battle of Fort Donelson

In the chilling winter of 1862, the American Civil War was about to witness one of its pivotal moments. The stage was set shortly after the Union's strategic capture of Fort Henry in Tennessee on February 6. This victory had not just boosted Union morale but also opened the vital Tennessee River for their troop movements. Approximately 2,500 Confederate soldiers, evading capture at Fort Henry, retreated to the nearby Fort Donelson, setting the scene for an epic confrontation.

The fall of Fort Henry presented the Confederates with a dire strategic dilemma. Union General Ulysses S. Grant's forces now effectively divided the Confederate armies of Generals P.G.T. Beauregard and William J. Hardee, stationed in Kentucky with significant troops. The vulnerable Fort Donelson, manned by just about 5,000 men, stood at the crossroads of potential Union onslaughts – a direct threat to Nashville, Tennessee, a crucial manufacturing hub.

Confederate General Albert Sidney Johnston, aware of the dire situation, convened a war council. In a move that signaled a retreat from their defensive stance in Tennessee, Johnston decided to reinforce Fort Donelson with an additional 12,000 men, despite his skepticism about its defensibility. This decision was a gamble, risking the loss of Middle Tennessee and Nashville but was seen as a necessary evil.

The choice of command at Fort Donelson fell to Brig. Gen. John B. Floyd, a controversial figure with more political than military experience. Floyd, a former U.S. Secretary of War under James Buchanan, was infamous in the North for his alleged corrupt and secessionist activities.

Meanwhile, on the Union side, Major General Henry W. Halleck, Grant's superior, was battling his own apprehensions. Despite Grant's recent success at Fort Henry, Halleck considered him reckless and was hesitant about advancing to Fort Donelson. Unbeknownst to Grant, there were discussions about possibly replacing him, underscoring the precarious nature of his command.

Grant, undeterred by these underlying currents, boldly declared his intention to capture Fort Donelson and return to Fort Henry. However, his optimism faced harsh realities – the treacherous twelve-mile march to Donelson, logistical challenges posed by the rising floodwaters, and damages sustained by his naval support in the previous battle. Yet, in a council of war on February 11, Grant's generals, with one exception, supported his plan for an assault on Fort Donelson. This council would be Grant's last during the Civil War, marking the beginning of his trademark decisive leadership style.

On the frosty morning of February 12, Union forces, buoyed by the imminent arrival of reinforcements and Union gunboats, began their march from Fort Henry towards Fort Donelson. The Union army, soon to swell to 25,000 men, advanced along the main roads, only to be hindered by the skilled cavalry maneuvers of Nathan Bedford Forrest, a Confederate commander acting under General Buckner's orders. Forrest's cavalry engaged in a sharp skirmish with a detachment from McClernand's division, briefly halting the Union advance before retreating under Buckner's directive.

As Forrest's cavalry withdrew, the Union troops edged closer to the Confederate lines, strategically positioning themselves to block any potential Confederate escape routes. Grant's army was strategically arrayed with McClernand's division on the right and C.F. Smith's division on the left. The

USS Carondelet, leading the naval support, arrived upstream and launched a barrage of shells at Fort Donelson, testing the fort's defenses before withdrawing.

Meanwhile, Confederate General Buckner, upon receiving orders from Generals Floyd and Pillow, contemplated a bold move to attack Union supply lines near Cumberland City. This strategy, however, risked leaving Fort Donelson dangerously outnumbered. General Pillow, questioning these orders, left to confer directly with General Floyd, temporarily placing Buckner in charge of the fort. But, alarmed by the distant artillery fire, Pillow hastily returned to resume command.

With Grant's forces approaching, Confederate leadership was in disarray. General Johnston instructed Floyd to reinforce Fort Donelson with any available troops from Clarksville, highlighting the fort's strategic importance.

On February 13, despite explicit instructions from General Grant to avoid a full-scale engagement, probing attacks were initiated against the Confederate defenses. On the Union left, General C.F. Smith, disobeying orders, sent two brigades to test the Confederate lines, maintaining pressure with continuous fire throughout the night. Similarly, on the Union right, McClernand defied orders, launching an attack aimed at a troublesome Confederate battery. This assault, led by Colonel Isham N. Haynie of the 48th Illinois, experienced leadership confusion and was ultimately repelled, with some of the wounded tragically caught in grass fires sparked by artillery.

In a strategic move to divert attention, General Grant directed Commander Henry Walke to navigate the Carondelet up the Cumberland River and bombard Fort Donelson. The Confederate forces, quick to respond, unleashed their long-range artillery, scoring a hit on the gunboat. Despite this setback, Walke courageously returned to his position, relentlessly continuing his shelling of the Confederate water batteries.

Meanwhile, General McClernand faced his own challenges. He endeavored to extend his line toward the river but was impeded by a robust Confederate artillery. Realizing his troops were stretched too thin to reach the river, McClernand's efforts prompted Grant to call for reinforcements. He promptly dispatched orders to General Wallace at Fort Henry, instructing him to bring additional forces to the fray at Fort Donelson.

The Confederate command at Fort Donelson underwent a shift as General Floyd assumed leadership, relegating the execution of battle strategies largely to Generals Pillow and Buckner. Despite a series of skirmishes throughout the day, the positions of both armies remained largely unchanged as night fell, with both sides enduring the bitter cold.

The weather, which had been predominantly rainy during the campaign, took a dramatic turn on the night of February 13. A severe snowstorm swept in, bringing punishing winds and plummeting temperatures down to 10-12 °F, blanketing the area with 3 inches of snow. The freezing conditions rendered guns and wagons immobile, stuck to the frozen ground.

Caught in the grip of this harsh winter weather and in close proximity to enemy lines, the soldiers on both sides were unable to light fires for warmth or cooking. The night was especially brutal, with many troops suffering without the comfort of blankets or overcoats. This stark setting of intense cold and proximity to the enemy heightened the misery and challenge for both the Union and Confederate forces as they prepared for the impending battle.

At 11:00 a.m. on February 14, inside the Dover Hotel transformed into a makeshift headquarters, General Floyd convened a critical council of war. The consensus was bleak: Fort Donelson was likely indefensible. A daring plan emerged: General Pillow would spearhead an escape, evacuate the fort, and head towards Nashville. As preparations for this breakout maneuver commenced behind the Confederate lines, they initially breached the Union defenses. However, Grant's swift response forced them to retreat back to Fort Donelson. Pillow, known for his combat aggressiveness, was visibly shaken by the setback, believing their element of surprise lost, and called off the breakout.

Simultaneously, a major shift in Union forces occurred on February 14. General Lew Wallace's brigade, fresh from Fort Henry, arrived around noon. Shortly thereafter, in the mid-afternoon, Admiral Foote's formidable flotilla reached the Cumberland River, reinforcing the Union with six gunboats and 10,000 troops aboard twelve transports. Wallace quickly organized these new arrivals into a third division, comprised of two brigades under Colonels John M. Thayer and Charles Cruft, taking up a central position facing the Confederate trenches. This allowed an extension of McClernand's right flank to Lick Creek, with Colonel John McArthur's brigade moving to close a critical 400-yard gap.

Admiral Foote, upon his arrival, was pressed by Grant to attack the Confederate river batteries immediately. Despite his reservations about acting without thorough reconnaissance, Foote positioned his gunboats close to shore by 3:00 p.m. and commenced bombardment, mirroring his tactics at Fort Henry. The Confederate gunners waited until the Union fleet was dangerously close—about 400 yards—before unleashing a fierce counterattack. The Confederate artillery inflicted severe damage: Foote was injured (ironically in his foot), the USS St. Louis lost its wheelhouse and drifted downstream, the USS Louisville was disabled, and the USS Pittsburgh began taking on water. The Union naval assault, devastated by the Confederate artillery, retreated downstream. The Confederate gunners had fired 500 shots, striking the USS St. Louis 59 times, the Carondelet 54 times, the Louisville 36 times, and the Pittsburg 20 times. Foote's underestimation of the Confederate defenses was evident, and historian Kendall Gott later suggested that a more cautious approach with longer-range bombardment or a night assault, similar to tactics used in the 1863 Vicksburg Campaign, might have been more effective. Once past the Confederate batteries, the fort would have been vulnerable.

The naval engagement was costly for the Union: eight sailors killed and 44 wounded, while the Confederates suffered no casualties. On land, Union soldiers, heavily armed and numerous, encircled the Confederates. Although the Union boats were significantly damaged, they still maintained control of the river. Realizing that any potential victory at Fort Donelson would now depend predominantly on his army, Grant informed Halleck that a siege might be necessary to secure the fort.

In the wake of their unexpected triumph against the Union navy, the Confederate generals at Fort Donelson harbored deep reservations about their long-term prospects in the fort. Another council of war convened late into the night, culminating in a decision to revisit their previously abandoned plan of escape. As the first light of dawn broke on February 15, the Confederates, led by General Pillow, commenced a bold assault on the Union's vulnerable right flank, held by McClernand's division.

The Union soldiers, weary from the bitter cold and sleepless night, were somewhat prepared for combat, but General Grant was caught off guard. Anticipating no significant land offensive from the Confederates, Grant had left the fort early that morning to meet with Flag Officer Foote aboard his flagship downstream. Before leaving, he instructed his generals not to initiate any engagements and failed to appoint a second-in-command in his absence.

Pillow's objective was straightforward: drive back McClernand's forces, seize control of the critical Wynn's Ferry and Forge Roads, and pave the way for a Confederate retreat towards Nashville. General Buckner was tasked with moving his division to guard the retreat. A single regiment from Buckner's division, the 30th Tennessee, was left to hold the trenches and delay any Federal pursuit. The Confederate attack gained early momentum, forcing McClernand's line back and clearing the escape route, marked by the infamous and unnerving rebel yell, a sound new to Union troops in the West.

The Confederate advantage was partly due to the inexperience and poor positioning of McClernand's troops, compounded by a flanking maneuver from Forrest's cavalry. Union Colonels Richard Oglesby and John McArthur's brigades bore the brunt of the assault, retreating in an orderly fashion for regrouping. At around 8:00 a.m., a beleaguered McClernand sent an urgent request for reinforcements to Lew Wallace. However, Wallace, in the absence of direct orders from Grant and reluctant to act without them, initially declined to provide assistance.

As McClernand's ammunition dwindled, the situation grew increasingly dire, though his forces had not yet descended into chaos. A second, more desperate plea reached Wallace, this time with a messenger in tears, warning of the dire situation and the potential collapse of the entire Union line. Wallace, moved by the gravity of the situation, finally dispatched Colonel Charles Cruft's brigade to McClernand's aid.

Cruft's brigade, stepping in for the weary Oglesby and McArthur's brigades, soon realized the severity of their predicament as they encountered Pillow's Confederates and faced being outflanked. Despite their efforts, they too began to falter, adding to the mounting tension and uncertainty on the Union right flank.

The Confederate advance at Fort Donelson was not without its challenges. By 9:30 a.m., as the front Union brigades were retreating, Nathan Bedford Forrest urged Bushrod Johnson to capitalize on this opportunity with an all-out attack. Johnson, more cautious, refrained from a full assault but continued to press forward with the infantry. Two hours into the conflict, General Pillow realized that General Buckner's forces were not engaging in tandem with his own. This led to a heated exchange between the two generals, after which Buckner's troops finally advanced. Their combined effort, targeting W. H. L. Wallace's brigade, successfully secured key sections of Forge Road and Wynn's Ferry Road, effectively opening a pathway to Nashville.

However, Buckner's initial hesitation had given Lew Wallace's Union troops enough time to bolster McClernand's faltering line before a complete collapse. Defying Grant's previous orders, Wallace's brigades, including Thayer's, moved to support McClernand, allowing for a critical regrouping and resupply of ammunition. The 68th Ohio was strategically left to guard the rear.

By 12:30 p.m., the Confederate offensive began to lose steam. Wallace's and Thayer's Union forces established a defensive line along Wynn's Ferry Road. Despite multiple assaults by the Confederates, this new Union line held firm, forcing the Confederates to withdraw to a ridge half a mile away. Although the morning had seen significant Confederate advances, pushing Union defenders back and opening their escape route, the momentum was stalling.

Meanwhile, General Grant, initially oblivious to the unfolding battle, was informed by an aide and hurried back to the front lines in the early afternoon. His first stop was with C. F. Smith on the Union left, where he directed additional troops to reinforce the Union right. After a treacherous 7-mile journey over icy terrain, Grant reached McClernand and Wallace. Distressed by the disarray and lack of cohesive leadership, Grant encountered McClernand's frustration about the need for a unified command. Grant, recognizing the urgency, decisively stated, "It seems so. Gentlemen, the position on the right must be retaken." This firm directive underscored Grant's resolve to regain control and momentum in the battle.

Unfazed by the Confederate onslaught, General Grant maintained his composure. En route back from the river, the sounds of battle reached him, prompting him to instruct Foote to start a naval bombardment. Grant hoped this show of force would bolster the morale of his potentially demoralized troops. Noticing that some Confederate soldiers, particularly those under Buckner, were equipped with knapsacks carrying several days' rations, Grant inferred a possible escape attempt rather than a full-scale assault. He confidently remarked to an aide, "The one who attacks first now will be victorious. The enemy will have to be in a hurry if he gets ahead of me."

Despite their successful morning advance and a clear escape route, to the surprise of Generals Floyd and Buckner, Pillow ordered his forces to retreat to their trenches by 1:30 p.m. A heated debate ensued between the Confederate leaders, with Floyd poised to override Pillow's decision. However, Pillow insisted on regrouping and resupplying before abandoning the fort, and his argument prevailed. Floyd also held the misconception that C. F. Smith's division was receiving substantial reinforcements, leading to the entire Confederate force withdrawing back into Fort Donelson, relinquishing their earlier territorial gains.

Seizing the opportunity, Grant instructed Smith to take Fort Donelson, to which Smith confidently responded, "I will do it." Smith's plan involved two brigades: Lauman's leading the main attack with Col. James Tuttle's 2nd Iowa Infantry at the forefront, and Cook's brigade providing support and diversion. This offensive quickly overran the outer Confederate entrenchments, manned by the 30th Tennessee from Buckner's division. Despite persistent Confederate counterattacks, Smith's forces held their ground, positioning the Union for a decisive move against Fort Donelson and its river batteries by the next dawn.

On the Union right, Lew Wallace organized an attacking formation with three brigades to recapture the terrain lost in the morning's battle. Wallace's former brigade of Zouaves, now under Col. Morgan L. Smith, along with others from McClernand's and Wallace's divisions, led this counteroffensive. Employing Zouave tactics, the troops advanced, alternating between rushing forward and dropping to the ground. By 5:30 p.m., Wallace's forces had successfully reclaimed the lost ground. By nightfall, the Confederate troops were pushed back to their original positions. Grant, preparing for the next day's assault, overlooked the need to secure the escape route initially opened by Pillow.

In the midst of these fierce engagements, John A. Logan, a key figure in the Union army, was gravely injured on February 15. His valor and contributions in the battle were later recognized with a promotion to brigadier general in the volunteer army.

The aftermath of the battle at Fort Donelson was grim, with nearly 1,000 soldiers from both sides killed and around 3,000 wounded still on the field. Tragically, some of these wounded soldiers succumbed to the freezing temperatures, a number of Union soldiers having discarded their blankets and coats earlier.

Despite the day's heavy losses, Generals Floyd and Pillow sent an overly optimistic report to General Johnston in Nashville, claiming a significant victory. However, General Simon Bolivar Buckner presented a starkly different view, highlighting their dire situation, especially with the continuous influx of Union reinforcements. During a late-night council of war at the Dover Hotel, Buckner grimly predicted that if C.F. Smith launched another attack, their defensive stand could last only about thirty minutes, and the cost in casualties could be devastatingly high.

The possibility of a large-scale escape was slim, as most river transports were occupied ferrying wounded soldiers to Nashville and unlikely to return in time. Floyd, concerned about being indicted for his alleged corruption as Secretary of War under President Buchanan, hastily relinquished his command to Pillow, who then passed it on to Buckner. Buckner agreed to stay and surrender the army. Pillow escaped by boat, while Floyd departed the following morning on a steamer with his Virginia infantry. Disgusted by this display of desertion, Nathan Bedford Forrest adamantly refused to surrender and led approximately 700 cavalrymen out of the fort, evading capture.

On the morning of February 16, Buckner reached out to Grant, requesting a truce and terms for surrender. Expecting leniency due to their past friendship, Buckner was met with Grant's stern, uncompromising stance. Grant's infamous reply, which earned him the nickname "Unconditional Surrender," reflected his resolve against the Confederate rebellion.

Despite Buckner's personal humiliation and the strategic blow to the Confederacy, Grant showed a moment of courtesy by offering financial assistance to Buckner, which was declined. The Confederate defeat was significant: over 12,000 men captured, substantial artillery and equipment lost, and control of the Cumberland River conceded, leading to Nashville's evacuation. This victory at Fort Donelson marked the first of three major Confederate army surrenders orchestrated by Grant during the Civil War.

The captured Confederate soldiers, numbering over 7,000, were transported to various prison camps in the North, including Camp Douglas in Chicago and Camp Morton in Indianapolis. Buckner himself was detained at Fort Warren in Boston until his exchange in August 1862. This decisive Union victory at Fort Donelson was a critical moment in the Civil War, profoundly impacting both military and political dynamics.

Battle of Valverde

In the tense winter days of mid-February 1862, Brigadier General Henry Hopkins Sibley, leading a Confederate brigade, inched perilously close to the Union stronghold of Fort Craig, halting his march a mere fifteen miles to the south on the evening of February 13th. Sibley, a seasoned tactician, quickly assessed the robust defenses of Fort Craig and deemed a direct assault too risky. Instead, he masterfully arrayed his troops in a strategic line over the ensuing three days, aiming to entice the Union forces into a more vulnerable, open-field confrontation. However, Colonel Edward Canby, commanding the Union forces, harbored deep reservations about the combat readiness of his largely volunteer soldiers and chose to remain fortified within the safety of the fort's walls, frustrating Sibley's plans.

The impasse could not last. The Confederates, grappling with dwindling rations, faced the stark reality of their situation. A strategic pivot was necessary. On February 18th, a council of war convened under Sibley's leadership reached a bold decision: the army would ford the Rio Grande, strategically repositioning itself on the river's eastern banks. Their objective was audacious - to sever the vital communication line between Fort Craig and the Union headquarters in Santa Fe, just six miles to the north at the Valverde ford.

By February 20th, under the concealment of undulating hills and the river's meandering course, the Confederate army found itself stealthily positioned opposite Fort Craig. Colonel Thomas Green, a figure of Confederate valor, endeavored to mount artillery on the dominating heights overlooking both the river and Fort Craig. But Canby, ever vigilant, had foreseen such a maneuver, thwarting Green's plans and relegating the Confederate troops to a parched encampment that night.

In a daring and unconventional midnight operation, Union Captain James Graydon launched a surreptitious attack. His plan involved mules, unassumingly loaded with barrels of gunpowder, their fuses lit, aimed at wreaking havoc within the Confederate lines. However, in an almost comical twist of fate, the loyal old army mules, perhaps sensing the danger, veered back towards the Union camp, detonating harmlessly away from their intended targets. The only casualties of this explosive escapade were the two mules themselves. Nonetheless, the ensuing chaos had an unexpected benefit for the Union: a panicked stampede of Confederate beef cattle and horses, desperately needed for sustenance and mobility by Green's troops, inadvertently found refuge within Union lines.

As dawn broke on February 21, Brigadier General Henry Hopkins Sibley initiated a critical phase of his campaign. He dispatched a vanguard, spearheaded by the valiant four companies of the 2nd Texas Mounted Rifles, under the seasoned command of Major Charles Pyron. Their objective was clear: to reconnoiter the strategic Valverde ford, a crucial crossing point on the Rio Grande. In a calculated move, Sibley ordered the 4th Texas Mounted Rifles, led by the astute Lieutenant Colonel William Read Scurry, to trail closely behind Pyron's contingent. The remainder of Sibley's brigade lingered in the camp, poised to follow as the situation developed.

Meanwhile, the Union forces, ever watchful, had been tipped off by their scouts about this Confederate thrust towards the north. Reacting swiftly, Colonel Edward Canby deployed a versatile force amalgamating infantry, cavalry, and artillery, entrusting its command to the capable Colonel Benjamin S. Roberts of the 5th New Mexico Infantry. The diverse composition of Roberts' force, while offering a balance of strength, inadvertently slowed their march. In a tactical adjustment, Major Thomas Duncan was dispatched with the cavalry to hasten ahead and secure the ford, leaving the slower-moving infantry and artillery to follow.

In a parallel strategy, Canby bolstered this initial deployment with additional reinforcements from Fort Craig's garrison. He astutely assigned several companies of New Mexico volunteers with a dual mission: to closely monitor the Confederate maneuvers, and to employ guerrilla tactics to harass, flank, and delay the enemy, thereby disrupting their movements as effectively as possible.

The moment of confrontation neared as Pyron's Confederate troops reached the eastern banks of Valverde ford. They were met with a daunting sight: Union forces, already entrenched, blocking their intended path. Faced with this challenge, Pyron urgently signaled for reinforcements from the 4th Texas. Meanwhile, his men skillfully utilized an old riverbed, transforming it into a formidable defensive position. Despite their numerical superiority, the Union cavalry, perhaps underestimating the strategic advantage held by Pyron's position, deployed in a skirmish line rather than launching a full-scale offensive to dislodge the Confederates. This decision, potentially a tactical misstep, constrained the Union artillery to the opposite, western bank of the Rio Grande, limiting its effectiveness in the unfolding battle scenario.

As the sun rose higher in the sky on that fateful day, Lieutenant Colonel William Read Scurry, with a determined resolve, arrived at the battleground with his regiment. He deftly positioned his troops to the right of Major Charles Pyron's forces, while artfully placing the regimental artillery on the Confederate left flank. Despite their swelling numbers, the Confederates faced a significant disadvantage: their armaments, consisting predominantly of short-range shotguns and pistols, proved ineffectual against the Union positions situated some three hundred yards distant. Furthermore, their howitzers were frustratingly out of range to counter the Union artillery ensconced on the far riverbank.

At Fort Craig, Colonel Edward Canby, sensing the escalating intensity of the battle, decisively ordered the bulk of his garrison to march towards Valverde, leaving a contingent of militia to secure the fort. Upon his arrival, Canby strategically relocated most of his command, including the artillery, to the eastern bank of the Rio Grande. He wisely left the First and Second New Mexico Volunteers, commanded by Colonel Kit Carson and Colonel Miguel Piño respectively, on the western bank as a strategic reserve.

The unfolding afternoon saw the arrival of the remainder of Sibley's Confederate force, notably the 5th Texas Mounted Rifles led by Colonel Thomas Green and a battalion of the 7th Texas Mounted Rifles under the command of Lieutenant Colonel John Sutton. Fatigued and parched, these reinforcements found themselves denied vital access to the river by the steadfast Union defense. Sibley, who had remained with the supply wagons during the morning's developments, made a crucial command decision, entrusting the brigade leadership to Colonel Green. Green, in turn, delegated command of the 5th Texas to Major Samuel Lockridge.

Around 2:00 pm, under Green's authorization, a company of Confederate lancers boldly attempted a charge, targeting what they believed to be a less experienced New Mexico company positioned on the Union's extreme right flank. However, the Union soldiers, unexpectedly hailing from a seasoned Colorado company, held their ground with unwavering resolve, repelling the Confederate charge with formidable efficiency. This encounter resulted in severe losses for the lancers, with a devastating toll of twenty killed or wounded, and the majority of their horses incapacitated or slain. Despite this setback, the lancer company, undeterred and resolute, rearmed themselves with pistols and shotguns, and rejoined the battle with renewed vigor.

As the battle at Valverde ford intensified and the clock struck 4:00 p.m., the Union forces, under the command of Colonel Edward Canby, seemed to be gaining the upper hand. Canby, a tactician of considerable acumen, realized that a head-on frontal assault would likely end in failure. Instead, he crafted a strategy to outflank the Confederates by launching an assault on their left flank. To execute this plan, he ordered a strategic redeployment of one of his batteries to a position closer to the Confederate line. Additionally, he maneuvered several companies to bolster his right flank, notably including Colonel Kit Carson's First New Mexico Regiment, which crossed the river to form an integral part of the new line. This repositioning, while potentially advantageous, inadvertently created vulnerabilities in the Union center and left the battery on Canby's left exposed.

Sensing an opportunity to disrupt Canby's preparations, Confederate Colonel Thomas Green ordered Major Henry Raguet to launch an attack on the Union right. However, the Union forces, anchored by the resolute 1st New Mexico Regiment, repelled this assault with a combination of frontal fire and a strategic flank attack, pushing back the Confederates.

At this pivotal juncture, Green commanded the Confederate right wing, under Lieutenant Colonel William Read Scurry, to mount a daring charge against the Union center and the vulnerable battery on its left. This assault, comprising 750 determined men arrayed in three successive waves, was driven by more than just military strategy; the Confederates were desperately seeking access to the Rio Grande's water, blocked by Union forces. The ferocity of the Confederate charge sent shockwaves through the Union lines, causing over half of the battery's support troops to flee in disarray. During this tumultuous attack, Major Samuel Lockridge sustained mortal wounds.

In a countermove, the Union cavalry charged, but the main Confederate force, undeterred, continued to press their assault on Canby's left flank. This relentless push resulted in the capture of six Union artillery pieces and the fragmentation of the Union battle line, precipitating a disorderly and panic-stricken retreat by both regular troops and New Mexico volunteers.

As the Confederates appeared poised for another attack, a defining moment of battlefield civility occurred. Canby sent a white flag into the fray, requesting a truce to allow for the collection and care of the dead and wounded. Sibley, in a display of gentlemanly conduct amidst the chaos of war, agreed to the truce.

In the aftermath, Canby managed to rally his troops, although he faced the defection of about 200 New Mexico volunteers. Recognizing the untenable situation, he ordered a strategic retreat back to Fort Craig, effectively leaving the road to Santa Fe open for the Confederates. This series of maneuvers and fierce combat underscored the strategic and human complexities of the Civil War, highlighting both the harsh realities of warfare and moments of unexpected honor.

Battle of Island Number Ten

Island No. 10, an ephemeral gem in the Mississippi River, boasts a fascinating history and unique geographical features. This island, once the tenth landmark south of the Ohio River junction, emerged as an enlarged sandbar, stretching about 1 mile in length and 450 yards at its widest. Standing about 10 feet above low water, it was more than just a piece of land; it was a testament to the river's ever-changing nature.

More captivating than the island itself is the river's dramatic course around it. Island No. 10 sat at the southern end of a dramatic 180° clockwise turn in the Mississippi, immediately followed by a counter-clockwise twist. This double bend, known as the New Madrid Bend, remarkably leaves the river almost parallel to its original course but shifted west by about 8 miles. The tightness of these turns is striking – the distance from one end of the bend to the other is a mere 9 miles by air, or 12 miles following the river's channel.

Across from New Madrid, Missouri, on the Kentucky and Tennessee shore, lay the area known during the Civil War as Madrid Bend. The town of New Madrid, lending its name to the bend, sits at the northern apex of this serpentine river path.

Behind Island No. 10, the mainland was a gateway to Tiptonville, Tennessee, accessible by a solitary road. This region, a blend of lakes, sloughs, and swamps, was nearly impenetrable, with the nearest high ground almost 10 miles east. The notable Reelfoot Lake, stretching up to 40 miles long and 10 miles wide in places, transformed dramatically with the seasons. Its northern end neared Tiptonville in low water, but in spring floods, it extended well beyond the bend.

This geographic complexity made Island No. 10 seemingly impregnable from a land assault via Tennessee. However, this also meant that the only escape or reinforcement route was the Tiptonville road.

The Missouri side of the river presented a different landscape. Though higher than the Tennessee side, it didn't offer the significant height advantage seen in other Confederate defenses. At high water, the river banks, about 30 feet above low water, didn't provide a commanding position over the river, unlike previous battles where shore-based guns played a crucial role.

The early stages of the Civil War in the Western theater were marked by a whirlwind of command changes within the Confederate forces, creating a complex web of leadership that often makes pinpointing responsibility for specific actions challenging. Central to this narrative is New Madrid, Missouri, a pro-Southern stronghold. It was under the jurisdiction of the Confederate Department No. 2, initially commanded by Major General Leonidas Polk. Brigadier General Gideon J. Pillow, one of Polk's subordinates, brought the strategic significance of the New Madrid Bend to the forefront.

Responsibility for fortifying the bend, however, didn't fall to either Pillow or Polk. Polk delegated this task to army engineer Captain Asa B. Gray, who struggled with inadequate resources. In a pivotal shift on September 15, General Albert Sidney Johnston superseded Polk, with the latter retaining a subordinate role. Like Polk, Johnston showed little active interest in Island No. 10.

The scenario transformed with the arrival of General P.G.T. Beauregard to command the Army of the Mississippi in early February. Beauregard, becoming Johnston's de facto second-in-command, immediately grasped

Island No. 10's strategic value, ordering the relocation of troops from Columbus to fortify it. However, his failing health prevented him from taking direct command. During his recovery, Beauregard, along with Johnston, was preoccupied with the upcoming Battle of Shiloh.

Major General John P. McCown then took the reins as the local commander at Island No. 10, a role he maintained until the Union Army captured New Madrid. On March 31, 1862, Brigadier General William W. Mackall replaced him.

Throughout these shifts, Flag Officer George N. Hollins led the Confederate Navy's vessels on the Mississippi River. His role was complicated by the river spanning two military departments, requiring collaboration with multiple commanders.

On the Union side, command structures were also evolving, but with less impact on strategic outcomes. From late February 1862, the Army of the Mississippi was under Major General John Pope. Initially part of the Department of the Missouri and later the Department of the Mississippi, both under Major General Henry W. Halleck, these changes were more about organization than strategy.

In this theater, the Union's naval forces, the Western Gunboat Flotilla, played a crucial role. Commanded by Flag Officer Andrew Hull Foote, a US Navy captain, the flotilla was organized under the U.S. Army, making Foote subordinate to Halleck.

The Union's Anaconda Plan, masterminded by General in Chief Winfield Scott, gained significant public attention and alerted the Confederate government to the potential threat of a naval invasion along the Mississippi River. In a strategic response, the Confederates established a network of defensive positions along the river, including Fort Pillow near Memphis and extensive fortifications in Columbus, Kentucky. Both were crucial in the defense strategy concerning Island No. 10.

The construction of defensive batteries around Island No. 10 started in mid-August 1861, under the direction of Captain Asa B. Gray. The initial focus was a battery on the Tennessee shore, about 1.5 miles above the island. Known as Battery No. 1 or the Redan Battery, it was strategically positioned to control the approach to the bend, forcing incoming vessels to face its guns for over a mile. However, its effectiveness was limited due to its low-lying, flood-prone location. The project's momentum was hindered when Major General Leonidas Polk shifted his attention to capturing and fortifying Columbus. Consequently, work on Island No. 10 proceeded slowly, suffering from a lack of resources and manpower.

The significance of the New Madrid Bend escalated in early February 1862, following the Union's capture of Fort Henry and Fort Donelson. Columbus found itself isolated and vulnerable to Union forces moving from the Tennessee River to the Mississippi. To prevent the loss of the garrison and its equipment, General Beauregard ordered a discreet withdrawal from Columbus. The relocation commenced on February 24, with troops from Columbus beginning to arrive at Island No. 10. Two days later, the island's new commander, Brigadier General John P. McCown, arrived and immediately focused on fortifying the position from Battery No. 1 to Point Pleasant, recognizing the heightened strategic importance of the area.

Under the leadership of Brigadier General John P. McCown and with sufficient resources at his disposal, the Confederate forces transformed Island No. 10 and the surrounding mainland into a significant barrier for any naval force attempting to navigate past it. By mid-March, a formidable array of artillery was in place: five batteries with 24 guns on the shore above the island, 19 guns across five batteries on the island itself, and the nine-gun floating battery New Orleans anchored at the island's western end. Additionally, two forts were established at New Madrid: Fort Thompson to the west, armed with 14 guns, and Fort Bankhead to the east, near St. John's Bayou's confluence with the Mississippi, equipped with 7 guns.

The Confederate Navy also played a vital role in bolstering this defensive position. Flag Officer George N. Hollins commanded a squadron of six unarmored gunboats stationed between Fort Pillow and Island No. 10. The armored ram CSS Manassas was initially intended for this location but was rendered unsuitable due to the shallow waters and was subsequently sent back to New Orleans after sustaining damage.

On the Union side, preparations for the New Madrid assault began even before Columbus was evacuated. Major General John Pope, commanding the Union Army of the Mississippi, started assembling his forces at Commerce, Missouri, on February 23, 1862. Breaking from the customary winter hiatus, Pope mobilized his 10,000-strong army, improving roads for their march. The army reached New Madrid on March 3, but was not immediately ready to challenge the Confederate fortifications. Anticipating a siege, Pope secured heavy artillery reinforcements, which arrived on March 12.

The Union naval forces, led by Flag Officer Andrew H. Foote, were initially delayed in joining the operation. The damages sustained at Fort Donelson were still under repair. However, by March 14, Foote's gunboats, though not fully combat-ready in his view, were dispatched from Cairo. The Union fleet was further strengthened with the addition of 14 mortar rafts, each equipped with a 13-inch mortar. These mortars, commanded by Army Captain Henry E. Maynadier, operated as a semi-autonomous unit, enhancing the Union's capacity to lay siege to the Confederate defenses.

Determined to avoid a costly frontal assault on the Confederate forts at New Madrid, Major General John Pope devised an alternative strategy. He dispatched a brigade under Colonel Joseph B. Plummer, who later became a Brigadier General, to take control of Point Pleasant, Missouri. Located on the river's right bank, almost directly opposite Island No. 10, Point Pleasant was a strategic position. Plummer's brigade faced resistance from Confederate gunboats but soon adopted a tactic of withdrawing out of range when the gunboats appeared, only to return once they departed. They successfully occupied Point Pleasant on March 6, enduring three days of shelling from the boats. During this time, the Confederate Army remained within their fortifications, offering no assistance to Flag Officer George N. Hollins.

The arrival of the siege guns on March 12 caught both McCown and Hollins off guard, paralleling the unexpected winter advance of Pope's army. These guns effectively blocked the river for the unarmored Confederate gunboats and hindered the movement of reinforcements from Island No. 10 to the artillery units at New Madrid.

On March 13, the Union's large guns commenced bombardment of the New Madrid defenses, maintaining fire throughout the day. McCown, anticipating that Pope would engage in a systematic assault on his forts and recognizing the depleted state of his artillery forces, decided not to wait for the inevitable. On the night of March 13-14, he ordered the evacuation of the town and its forts. A heavy rainstorm concealed their movements, allowing the withdrawal to proceed smoothly. Despite some confusion, most of the troops were successfully relocated, although they had to spike and abandon the guns in the forts.

In the aftermath of New Madrid's fall, several units from the bend area were repositioned to Fort Pillow, almost 70 miles south by air, but nearly double that distance following the river's course. McCown was succeeded in command at the island by Brigadier General William W. Mackall. Although this change might appear as a demotion due to McCown's performance at New Madrid, he was actually promoted to major general.

The Union's siege of Island No. 10 commenced on March 15 with the arrival of gunboats and mortars. Major General John Pope, stationed in New Madrid, and Flag Officer Andrew H. Foote, positioned upstream of the bend, faced strategic coordination challenges due to their separation by the island.

Their approaches to the operation differed from the outset: Pope favored immediate action, while Foote preferred a gradual subjugation through bombardment.

Foote's strategy was further complicated by unclear and sometimes contradictory directives from Major General Henry W. Halleck, who was preoccupied with preparations for the Tennessee River campaign leading to the Battle of Shiloh. Early on, around March 17, Pope suggested that a few gunboats attempt to bypass the Confederate batteries, allowing Union forces to cross the river and encircle the garrison. Foote, however, was cautious, fearing the capture of a gunboat by the Confederates could pose a significant threat to Northern cities along the Mississippi and its tributaries. His judgment was possibly influenced by a lingering wound from Fort Donelson, causing him ongoing pain and mobility issues.

The ensuing two weeks saw intermittent action, predominantly long-range bombardments from the mortars, with occasional responses from Confederate batteries. The mortars, initially expected to be highly effective, fell short of these expectations, inflicting minimal damage on the enemy. A notable incident occurred on March 17 when a gun aboard the USS St. Louis exploded, resulting in casualties among the crew.

Following Foote's refusal to send gunboats past Island No. 10, a member of Pope's staff proposed the construction of a canal to circumvent the Confederate batteries. Though completed in two weeks, the canal was too shallow for gunboats. Nevertheless, it proved beneficial for the movement of transports and supply vessels, allowing Pope to rely less on land-based supply lines.

Persisting in his request for a gunboat to support his planned river crossing into Tennessee, Major General John Pope prompted Flag Officer Andrew H. Foote to hold two councils of war among his captains. The initial council on March 20 reaffirmed Foote's reluctance to risk running past the batteries.

However, a subsequent message from Major General Henry W. Halleck, urging Foote to assist Pope, led to another council on March 29. This time, Commander Henry Walke, captain of the USS Carondelet, volunteered for the risky mission. Preparations for the journey included covering the Carondelet with rope, chain, and assorted materials, attaching a coal barge for additional protection, and rerouting her steam exhaust to reduce noise. The Carondelet awaited a suitably dark night for her covert passage.

To minimize risk, a combined force of sailors and soldiers from the 42nd Illinois Infantry, led by Colonel George W. Roberts, neutralized Battery No. 1 on April 1 by spiking its guns. On April 2, a concerted attack by the flotilla damaged the floating battery New Orleans, causing it to drift out of action. Favorable conditions on April 4, including a moonless night and a thunderstorm, allowed the Carondelet to proceed undetected until she neared Confederate Battery No. 2. Despite a brief flare-up from her smokestacks, she successfully navigated past the batteries with minimal damage. Two nights later, the USS Pittsburg followed suit.

With the gunboats past the Confederate defenses, Pope could safely transport his army across the river without fear of Confederate naval interference and suppress enemy fire during the landing. On April 7, Pope executed his plan, using the gunboats to neutralize the batteries at Watson's Landing, his chosen attack site. The troop transports then crossed the river unopposed.

Brigadier General William W. Mackall, realizing his untenable position, ordered his mainland troops to move towards Tiptonville. Pope, informed by his scouts of this movement, redirected his forces to intercept them. The ensuing chase, rather than a battle, saw Mackall's forces hindered by Union gunboat interference, allowing Pope's army to reach Tiptonville first. Trapped and facing inevitable defeat, Mackall surrendered.

Simultaneously, the demoralized garrison at Island No. 10 also capitulated to Flag Officer Foote and his gunboats. This series of events effectively opened the Mississippi River up to Fort Pillow, marking a significant Union victory in their river campaign.

Battle of Pea Ridge

The Confederate strategy during the winter of 1862 was a daring and ambitious endeavor, crafted with the grand vision of reshaping the Civil War's landscape. Their goal? To sweep through Missouri with a bold northern advance, conquer the pivotal city of St. Louis, and seize control of the critical gateway to the West. This move was not just about gaining a strategic stronghold; it was about dominating the bustling commercial hub and the vital arteries of the Mississippi and Missouri Rivers. Such a victory would not only bolster the Confederacy's position in the war but also cement its influence over crucial transportation and trade routes.

At the heart of this grand plan stood Confederate Major General Earl Van Dorn, driven by a clear understanding of the strategy's immense significance. For Van Dorn, this wasn't merely a military campaign; it was a chance to etch his name in the annals of Southern history and possibly tilt the war towards Confederate victory. His words, "I must have St. Louis... Then Huzza," echoed the high stakes and his unyielding determination.

Missouri, a state teetering on the edge of North and South, became the focal point of this winter campaign. Its political, economic, and military importance was undeniable to both the Union and the Confederacy. Guarding the western boundary of the Confederate States, Missouri was a linchpin in maintaining the delicate balance of power. The Mississippi River, with its crossings and ferries, was more than a waterway; it was the lifeline connecting the eastern and western segments of the Confederacy. Its control was essential for sustaining commerce and movement of resources.

The prize was St. Louis, a city that symbolized and potentially secured the Confederacy's hold over the border state of Missouri. More than just a strategic location, St. Louis was a bustling industrial and commercial nucleus, standing at the confluence of the nation's two great rivers. Its capture would have been a triumph for the Southern cause and a testament to the audacity and ambition of General Van Dorn and his forces.

General Earl Van Dorn of Mississippi embodied the quintessence of boldness and aggression. A product of West Point, his military pedigree was established through valiant services and multiple injuries in the Mexican-American War of 1846-48, and engagements against Native American tribes in the southwest. Van Dorn rose to command the Confederate forces in Arkansas, succeeding Sterling Price after his retreat from Missouri in the winter of 1861-62. Demonstrating his strategic acumen, Van Dorn united Generals Sterling Price and Ben McCulloch under a daring vision to reclaim Missouri for the Confederacy, persuading even General Albert Sidney Johnston, who oversaw all Confederate forces west of the Appalachians, of the viability of his ambitious plan.

Van Dorn's vision extended beyond the mere recapture of Missouri. His grand strategy aimed to reshape the Civil War's course. He envisioned a northerly advance into Missouri, capturing St. Louis, and thereby reinstating Confederate control. The next phase of his strategy was to pivot eastward from St. Louis, cross the Mississippi River, and launch a surprise attack on Major General Ulysses S. Grant's Union forces in Tennessee. This move was intended to trap Grant's forces between Van Dorn's and Johnston's, potentially leading to a critical Confederate triumph in the West.

This envisioned scenario would have placed Grant in a precarious position, potentially overwhelmed and encircled in southern Tennessee. Van Dorn and his troops would assail from the north and northwest, with additional

Confederate forces attacking from the south and east. However, this grand plan never materialized. Instead, Van Dorn's forces encountered a significant setback at Pea Ridge, halting their march towards Missouri and the envisioned encirclement of Union forces in Tennessee.

Van Dorn's force, numbering approximately 16,500, included divisions under Price and McCullough, along with 2,000 to 3,000 Native American troops, predominantly Cherokees. These Native American allies joined the Confederacy in hopes of better treatment and the possibility of achieving independent status within the Southern Confederacy, including retaining their slaves. They faced about 10,000 Union troops led by General Samuel R. Curtis, another West Point graduate and Mexican-American War veteran, who had previously served as an Iowa Congressman.

In early 1862, Missouri's allegiance to the Union was uncertain. Although General Sterling Price's Confederate forces had initially triumphed at Wilson's Creek in August 1861, they were subsequently driven out of Missouri that winter. Yet, Union control remained tenuous, given the state's pro-slavery factions. Control over Missouri was pivotal, both militarily and politically, and was of utmost importance to both President Abraham Lincoln and Confederate President Jefferson Davis. Van Dorn's and Johnston's plans to press Grant from multiple directions hinged on the success of Van Dorn's Missouri campaign and the defeat of the Union troops barring the way to St. Louis. However, Confederate ambitions and Van Dorn's quest for glory were thwarted on March 7 and 8, 1862, by Union forces at the Battle of Pea Ridge/Elkhorn Tavern.

The Battle of Pea Ridge/Elkhorn Tavern, fought in the early stages of the American Civil War, holds a crucial place in the annals of the conflict, particularly in the Western Theater. While its significance was somewhat eclipsed at the time by the iconic naval engagement between the Monitor and the Merrimack (CSS Virginia) at Hampton Roads on March 9, 1862, the implications of Pea Ridge were profound both politically and militarily. This

Federal victory solidified Union control over Missouri, enabling it to serve as a strategic base for subsequent campaigns into Arkansas. More importantly, it disrupted the ambitious Confederate plan orchestrated by Generals Van Dorn and Johnston, which aimed to encircle and defeat Ulysses S. Grant's forces in Tennessee. This disruption set the stage for the consequential Battle of Shiloh in April.

The winter of 1861-1862 had been particularly harsh for Confederate forces in the West. The Union, under Grant's command, posed an escalating threat along the Tennessee and Mississippi Rivers. Grant's successful assaults on Forts Henry and Donelson in February led to the Confederate evacuation of Nashville and marked a significant shift in control over Kentucky and most of Tennessee to Union hands. Confederate General Albert Sidney Johnston faced the additional woes of combat losses and disorganized retreats, leaving his forces fragmented and vulnerable to the advancing Federals, including Brigadier Generals Don Carlos Buell and John Pope.

In Missouri, Confederate morale had plummeted from the highs following their victory at Wilson's Creek in August 1861. Federal forces, initially marshaled by Major General John Charles Frémont and later commanded by Brigadier General Samuel R. Curtis, had effectively driven Sterling Price's Confederate troops southward out of Missouri. By late February 1862, Johnston's positions to the east of the Mississippi were collapsing, and the Confederate stronghold west of the river had been pushed back to the Missouri-Arkansas border.

In early March 1862, Confederate forces, bolstered by optimism, advanced north from Arkansas towards Missouri. Major General Earl Van Dorn led a formidable force of approximately 16,500 men. This force was a composite of the remnants of Major General Sterling Price's units, which had been defeated and driven south from Missouri, Brigadier General Ben McCulloch's troops, who had achieved victory at Wilson's Creek, and a contingent of 2,000 to 3,000 Native American warriors from the Five Civilized Nations in the

Indian Territory, now united and poised to change the tide of the war in the West.

General Earl Van Dorn demonstrated both political acumen and military foresight in the lead-up to the Battle of Pea Ridge. His first major achievement was securing the endorsement of General Albert Sidney Johnston to pursue an ambitious campaign through Missouri, aiming to capture the key city of St. Louis for the Confederacy. Equally significant was his success in uniting two prominent Confederate commanders under his leadership: Sterling Price, known for his independent command aspirations, and Ben McCulloch, celebrated for his victory at Wilson's Creek. This unification formed a formidable Confederate force, numbering 16,500, surpassing the 11,000 Union troops under Brigadier General Samuel R. Curtis in the region.

Van Dorn's strategic vision for reclaiming Missouri involved a bold maneuver: advancing north from Arkansas, then veering west to outflank the Union forces, sever their supply lines, and attack from behind. This plan was not just about Missouri; it was a precursor to a larger scheme Van Dorn envisioned against Grant's forces east of the Mississippi, following his projected triumph in St. Louis.

The march began on March 4, 1862, amidst challenging conditions with heavy snowfall and blizzard-like weather. The arduous journey through the Boston Mountains tested the resolve of Van Dorn's troops. Meanwhile, anticipating the Confederate advance, Curtis moved his Union forces southward to confront the threat.

Curtis, aware of his numerical disadvantage, strategically positioned his forces along Little Sugar Creek, near Elkhorn Tavern in Leetown. His right flank, the target of Van Dorn's intended outflanking maneuver, was bolstered by the natural barriers of Elkhorn Mountain and Pea Ridge. This position, reinforced by the creek and the surrounding terrain, provided a strong defensive setup for the Union troops.

Upon encountering the Union positions on the evening of March 6-7, 1862, Van Dorn recognized that a stealthy bypass of Curtis's forces was impractical. He resolved to engage Curtis directly, capitalizing on his numerical superiority and the static nature of the Union entrenchments. The same terrain that lent protection to the Union right flank also offered Van Dorn an opportunity to obscure his movements west of the Union lines.

Van Dorn's confidence was further boosted on March 6 by a minor skirmish in which his advance guard engaged and overcame a small Federal detachment led by Brigadier General Franz Sigel. Although Sigel retreated, losing a few hundred men, the encounter had limited strategic impact since Sigel was primarily focused on joining the main body of Union troops.

In a daring move following the encounter with Sigel's detachment, General Earl Van Dorn planned to circumvent the entrenched Union positions by leading his Confederate troops along the Bentonville Detour during the night of March 6-7. This maneuver aimed to position the Confederates behind the Union lines, effectively neutralizing the advantages of the Federal entrenchments and their strategic placement behind Little Sugar Creek. Van Dorn's strategy involved using the divisions under Generals Price and McCulloch in a pincer movement, attacking the Union flanks from the rear in a surprise double envelopment. This tactic promised to trap the outnumbered Union forces with no avenue for escape.

However, this bold strategy was not without its ironies. Firstly, the Southern troops, split into two wings for the attack, would find themselves in an unusual position: north of their Union adversaries, launching a southern assault. Secondly, in his eagerness to cut off the Union forces from their supply lines, Van Dorn inadvertently severed his own lines of communication and supply from Arkansas. This oversight left his troops without easy access to their supply train, positioned in front of the Federal entrenchments.

The Battle of Pea Ridge/Elkhorn Tavern commenced on March 7, 1862.

Brigadier General Samuel R. Curtis had consolidated his forces, now numbering around 10,500 after the skirmishes on March 6, in a well-chosen defensive position along Little Sugar Creek, with the natural barrier of the creek and the protection of Pea Ridge behind them. Curtis, characterized by a traditional military approach, prepared his troops for defense, anticipating Van Dorn's offensive. Despite his old-school tactics, Curtis displayed remarkable adaptability later in the battle, countering the Confederate envelopment strategy and judiciously deploying his reserves at a critical moment, thereby securing a Union victory.

Initially, Van Dorn appeared confident of success. With numerical superiority and the element of surprise on his side, he maintained the illusion of presence in front of the Union lines on the night of March 6-7 while maneuvering his troops to the rear of the Federal position. He directed Price's divisions to undertake a longer route to flank the Federal left (east) wing, while McCulloch's forces, composed of units from Arkansas, Texas, Louisiana, and Native American warriors, were assigned a shorter route to position themselves behind the Federal right (west) wing. This coordinated movement was intended to create the envisaged double envelopment, propelling the Confederate forces to victory and paving the way for a march towards St. Louis.

By the morning of March 7, Curtis realized the absence of Confederate forces from their previous positions. Initially uncertain of their whereabouts, he soon received reports from his scouts of Confederate troops moving through the high ground along Pea Ridge, heading towards his rear. The challenging terrain and winter conditions had slowed down the Confederate advance during the night, causing delays in their assault positioning just miles behind the Union lines.

Faced with the unexpected Confederate maneuver, Brigadier General Samuel R. Curtis had several options, including a retreat across Little Sugar Creek or withdrawal toward Arkansas or Missouri. However, Curtis chose to confront the challenge head-on. He ordered his army to perform an about-face, a maneuver fraught with difficulties. Such a reversal can disorient troops, as familiar positions and directions are reversed, potentially leading to confusion. Despite these challenges, Curtis and his officers successfully executed the turn, maintaining order and discipline within their ranks.

By 10:30 a.m., as Confederate forces under General Sterling Price advanced down the Telegraph Road and approached the Union positions near Elkhorn Tavern at the eastern end of Pea Ridge, Union forces led by Colonel Eugene Asa Carr were prepared. Initially, Carr's men launched an attack against the numerically superior Confederate troops but were soon overwhelmed by the intensity of the Confederate attack. Carr, showing resilience, reorganized his forces multiple times, forming new defensive lines and requesting reinforcements from Curtis. The area around Elkhorn Tavern became the epicenter of fierce fighting on March 7.

Simultaneously, the Confederate wing under General Ben McCulloch engaged the Union's left (western) flank near Leetown. Curtis had tasked Colonels Peter Osterhaus and Jefferson Davis (not the Confederate president) with defending this position. Like their counterparts at Elkhorn Tavern, these Union forces were ready to confront the advancing Confederates but soon found themselves heavily outnumbered and struggling to maintain their position.

Throughout both flanks of the battle, the Confederates leveraged their numerical superiority, fielding approximately 16,500 men and 60 artillery pieces against the Union's 11,000 soldiers and 50 guns. The battle, particularly in its early stages near the western wing, often resembled an extended artillery duel. Despite the Union forces' tenacious defense, the Confederates initially gained the upper hand in these artillery exchanges, pressing hard against the Union lines without breaking them.

Curtis faced the urgent task of reinforcing both flanks: Carr's position near Elkhorn Tavern on the right (east) and the Osterhaus/Davis front near Leetown on the left (west) at the base of Pea Ridge. Osterhaus, in particular, was in a precarious situation, having lost ground and military equipment. Brigadier General Franz Sigel was dispatched to bolster Osterhaus's position. Meanwhile, Carr's forces were steadily pushed back from Elkhorn Tavern by Price's relentless assaults. Despite the intense pressure, neither Union flank succumbed to the Confederate advances.

The tide began to turn in favor of the Union forces, largely due to the passage of time and two critical tactical errors made by Confederate General Earl Van Dorn earlier in the engagement.

Firstly, the Confederate forces found themselves critically low on ammunition. Van Dorn's earlier decision to bypass the Union lines had inadvertently placed his supply lines behind the enemy, leaving his troops without easy access to much-needed ammunition. The supplies were now on the south side of Little Sugar Creek, separated from the Confederate forces by the challenging terrain and the entrenched Union army.

Secondly, the Confederate troops were reaching their physical limits. They had endured several days of marching through harsh winter conditions and challenging terrain, without adequate rest or food. Their night march on March 6-7, intended to position them for a surprise attack on the Union rear, had instead led them to face a well-prepared and resolute Union front. The Confederates, expecting to confront a surprised and overwhelmed enemy, met instead a determined force ready to fiercely defend every inch of ground.

Compounding these difficulties, the Confederate forces faced setbacks in their ranks. Their Native American allies, initially successful against the Osterhaus/Davis divisions on the western flank, refrained from further direct assaults after their initial engagement, eventually withdrawing from the battle. This decision was guided by their reluctance to engage in frontal assaults against fortified positions, a common tactic in Civil War battles.

Additionally, the loss of McCulloch and his senior officers proved devastating, particularly on the western side of Pea Ridge. McCulloch's death was a significant blow to the morale of his troops, and the absence of key leadership created a critical gap in command.

On the eastern flank near Elkhorn Tavern, Price's men faced formidable resistance from a Union force half their size. Van Dorn, positioned with Price's units, grew increasingly desperate as the day wore on. In a bold but risky move, he ordered a late afternoon assault on March 7, despite the exhausted state of his troops and the critical shortage of ammunition. The Confederate artillery managed to inflict significant damage on Union positions, but the relentless assault forced Carr to establish yet another line of defense in an effort to repel the advancing Confederate forces.

As dusk settled on March 7, Brigadier General Samuel R. Curtis's strategic patience began to yield dividends. While Colonel Eugene Asa Carr's situation at the Union right (east) was precarious, Curtis sensed a weakening in the Confederate threat on his left (west). He sent his reserve division under Brigadier General Alexander Asboth to bolster Carr's position, enabling them to establish a robust fourth defensive line. The exhausted Confederates, having expended their last reserves of energy in the day's assaults, succumbed to fatigue and rested on the battlefield as night fell.

Throughout the night, Curtis, who had judiciously conserved his reserves during the previous day's battles, now correctly assessed that the Confederate forces were severely drained. He relied on the advantages of interior lines, disciplined maneuvering, and the valor of his troops, who had withstood a day of relentless assaults despite being outnumbered and outgunned. Curtis reinforced his right flank, anticipating further action near Elkhorn Tavern.

The Confederate forces, split between Price's contingent on the Union right and the remnants of McCulloch's forces on the Union left, had drawn closer together during the day's engagements. Curtis, noting their defensive posture and inwardly curved lines, surmised that the Confederates were unlikely to initiate offensive actions the next day. He shifted Jefferson Davis' division to join forces with Carr and Asboth on the right, while Sigel and Osterhaus held the left flank against the weary Confederate troops.

On March 8, the Federal troops started the day with a morale-boosting hot breakfast and the confidence gained from holding their ground against superior numbers. In contrast, the Confederates were low on both food and ammunition, diminishing their capacity for an effective offensive.

Van Dorn initiated the day's hostilities with an unfocused artillery barrage, more a test of Union resolve than a prelude to an assault. Recognizing his numerical advantage but also the previous day's toll on his troops, Van Dorn was reluctant to retreat but saw no clear path to victory. He nonetheless ordered another assault.

Curtis quickly discerned the waning strength of the Confederate artillery, particularly on the left. He commanded Sigel's artillery to advance, which significantly damaged the Confederate batteries. As the Confederate artillerymen retreated or lost their cannons, Union infantry advanced up the ridge, pushing the Confederates back. Energized by Sigel's success, the Union forces on the right mirrored the left's aggressive advance.

Curtis, maintaining command, ordered a coordinated assault, avoiding a disorganized charge. Sigel's forces on the left advanced eastward, converging with the right wing. Their combined assault reclaimed ground lost the previous day and forced the exhausted Confederates into a retreat along the entire front. The once-formidable Confederate force began to disintegrate, signaling a swift and somewhat anticlimactic Union victory.

For Van Dorn, the immediate concern was the disintegration of his forces. His men, demoralized and depleted, retreated chaotically. The Native American contingents dispersed into the wilderness, while the Confederate soldiers scattered in disarray, abandoning equipment and artillery in their haste to evade the victorious Union forces. Van Dorn managed to rally a small portion of his force and retreated back to Arkansas, but the majority of his troops dispersed, significantly impairing the Confederacy's military presence in the region for the foreseeable future.

Battle of Hampton Roads

In the dramatic days following the outbreak at Charleston Harbor, President Abraham Lincoln took a decisive step in the Civil War saga. On April 19, 1861, he announced a sweeping blockade of ports in the Confederate states. The tension escalated when Virginia and North Carolina joined the Confederacy, prompting Lincoln to extend the blockade to their ports as well. Meanwhile, in a bold move, local troops swiftly took control of the Norfolk area and the strategic Gosport Navy Yard in Portsmouth.

The scene at the Navy Yard was a mix of loyalty and conflict. Captain Charles S. McCauley, a Unionist, found himself paralyzed by the advice of his mostly secessionist subordinates. Despite orders from Secretary of the Navy Gideon Welles to relocate the ships, McCauley hesitated until April 20, when he ordered the scuttling of the yard's ships and the destruction of its facilities.

This act led to a fiery spectacle as at least nine ships were set ablaze, including the formidable USS Merrimack. Although the Merrimack was burned to the waterline, her engines remained largely intact. The Confederates, without firing a single shot, had captured the South's largest navy yard, the hull and engines of what would become an iconic warship, over a thousand heavy guns, and substantial gunpowder supplies.

The Confederacy's grip on Norfolk and Portsmouth's navy yard meant they controlled Hampton Roads' southern side. To protect the yard, they fortified positions at Sewell's Point and Craney Island. The Union, however, maintained control over Fort Monroe on the Virginia Peninsula and constructed Fort Wool on the nearby Rip Raps island, asserting their dominance over Hampton Roads' entrance.

This strategic positioning enabled the Union to effectively enforce the blockade initiated on April 30, 1861, severely limiting Norfolk and Richmond's access to the sea. The Union's formidable warships, protected by the guns of Fort Monroe and nearby batteries, held a firm stance in the roadstead, presenting a formidable challenge to the Confederacy. For most of the war's first year, the South struggled to counter this blockade.

The advent of steam propulsion marked a turning point in naval warfare, reigniting interest in armored warships. This interest wasn't new; armor experiments had been conducted during the Crimean War, just before the American Civil War. The British and French navies led the charge, each constructing their own armored ships. In 1860, the French Navy launched La Gloire, a groundbreaking ocean-going ironclad, and Great Britain wasn't far behind with the HMS Warrior, the first armor-plated, iron-hulled warship. Despite these advancements, the United States Navy remained skeptical about adopting this emerging technology.

The onset of the Civil War in 1861 changed the naval landscape. Confederate Secretary of the Navy Stephen R. Mallory, recognizing the limitations of the Confederacy in matching the Union's shipbuilding capabilities, saw armor as a game-changer. He envisioned a strategy not of quantity, but of quality — creating fewer ships that were superior in design and defense to those of the Union. To bring this bold vision to life, Mallory assembled a team of innovative minds, including John M. Brooke, John L. Porter, and William P. Williamson, who were instrumental in turning the idea of armored Confederate vessels into a reality.

Mallory's team faced a significant challenge in their quest for engines robust enough to power the heavy ironclads they envisioned. Their search across the South led them to realize that no existing facility could immediately meet their needs. The Tredegar Iron Works in Richmond, the most capable of them all, estimated a year to build such engines from scratch. It was then that Williamson proposed a clever solution: repurpose the engines from the Merrimack, a ship recently salvaged from the Elizabeth River. This idea was quickly accepted and further developed to modify their ironclad design to fit the Merrimack's hull, with Porter drafting the new plans for Mallory's approval.

By July 11, 1861, the innovative design was green-lit, and the team wasted no time in getting to work. They began by towing the Merrimack's charred hull to the graving dock that had survived Union efforts to destroy it. During its transformation, the vessel was equipped with a formidable iron ram and an impressive arsenal of 10 guns, including Dahlgren smoothbores and Brooke rifles, capable of piercing thick armor.

The Tredegar Iron Works was tasked with producing ammunition, focusing on explosive shells as they expected the CSS Virginia to primarily encounter wooden ships. The ship's armor, initially planned to be one inch thick, was significantly upgraded to double layers of two-inch plates, backed by a substantial 24 inches of iron and pine, creating a formidable defensive shell with 14 strategically placed gunports.

However, the ambitious nature of the project, coupled with the logistical challenges inherent in the Southern transportation infrastructure, led to delays. These setbacks pushed the launch of the CSS Virginia to February 3, 1862, with its commissioning occurring two weeks later.

The news that the Confederates were crafting an ironclad warship brought a wave of concern to the Union. Secretary of the Navy Gideon Welles, realizing the urgency of the situation, awaited congressional authorization to start building armored vessels. This approval came on August 3, 1861. Welles then formed a special commission, dubbed the Ironclad Board, comprising three experienced naval officers: Captains Joseph Smith, Hiram Paulding, and Commander Charles Henry Davis. Tasked with evaluating submitted designs, the board sifted through seventeen proposals, ultimately deciding to back three of them. The first to be completed, showcasing the most innovative design, was the USS Monitor, brainchild of Swedish engineer John Ericsson.

Built in Ericsson's Brooklyn shipyard, the USS Monitor was a marvel of naval engineering, boasting revolutionary design elements, particularly in armor and armament. Breaking from traditional warship design, which featured numerous smaller guns, Ericsson equipped the Monitor with just two large-caliber guns. He had initially hoped for 15-inch guns but settled for 11-inch Dahlgren guns due to availability issues. These were mounted in an innovative cylindrical turret, protected by thick iron armor and powered by a steam engine for rotation, a design allowing control by a single operator. Ericsson, cautious of the risks, instructed that only half the standard black powder charge be used in the turret to reduce the risk of explosions.

During trials, it was found that even with reduced charges, the Monitor's guns could penetrate armor plating, a capability that would prove crucial in battle. However, the ship's design had a notable drawback: the pilot house, positioned forward of the turret on the main deck, hindered the guns' forward firing capability and was somewhat isolated from the ship's main operations. Despite these challenges and its late start, the Monitor was completed just days before its Confederate counterpart, the Virginia.

The Confederate naval command structure during the Civil War was notably unconventional. Lieutenant Catesby ap Roger Jones, instrumental in transforming the Merrimack into the Virginia, was notably disappointed when he wasn't appointed as her captain. Instead, he served as the executive officer. Normally, a captain from the Confederate States Navy, chosen through a strict seniority system, would lead such a ship. However, Secretary Mallory, seeking a more aggressive leader, preferred Franklin Buchanan. To bypass the seniority issue, Mallory appointed Buchanan as the flag officer overseeing Norfolk and the James River defenses, thereby giving him de facto control over the Virginia's movements. Consequently, the Virginia entered battle technically without a captain.

On the Union side, the North Atlantic Blockading Squadron was commanded by Flag Officer Louis M. Goldsborough. He had planned for his frigates to engage the Virginia in a strategic crossfire. However, this plan failed when four of his ships ran aground in the constrained waters of the roadstead, one intentionally. During the actual battle, Goldsborough was absent, coordinating with the Burnside Expedition in North Carolina. This left command to his second-in-command, Captain John Marston of the USS Roanoke. As Roanoke was among the ships grounded, Marston's influence on the battle was minimal, and his role is often overlooked in historical accounts.

The historic battle commenced on the morning of March 8, 1862, with the formidable CSS Virginia leading the charge into Hampton Roads. Captain Buchanan was eager to engage in combat. Accompanied by the Raleigh and Beaufort from the Elizabeth River, the Virginia was soon joined by the James River Squadron, comprising Patrick Henry, Jamestown, and Teaser. Their approach was marked by an early setback when Patrick Henry sustained damage from Union fire at Newport News, causing a temporary retreat for repairs before rejoining the fray.

At that time, the Union fleet in the roadstead included five warships, namely the sloop-of-war Cumberland, the frigate Congress, anchored near Newport News, and the sail frigate St. Lawrence, steam frigates Roanoke and Minnesota, positioned near Fort Monroe, along with the storeship Brandywine. The appearance of the Virginia prompted these Union ships to mobilize, but soon, St. Lawrence, Roanoke, and Minnesota found themselves grounded, rendering them largely ineffective in the ensuing battle.

The CSS Virginia set her sights on the Union squadron, initiating the battle with an exchange of fire between the Union tug Zouave and the Confederate Beaufort, though this initial skirmish had little impact. The real action began when Virginia came into close range of Cumberland, effortlessly deflecting the Union ship's gunfire with her iron armor. Some shots from Cumberland managed to lightly damage Virginia, but they were largely ineffective.

In a bold maneuver, Virginia rammed Cumberland below the waterline, causing the Union ship to sink rapidly while still engaged in combat. This tragic moment resulted in the loss of 121 seamen, with the total casualties nearing 150 due to the wounded.

The ramming nearly spelled disaster for Virginia as well. Her bow ram became lodged in Cumberland's hull, and as the Union ship began to sink, it threatened to drag the Confederate ironclad down with it. A precarious moment ensued when one of Cumberland's anchors hovered over Virginia's foredeck, posing a risk of sinking both vessels. Fortunately for Virginia, she managed to break free, albeit with her ram breaking off in the process.

After the engagement with the Cumberland, Captain Buchanan directed the CSS Virginia's firepower towards the Congress. Anticipating a fate similar to the Cumberland's, Lieutenant Joseph B. Smith, commanding the Congress, grounded his ship in shallow waters. However, the James River Squadron, under John Randolph Tucker's command, had arrived to reinforce Virginia in the attack. After enduring a relentless assault for an hour, the severely damaged Congress was forced to surrender.

During the evacuation of Congress's crew, a Union battery on the shore opened fire on the Virginia. In response, Buchanan ordered a barrage of hot shot – red-hot cannonballs – against the Congress. This action set the Congress ablaze, and by midnight, the flames reached her ammunition magazine, causing a catastrophic explosion that sank the ship, resulting in over 110 casualties and numerous injuries.

Meanwhile, Virginia had not emerged from the battle unscathed. Her smokestack was heavily damaged by fire from the Cumberland, Congress, and Union shore troops, which significantly reduced her speed. Additionally, two of her guns were disabled, several armor plates were loosened, and there were casualties among her crew, including Buchanan, who was injured by a rifle shot.

The James River Squadron then shifted its focus to the Minnesota, which had run aground after leaving Fort Monroe to engage in the battle. Virginia, despite her damages, joined in the attack. However, due to her deep draft and the receding tide, she couldn't get close enough to be effective, and the onset of darkness hampered the squadron's ability to aim properly. The attack was consequently postponed, with Virginia retreating to Confederate-controlled waters for the night, planning to resume the offensive the following day.

This series of events marked the United States Navy's most significant defeat until World War II and sent shockwaves through Washington. Panic set in, with Secretary of War Edwin Stanton voicing fears that Virginia could attack coastal cities and even threaten the White House. Secretary of the Navy Welles, however, reassured the Cabinet of their safety, pointing out Virginia's inability to navigate the Potomac River and informing them of the Union's own ironclad, the Monitor, which was en route to confront the Virginia.

During the lull in battle, both sides took the opportunity to regroup and prepare for the next day's confrontation. The CSS Virginia landed her wounded, including Captain Buchanan, and underwent swift repairs. With Buchanan incapacitated, command for the following day's action fell to his executive officer, Lieutenant Catesby ap Roger Jones. Jones, matching Buchanan in aggressiveness, geared up for the battle's renewal. Meanwhile, the Union ironclad USS Monitor, under the command of Lieutenant John L. Worden, arrived at Hampton Roads. The Monitor's deployment was a strategic move to shield the Union fleet and thwart the Virginia's threat to

Union cities. Worden was specifically instructed to defend the grounded USS Minnesota, positioning the Monitor protectively nearby. Captain Gershom Jacques Van Brunt of the Minnesota expressed relief at the arrival of this formidable ally.

At dawn on March 9, 1862, the Virginia, accompanied by the James River Squadron, set out from Sewell's Point to target the Minnesota, still stuck. However, they were confronted by the Monitor, an unfamiliar sight to the Confederates, initially mistaken for a floating boiler from the Minnesota. It quickly became evident to Jones that a battle with this peculiar adversary was inevitable.

The Virginia initiated the battle, firing the first shot at the Monitor, but missing and hitting the Minnesota instead. The Minnesota responded with a broadside, marking the start of an intense and prolonged engagement. Captain Van Brunt, prepared for the clash, recounted, "All hands were called to quarters, and when she approached within a mile of us I opened upon her with my stern guns and made a signal to the Monitor to attack the enemy."

After hours of intense combat at close quarters, the CSS Virginia and the USS Monitor found themselves in a stalemate. The armor on both vessels held up remarkably well, partly due to limitations in their offensive capabilities. Virginia's Captain Buchanan hadn't anticipated battling another ironclad and was thus armed only with explosive shells, not armor-piercing ammunition. On the Monitor's side, the standard service charge of 15 pounds of powder for its guns was insufficient to penetrate the Virginia's armor. Post-battle tests revealed that the Dahlgren guns could have been effectively and safely used with charges up to 30 pounds. During the battle, the Monitor almost breached Virginia's armor, but a misfire thwarted this opportunity. In a twist of fate, Virginia ran aground at 10 AM, becoming vulnerable to Monitor's fire, yet she managed to break free and reengage.

During the engagement, Acting Master Louis N. Stodder and officers Stimers and Truscott were strategizing inside the Monitor's gun turret when it took a direct hit. The impact knocked Stodder unconscious, making him the first casualty of the battle. He was replaced by Stimers after regaining consciousness an hour later.

The battle reached a turning point when a shell from the Virginia struck Monitor's pilot house, showering fragments into Lieutenant John L. Worden's eyes, temporarily blinding him. This forced the Monitor to withdraw temporarily, leaving Lieutenant Samuel Dana Greene to assume command and reenter the battle. During this brief withdrawal, the crew of the Virginia mistakenly believed their adversary was retreating. Although the grounded Minnesota remained a target, the receding tide made her inaccessible, and the Virginia, too, required extensive repairs.

Believing he had secured a victory, Jones ordered the Virginia back to Norfolk. Simultaneously, the Monitor, rejoining the battle, found the Virginia withdrawing. Greene, under orders to prioritize the Minnesota's safety and not to risk his vessel unnecessarily, chose not to pursue.

Over the course of the two-day battle, the USS Minnesota unleashed a formidable barrage, firing a total of 78 rounds of 10-inch solid shot, 67 rounds of 10-inch shells with 15-second fuses, 169 rounds of 9-inch solid shot, 180 9-inch shells with 15-second fuses, 35 8-inch shells with 15-second fuses, and using 5,567.5 pounds of service powder. The ship suffered casualties, with three crew members—Alexander Winslow, Henry Smith, and Dennis Harrington—losing their lives, and 16 others injured. From the Monitor's crew, Quartermaster Peter Williams received the Medal of Honor for his bravery during the confrontation.

Post-battle, the CSS Virginia underwent nearly a month of repairs and improvements in drydock, emerging on April 4. Although Captain Buchanan, still recuperating, had hoped for Lieutenant Catesby ap Roger Jones to be his successor, the naval seniority system led to Commodore Josiah Tattnall

III's appointment. The Monitor, relatively unscathed, continued its service, although Lieutenant Samuel Dana Greene, like Jones, was replaced due to his youth, first by Lieutenant Thomas Oliver Selfridge Jr., and shortly thereafter by Lieutenant William Nicholson Jeffers.

By late March, the Union blockade was reinforced with retrofitted civilian vessels like the SS Vanderbilt, SS Arago, SS Illinois, and SS Ericsson, equipped with rams and some iron plating. Additionally, by late April, new ironclads like the USRC E. A. Stevens and USS Galena joined the blockade.

In the ensuing period, both sides sought to draw the other into a disadvantageous battle, but neither captain took the bait. Jeffers, in particular, was under strict orders not to risk the Monitor.

The demise of the Virginia came first. With Norfolk's strategic value diminished due to the unbroken blockade, plans were made to relocate her near Richmond. However, when Confederate General Benjamin Huger abandoned Norfolk on May 9 without Navy consultation, the Virginia found herself trapped. Unable to navigate the shallow James River, Tattnall chose to scuttle her rather than risk capture. She was set ablaze near Craney Island, burning for a day and night before her magazine detonated.

The Monitor's end came later that year. Ordered to Beaufort, North Carolina, for blockade duty, she encountered rough seas while being towed on December 31, 1862. Overwhelmed by the waves and with her engines extinguished, she sank, taking 16 of her crew with her, while the rest were rescued by the USS Rhode Island.

In the immediate aftermath of the Battle of Hampton Roads, both the Confederate and Union sides claimed victory, but these assertions, rooted in misinterpretations of each other's actions, are viewed by contemporary historians as misguided. The consensus among modern scholars is that the iconic clash between the Monitor and the Virginia ended in a draw. While the Southern fleet did inflict considerably more damage than it sustained, typically a marker of tactical victory, this did not translate into a strategic triumph. From a broader perspective, considering the loss of men and ships, the Union Navy faced a significant setback. However, the crucial blockade remained intact, suggesting that the Confederate assault ultimately failed to achieve its strategic objectives.

In the period following the battle, both Confederate and Union media seized the opportunity to claim victory for their respective sides. A Boston newspaper headline suggested a Union triumph by proclaiming, "The Merrimac Driven back by the Steamer!", while Confederate reports highlighted their initial success against the Union's wooden ships. These claims, though not fully accurate, served as morale boosters, tapping into the public's fascination with the groundbreaking ironclad ships.

Strategically, the battle's implications are still debated. The blockade not only continued but was strengthened, effectively containing the Virginia in Hampton Roads. This outcome is seen by some as a strategic victory for the Union since it neutralized a significant Confederate threat. However, Confederate proponents argue that the Virginia had a broader military impact beyond the blockade, particularly in the Tidewater Virginia region. Her presence alone effectively closed the James River to Union forces and imposed constraints on the Union Army's Peninsula Campaign under General George B. McClellan. McClellan's concerns about the Virginia interfering with his York River positions, though ultimately unfounded, influenced his strategic decisions until the destruction of the Virginia.

The Battle of Hampton Roads garnered significant attention from naval powers worldwide, marking a pivotal moment in naval warfare. The USS Monitor, emerging from this battle, became the prototype for a new class of warships known as monitors, symbolizing a fundamental shift in naval design. This class of warship, alongside the HMS Dreadnought, was so influential that their names were adopted for entire classes of subsequent vessels. The success of the Monitor inspired the construction of numerous similar vessels, including river monitors that played a crucial role in Civil War battles along the Mississippi and James Rivers.

In response to the Monitor's success, the United States quickly began constructing ten additional monitors based on an expanded version of Ericsson's design, known as the Passaic-class monitors. By the war's end, over 20 additional monitors had been built by the Union. Despite their effectiveness in river combat, these monitors had limitations in open seas due to their low profile and heavy turrets.

The "Monitor mania" spread internationally. Russia, concerned about the potential spread of the American Civil War to its territory in Alaska, quickly built ten sister ships following Ericsson's plans. This global fascination with the Monitor's design led to widespread adoption of revolving turrets in naval architecture, a feature that would eventually become standard in modern battleships.

The vulnerability of wooden hulls against armored ships, as demonstrated in the battle, caught the attention of naval powers like Britain and France, reinforcing their decision to transition to armored fleets. Another design aspect influenced by the battle was the incorporation of rams into hull designs, spurred by the ease with which the Virginia sank the Cumberland. The French armored ram Taureau, launched in 1863, was the first purpose-built ram in the modern era, with its armament primarily serving to pave the way for ramming attacks. This design feature persisted in naval architecture almost until the outbreak of World War I, illustrating the lasting impact of the Battle of Hampton Roads on naval warfare and design.

Battle of New Bern

New Bern, nestled on the southwestern bank of the Neuse River in North Carolina, presents a scene of historical significance and natural beauty. About 37 miles from where the river joins the expansive Pamlico Sound, the area is marked by its broad, navigable waters, once bustling with vessels during its colonial seaport days. By the Civil War era, although surpassed by Morehead City and Beaufort in seaport prominence, New Bern remained a crucial military site. The Atlantic and North Carolina Railroad, a vital artery connecting the coast to the interior, ran directly through this city. Significantly, at Goldsboro, this line intersected with the Wilmington and Weldon Railroad, a lifeline for the Confederate Army of Northern Virginia.

The landscape around New Bern is characterized by low, flat terrain, often interspersed with marshy areas. In 1862, this land was predominantly open pine forest, punctuated occasionally by low hills and deciduous woodlands, divided by meandering ravines. The Trent River, a notable waterway, forms a natural boundary to the south of New Bern. Slocum's Creek, another notable creek, was earmarked as the landing site for Federal forces during their assault.

The battle for New Bern unfolded primarily between the Trent River and Slocum's Creek. The strategically placed railroad, just a mile inland from the river, traversed this landscape on embankments and through cuts, eventually crossing the Trent River into the city. Parallel to this was a county road, unpaved in the style of the era, linking New Bern with Morehead City and Beaufort. This road, a silent witness to the Union soldiers' struggles, ran between the railroad and the river before intersecting the railroad track north of the battlefield, continuing northwest to cross the Trent River via a drawbridge.

After North Carolina seceded from the Union, its coastal defenses suffered due to the Confederate government in Richmond focusing more on other areas. Initially overseen by Secretary Leroy P. Walker and later by Judah P. Benjamin, the War Department prioritized the Virginia campaigns, especially protecting Richmond, the Confederate capital. Consequently, when Union forces captured Hatteras Island in August 1861, North Carolina had only six infantry regiments to defend its entire coastline.

The Confederacy had organized its coastal defenses into distinct districts for better command and control. The northern sector, stretching from near Cape Lookout to the Virginia border, was under Brig. Gen. Daniel H. Hill's command. He established defensive lines around New Bern, with a key focus on two primary lines south of the city, across the Trent River. The first line, known as the "Croatan Works," comprised breastworks near Otter Creek, extending inland towards the railroad. Closer to New Bern, about six miles away, stood another significant defense line anchored by Fort Thompson on the river. This fort, equipped with 13 guns, including three facing landward, was a formidable obstacle.

In addition to these fortifications, Hill ordered the construction of river batteries to thwart naval attacks. The Confederates also obstructed the river with two barriers. The first, located a mile and a half below Fort Thompson, was a double row of submerged piles topped with iron and backed by 30 torpedoes, each loaded with around 200 pounds of powder. The second barrier, opposite Fort Thompson, comprised a line of hulks and chevaux de frise, designed to funnel ships under the fort's guns.

Hill anticipated reinforcements to strengthen his defenses, but he was reassigned to Virginia before they arrived. His successor, Brig. Gen. Lawrence O'B. Branch, took over a restructured district extending from Cape Lookout to Pamlico Sound's limits. The area from there to the Virginia border, including the strategic Roanoke Island, fell under Brig. Gen. Benjamin Huger, who was primarily concerned with defending Norfolk and its surroundings.

The Union Army, led by Brig. Gen. Ambrose E. Burnside's Coast Division, in collaboration with a Union gunboat flotilla from the North Atlantic Blockading Squadron under Flag Officer Louis M. Goldsborough, successfully captured Roanoke Island on February 7–8, 1862. This victory was swiftly followed by the Union gunboats eliminating the Confederate Navy's Mosquito Fleet in a strike on Elizabeth City. After these battles, Goldsborough departed for duties at Hampton Roads, leaving Commander Stephen C. Rowan in charge of the naval forces. These victories granted the Union uncontested movement in Albemarle and Pamlico Sounds, making every city and town within their reach, particularly New Bern, vulnerable to attack. Burnside quickly set his sights on capturing New Bern.

Despite the strategic importance of New Bern, the Confederate leaders in Richmond did little to reinforce its defenses. Even a month after the fall of Roanoke Island, no additional troops were sent to bolster New Bern's defenses. General Branch, the local commander, had roughly 4,000 troops at his command, fewer than the 6,130 he estimated necessary to defend the city effectively. Many of these troops were poorly equipped militiamen, and their numbers were often diminished by illness.

Facing this manpower shortage, Branch made the strategic decision to consolidate his defenses, focusing on the line at Fort Thompson and abandoning some of the extensive breastworks established by his predecessor. The Fort Thompson line, initially extending from the river to the railroad, ended near a brickyard, a key location in the upcoming battle. To mitigate the risk of being outflanked on firmer ground, Branch extended the line beyond the railroad, doubling its length and anchoring it in a swamp.

However, in his haste and due to a critical shortage of labor, Branch made a significant tactical error in the layout of the extended line. He incorporated a small creek into the defense, creating a dogleg at the center where the creek intersected the railroad, about 150 yards up from the brickyard.

On March 11, 1862, the soldiers of the Union's Coast Division embarked from Roanoke Island. The following morning, they set sail, accompanied by 14 Navy gunboats and their own gunboat. One Navy vessel was tasked with guarding the Pamlico River's mouth against rumored Confederate threats. The fleet navigated Pamlico Sound, entered the Neuse River, and anchored by Slocum's Creek at dusk. The infantry disembarked south of the Confederate forces at Fort Thompson, who numbered around 4,000 and were positioned behind makeshift defenses.

Aware of the Union's presence, Confederate General Branch immediately mobilized his troops. He dispatched Col. James Sinclair's 35th North Carolina Infantry to Otter Creek, instructing them to hinder enemy landings there. Colonel Zebulon Vance's 26th North Carolina was positioned in the Croatan work, while other units covered the river upstream, and reserves were stationed at the railroad and Beaufort road intersection.

At dawn on March 13, Union troops began disembarking, quickly overcoming a small Confederate force at the landing. Burnside spent the morning deploying men and equipment, including Navy and Army howitzers. Dense fog later hindered communication with the fleet, preventing the landing of additional artillery.

By noon, the Union soldiers started advancing towards Confederate lines, just as heavy rain began, turning roads into muddy quagmires. The 51st Pennsylvania Infantry was called in to assist the exhausted gunners with their howitzers, a task remembered as particularly grueling.

As the Union troops trudged forward, the gunboats moved ahead, bombarding potential Confederate positions. Mistaking this for a prelude to an assault on the Croatan work, Confederate Col. R. P. Campbell ordered a retreat to the Fort Thompson line. Consequently, the Union forces found the first Confederate breastworks deserted.

The Coast Division continued its advance, with Foster's Brigade (First) following the county road on the right, Reno's Brigade (Second) paralleling the railroad on the left, and Parke's Brigade (Third) trailing behind the First. They engaged enemy pickets about a mile and a half from the Confederate-held Fort Thompson line. As daylight faded, Burnside ordered a halt, arranging the brigades for overnight bivouac: the First Brigade near the road on the right, the Second near the railroad on the left, and the Third behind the First. The howitzers arrived at the scene around 3:00 a.m. the following morning.

On the morning of March 14, engulfed in dense fog, General Burnside commanded his forces to advance towards the Confederate positions. Lacking full knowledge of the Confederate deployment, the Union believed the enemy line stretched from the river to the brickyard. Based on this assumption, Burnside directed the First Brigade to confront the enemy's left flank, while the Second Brigade aimed to flank the right at the brickyard. The Union positioned eight howitzers across the county road, with the Third Brigade held in reserve.

From the naval front, Commander Stephen C. Rowan's gunboats provided support, bombarding the Confederate positions. Although the forests obscured their view, this naval gunfire unsettled the North Carolinians, but its imprecision led Burnside to eventually request a change in the gunboats' firing direction.

Meanwhile, Confederate General Branch had his forces ready along the line. From Fort Thompson on the left to the brickyard on the right, he positioned the 27th, 37th, 7th, and 35th North Carolina regiments, with the 33rd Regiment in reserve. The 35th's right flank, fortified at a brickyard kiln, faced the First Brigade of the Union Army, comprising the 25th, 24th, 27th, and 23rd Massachusetts regiments, and the 10th Connecticut, aligned from the river to the railroad. The Union's howitzers, dragged along with great effort, were positioned along the Beaufort Road in the center of this line.

Unbeknownst to the Federal forces, the Confederate line extended beyond the railroad, manned by the 26th North Carolina regiment and a few cavalry companies. A militia battalion, poorly trained and equipped with shotguns and hunting rifles, covered a vulnerable gap in the line near the railroad. To reinforce this weak point, Branch ordered a two-gun battery of 24-pounders to the kiln, but they were not operational at the onset of the attack.

On the Union's left, General Reno, unaware of the Confederate line's extension, ordered a portion of the 21st Massachusetts to assault the brick kiln, supported by the 9th New Jersey and the 51st New York, with the 51st Pennsylvania in reserve. Although initially successful, the Union forces soon faced intense fire from the entire Confederate line and were compelled to retreat.

In a decisive moment, General Burnside called his Third Brigade to reinforce General Reno's Second Brigade. The 4th Rhode Island, replacing the ammunition-depleted 21st Massachusetts, was led by Colonel Isaac P. Rodman. Encouraged by Lieutenant Colonel William S. Clark of the 21st Massachusetts, Rodman independently decided to launch another attack on the brick kiln. This charge, informed by a clearer understanding of the enemy's position, proved successful. The 4th Rhode Island captured nine brass field pieces and outflanked the Confederate entrenchments.

The Confederate line quickly crumbled. The breakdown began with the inexperienced militia fleeing, leaving gaps that exposed adjacent units. Despite General Branch's orders to send reserves to fill the breach, they arrived too late. As the Union forces pressed on, each Confederate regiment withdrew in succession to avoid being overrun. Branch ordered a retreat, which quickly turned into a chaotic rout. The retreating Confederates hurried across the Trent River into New Bern, hastily burning the bridge behind them, trapping some of their own forces and destroying the railroad bridge with a fire raft.

Meanwhile, Commander Rowan's naval forces advanced up the river, supporting the ground troops. They incurred minor damage bypassing the lower barrier and positioned themselves to shell Fort Thompson. When the fort was evacuated, they passed the second barrier and headed towards New Bern. As Branch had ordered all Confederate river batteries to retreat, their guns were spiked and abandoned. The Union fleet shelled the retreating Confederate troops in New Bern, preventing them from regrouping. The Confederate forces couldn't regroup until reaching Kinston.

The battle resulted in 64 Confederate deaths, 101 wounded, and 413 captured or missing, compared to the Union's 90 killed, 380 wounded, and one captured.

Following the battle, New Bern fell under Union control and remained so for the rest of the Civil War. Burnside promptly shifted focus to capturing the port at Beaufort, defended by Fort Macon. The Union forces quickly occupied Morehead City and Beaufort, with the siege of Fort Macon commencing shortly thereafter. This victory marked a significant turning point for the Union in controlling North Carolina's coast. New Bern's capture not only held strategic importance but also provided space for refugee camps, housing, and employment, further bolstering the Union's foothold in the region.

First Battle of Kernstown

Winchester, Virginia, stood as a pivotal crossroads in the heart of the lower Shenandoah Valley. This bustling hub of trade and transportation, nestled in northern Virginia, was more than a mere town—it was a strategic chessboard in the American Civil War. Its streets intertwined with the Valley Turnpike, the region's sole macadamized artery, while the nearby Potomac River whispered tales of commerce along the Chesapeake and Ohio Canal.

But with the dawn of 1861, Winchester transformed. No longer just a center of trade, it became a vital strategic stronghold. Its position was a double-edged sword: for the North, it was a gateway to protect Washington D.C. from Confederate advances; for the South, it was a stepping stone for an audacious thrust across the Potomac into Maryland.

Winchester's geographical quirks added to its allure. Travelers venturing north paradoxically moved 'down' the valley, following the southeast-northwest flow of the rivers. This was more than just a curiosity—it was a tactical quirk that shaped military strategies.

Enter Confederate Major General Thomas Jonathan "Stonewall" Jackson, a mastermind tasked with controlling this pivotal region in the spring of 1862. Guided by the strategic insights of General Robert E. Lee, advisor to Jefferson Davis, Jackson's mission was clear: bind the Union forces under Major General Nathanael Prentice Banks in the valley's embrace, preventing them from bolstering their comrades in eastern Virginia.

The stage was set for a daring gamble. Outnumbered by Banks, Jackson spied a fleeting chance as the Union troops retreated towards Winchester. Banks, intent on reinforcing Major General George Brinton McClellan's impending assault on Richmond, was unwittingly walking into Jackson's trap. In this chess game of war, Winchester was the board, and its fate hung in the balance, influenced by the cunning, courage, and decisions of those who dared to maneuver its pieces.

In the unfolding drama of the 1862 Valley Campaign, Brigadier General James Shields, a fiery Irishman serving under Banks, emerged as a key player. His bold leadership on March 23 would deliver to Jackson his sole setback that spring and summer. Yet, in this defeat, Jackson's strategic acumen shone brighter than Shields' momentary triumph. This was the backdrop to the Battle of Kernstown, the first of two pivotal clashes in this area, setting the stage for a pivotal season of conflict.

Jackson, a man of deep convictions, held a strong aversion to combat on Sundays. On March 22, 1862, his army was encamped at Strasburg, Virginia, under a cloudy sky. That morning, forces from the 2nd and 27th Virginia Infantry joined Colonel Turner Ashby, venturing towards Winchester to gauge the Union's strength. Meanwhile, Jackson's remaining troops enjoyed a brief respite, cooking breakfast and preparing for the march towards Winchester, 20 miles north along the Valley Turnpike.

Meanwhile, 13 miles north of Jackson's camp, the determined Colonel Ashby encountered the Union division led by Brigadier James Shields. However, Shields had been incapacitated by a Confederate artillery shell the previous day, leaving Colonel Nathan Kimball, an Indiana native, in command. Kimball, underestimating the Confederate threat, believed Ashby's cavalry to be the sole Southern presence in the area, unaware of the approaching 3,600 Confederate infantry.

Near the village of Kernstown, a settlement named after Adam Kern Sr., a 1766 immigrant to Frederick County from Pennsylvania, the Union forces were assembling. Kernstown, which grew around the "Great Wagon Road" (later the Valley Turnpike), was now the setting for a significant military encounter. Here, 7,000 Union soldiers, including five artillery batteries and 750 cavalrymen, were positioned strategically. Colonel Jeremiah Cutler Sullivan from Indiana led the Second Brigade to the east of the Valley Turnpike, with Kimball's First Brigade behind. In reserve, near Winchester's southern outskirts, stood Colonel Erastus Bernard Tyler from New York with his Third Brigade.

Back in Winchester, Brigadier General James Shields, nursing an injury, relayed orders to Colonel Nathan Kimball. Shields, confident in his directives, instructed Kimball to either drive away or capture the enemy, assuming they were facing merely Colonel Turner Ashby's reconnaissance unit. At 9:00 a.m., Colonel John Sanford Mason of the 4th Ohio Infantry was dispatched by Shields to scout ahead. He returned within the hour, mistakenly assuring the Union leadership that they were up against nothing more than Confederate cavalry. This led Major General Nathaniel Prentice Banks, commander of the Union V Corps, to conclude that Jackson wouldn't risk a confrontation, allowing Banks' other divisions to march eastwards through the Blue Ridge Mountains to join Major General Irwin McDowell for General George McClellan's campaign.

However, this assessment was a miscalculation. Mason's reconnaissance had failed to breach Ashby's cavalry screen, leaving the true Confederate strength hidden. While the Union forces believed the situation to be under control, the reality on the Valley Turnpike told a different story. Jackson's infantry, known for their swift marching, were closing in. Ashby, meanwhile, kept up his skirmishes with the Union soldiers, unaware of Jackson's erroneous belief that his forces outnumbered Kimball's.

Ashby's skirmishing continued into the next day. He positioned his horse-artillery, commanded by Captain Robert P. Chew, near Hoge's Run. Chew's crew prepared to fire with a long-range Blakeley rifle, a British-made artillery piece. Ashby's forces, including the 7th Virginia Cavalry, began moving towards Kernstown.

As Jackson's main force approached Kernstown in the early afternoon, they paused briefly in Bartonsville. Jackson initially planned to rest his troops, survey the Union lines, and prepare for battle the next day. However, observing his men's spirits and considering the Union's advantageous position on higher ground, Jackson decided to attack that day, setting aside his usual practice of avoiding combat on Sundays.

Jackson, responding to the call of duty, quickly formulated his attack plan. Notably, he did this without consulting Ashby, who was more familiar with the immediate tactical situation. By 1:30 p.m., Jackson had set his plan in motion, ready to challenge the Union forces in what would become a crucial encounter in the Valley Campaign.

Jackson, surveying the battlefield with a strategic eye, noticed the elevated terrain of Sandy Ridge to the west of his position. This ridge, running parallel to the Valley Turnpike, offered a tactical advantage: if seized, it could enable the Confederates to outflank the Union line, positioned on the opposing elevation of Pritchard's Hill.

In response, Jackson directed Colonel Jesse Spinner Burks' Brigade, stationed along the Turnpike, to assist Ashby. Concurrently, the brigades under Colonel Samuel Vance Fulkerson and the Stonewall Brigade led by Brigadier General Richard Brooke Garnett advanced towards the historic Opequon Church. As the Confederate forces approached this 18th-century landmark, symbolizing early European settlement in the Shenandoah Valley, they encountered Federal infantry and cavalry. Jackson swiftly ordered Captain Joseph Carpenter to deploy his artillery, swiftly dispersing the Union troops.

Clearing the area around the church, the Confederate troops veered left onto a country lane, with the 37th Virginia Infantry, hailing from Washington County, in the lead, followed by the 23rd Virginia Infantry from the capital region. After navigating through the woods, they emerged onto an open, unguarded field. Fulkerson, halting the advance, awaited further instructions, which soon arrived: form battle lines and silence a nearby Federal battery.

Fulkerson's brigade moved into action, tearing down a wooden fence to advance across the field towards the Federal artillery. As they charged, the 33rd Virginia, part of Garnett's command, initiated their attack. Across the field, atop Pritchard's Hill, the Union defense, including Lieutenant Colonel Philip Daum's 1st Ohio Artillery and infantry units from Ohio and Pennsylvania, braced for the Confederate onslaught. Some Union artillerists, initially shaken, were sternly rallied by their commanding officer.

As the Virginians charged, they were met with a barrage of small arms fire. Fulkerson's men, attempting to reach a tree line for cover, found themselves veering into an open meadow under intense fire. Fulkerson later described the Union firepower as overwhelming, even for seasoned troops. Having advanced half a mile and realizing the futility of taking the Union guns on Pritchard's Hill, Fulkerson decided instead to attempt a flanking maneuver, adapting to the challenging situation on the battlefield.

As the battle intensified, the Confederate formation took on a wedge shape. On one side, the artillery batteries of Captains Carpenter, McLaughlin, and Waters were positioned. On the other side stood Fulkerson's Brigade, while in the center were two regiments from Burks' Brigade and the entirety of the Stonewall Brigade under Garnett.

During a brief pause in the fighting, Jackson's aide, Alexander "Sandie" Pendleton, returned from scouting the Union position with alarming news: the enemy was strongly positioned and possibly numbered around 10,000. This contradicted Ashby's earlier assumption of facing only a small Union rearguard. Realizing the potential danger to his troops, Jackson's response was resolute and unflinching: "Say nothing about it, we are in for it," he declared, a statement that would later be recalled by Pendleton in a letter to his mother.

On the Union side, the realization dawned that they were facing more than just Ashby's forces. Kimball, understanding the advantage of his defensive position, prepared to counter the Confederate maneuvers. Despite his injury, Shields continued to direct reinforcements to support Kimball, including the 13th Indiana and 39th Illinois from Sullivan's "Second Brigade."

The battle reignited with the 27th and 21st Virginia Infantry engaging in a back-and-forth with Union forces, all under Jackson's watchful eye. As the Confederates attempted to flank the Union line, Kimball called in Colonel Erastus B. Tyler's brigade, which was positioned south of Milltown. Tyler's men, using Cedar Creek Grade Road to reach Sandy Ridge, advanced in column formation through the woods.

Tyler, leading his brigade, didn't form a battle line but instead charged forward with a command to "Charge Bayonets." The Union troops surged towards the 27th Virginia Infantry, which was sheltered behind a stone wall. To compensate for their limited numbers, the 27th Virginia, led by Colonel John Echols, stretched out their line, while Carpenter's artillery provided support. The Confederates not only fired at their adversaries but also taunted them, adding psychological warfare to the physical battle.

In the heat of battle, as Tyler's Union forces advanced, the leading regiments - the 7th Ohio and 7th Indiana - dropped to the ground in a sharp depression to minimize exposure to enemy fire. The air was filled with the deafening sound of Confederate gunfire, temporarily halting the Union advance. It took the efforts of line officers and sergeants to rally the troops and move them forward again, amidst the chaos and the unnerving whizz of bullets.

The Union charge was faltering. The 110th Pennsylvania, positioned further back in the column, was particularly affected, with an officer recalling how they broke ranks and scattered at the first sign of enemy fire.

Amidst this disarray, over 300 Pennsylvanians made an untimely retreat, further disrupting the formation. Tyler, at the front, struggled to correct his tactical error as his troops neared within a hundred yards of the Confederate line. The confusion was exacerbated as not all of Tyler's men could hear his commands, resulting in a disjointed Union formation.

On the Confederate side, Colonel Echols' commanding presence provided stability to his outnumbered troops. However, as they began to run low on ammunition and face the pressure of the larger Union force, Echols was severely wounded and had to relinquish command to Lieutenant Colonel Andrew Jackson Grigsby. Echols' departure demoralized the 27th Virginia, causing them to start retreating.

As the 21st Virginia under Colonel John M. Patton joined the fray, bolstering the Confederate line, Tyler sought to outflank the Confederates. He deployed Colonel Joseph Thoburn and the 1st West Virginia, who dashed across open terrain towards another stonewall, aiming to flank the Confederate position.

Just as the Union forces neared their strategic objective, two Confederate regiments from Fulkerson's Brigade – the 23rd and 37th Virginia – emerged from their concealed position in the woods on Sandy Ridge. Their timely intervention provided crucial support to both the 21st and 27th Virginia Infantries. Despite being within range of the 7th Ohio's fire, Fulkerson's regiments miraculously avoided any casualties.

From their elevated position, the Confederate regiments commanded by Fulkerson had a tactical advantage, able to quickly respond to Union movements in the fields below. Reaching a crucial stonewall just before the Union troops, they used it as a platform to unleash a devastating volley of fire on the Union soldiers, who were exposed and vulnerable only forty yards away.

One Confederate soldier later reflected on the intensity of the engagement with a candid remark, suggesting that if he ever inflicted casualties during the war, it was likely in this fierce encounter.

Meanwhile, Colonel Joseph Thoburn, leading the Union charge, was hit by three bullets, one severely injuring his arm. Despite his wounds, he continued to direct his troops from a seated position. A few of his men managed to breach the wall but were quickly repelled by the 37th Virginia, which had been ordered to clear the Union soldiers from their position. The Union forces were ultimately pushed back, retreating towards the woods across the field they had charged over.

This intense skirmish, which seemed to last much longer to those involved, was in fact a brief but brutal ten-minute confrontation. By 4:00 p.m., the Confederate line on Jackson's left flank was composed of Fulkerson's troops on the left, followed by a gap, and then the 27th and 21st Virginia regiments positioned on Sandy Ridge, utilizing a stonewall for cover. Brigadier General Richard Brooke Garnett, arriving at Sandy Ridge, assessed the situation amidst the ongoing conflict, which included clashes between Sullivan's Union forces and Ashby's Confederate cavalry.

Garnett, after surveying the scene, directed the 33rd Virginia to hold position across an open field from where the 21st and 27th Virginia were engaged with Tyler's forces. He was uncertain if the Virginian regiments could repel the Union attack and was unaware of Fulkerson's successful counter against Thoburn's advance amidst the chaos of battle.

By 4:15 p.m., Garnett repositioned the 33rd Virginia to reinforce the right flank of the 21st Virginia. Simultaneously, the 4th Virginia, which had been exchanging fire from the safety of nearby woods, braved the sporadic shots from Tyler's retreating troops. Following Garnett's orders, they moved to occupy the gap, positioning themselves between the 27th and 23rd Virginia regiments. This maneuver strengthened the Confederate line, filling in the crucial gap and creating a more formidable defense against the Union forces.

The battlefield was set with approximately 1,700 Union soldiers from Tyler's Brigade facing off against 1,200 Confederates from Fulkerson's and Garnett's Brigades. As the late afternoon approached, the skirmish devolved into chaos. Amidst the roar of artillery, musket fire, and the indiscriminate fall of soldiers, the scene became a blur of confusion. Regimental commands on both sides were intermingled, exacerbated by Jackson's unorthodox tactic of reassigning regiments on the fly, often disregarding the established brigade structures.

Just before 5:00 p.m., additional Confederate forces arrived, including the 2nd Virginia and the Irish Battalion from Burks's Brigade, evening out the numbers to 1,700 on each side. Meanwhile, the Union side received a much-needed boost. Anticipating the need for reinforcements, Kimball had earlier sent for a brigade from Brigadier General Alpheus Williams's Division, which was initially headed east but was delayed by a broken bridge.

With reinforcements en route, Kimball focused on consolidating his control over the battlefield, ensuring smoother communication and gathering reports from the front lines near Sandy Ridge.

The intensity of the battle was described by Major Frank Jones of the 2nd Virginia as "the most terrific fire of musketry that can be imagined," lasting over an hour and a half. Pennsylvania, Indiana, and Ohio regiments clashed fiercely with their Virginian counterparts, while Jackson worked to strengthen his left flank with additional reserves.

These reinforcements included the 5th, 42nd, and 48th Virginia regiments. The 5th Virginia took a crucial position on the right of the stonewall, near the Valley Turnpike, while facing the threat of Union troops maneuvering on their flank. However, they were soon ordered to relocate to Sandy Ridge, positioning themselves in a strategic woodlot.

The 42nd Virginia, previously supporting Ashby on the right, was redirected to the left flank. They, along with two Confederate artillery units, mounted a vigorous defense of Sandy Ridge, providing cover for other units running low on ammunition to disengage.

Garnett, overseeing the battlefield dynamics, received reports of dwindling ammunition across his brigade. Faced with this critical situation, he made the decisive call for a strategic retreat. The Stonewall Brigade, along with the 21st and 27th Virginia, began to withdraw, marking a significant shift in the battle as the day drew to a close.

In another part of the battlefield, General Jackson was unaware that a significant portion of his infantry had been ordered to withdraw. Confronted with retreating soldiers, he demanded to know why they were falling back. Upon learning it was due to a lack of ammunition, Jackson's response was emphatic: "then go back and give them the bayonet." He even commandeered a drummer boy to rally the troops, but to no avail; the Confederate retreat continued.

This retreat left Fulkerson's right flank exposed. The Virginian regiments, which had been heavily engaged throughout the day, also began to abandon their positions. In the ensuing chaos, some Confederate infantry managed to evade Union cavalry by taking a route to the right, while others, less fortunate, were captured after heading left into the Federal horsemen.

Jackson, moving up the Valley Turnpike, eventually encountered Garnett and inquired about the retreat. Despite Garnett's insistence that reinforcements were imminent and that troops could still fight with bayonets despite the lack of ammunition, the retreat continued. This decision would later have significant consequences for both Garnett and Jackson, unresolved even by the time of Jackson's death in May 1863.

The battle's toll was heavy. Of the approximately 8,500 Union soldiers engaged, around 600 were casualties. Jackson's force of over 3,500 suffered over 700 casualties, including those killed, wounded, or missing. The Union, holding the field at the battle's end, could claim a tactical victory in terms of 19th-century warfare standards.

However, the impact of the Battle of Kernstown extended far beyond immediate military outcomes. It had significant strategic implications, affecting decisions in both Washington D.C. and Richmond. Jackson's presence in the Shenandoah Valley, as directed by Confederate General Joseph Eggleston Johnston, was intended to prevent Union forces from reinforcing McClellan. This strategy was based on the belief that Jackson's proximity to Winchester would deter Union troop movements. Johnston's dispatch to Jackson, sent just days before the battle, underscored the importance of Jackson's role in the valley to keep the Union army engaged and away from McClellan. Both Johnston and Jackson recognized that even the mere threat of Confederate activity in the Shenandoah Valley could influence Union military planning.

In the aftermath of the Battle of Kernstown, the Union soldiers found themselves immersed in a flurry of activity. Their days were filled with tending to the wounded, managing Confederate prisoners, and reflecting on the harrowing experience they had just endured. Officers busied themselves with strategizing the next moves and pondering the motives behind Jackson's decision to engage in battle. Was it possible that Jackson had more forces at his disposal than they had initially estimated?

Amid this bustle, David Hunter Strother, an illustrator and writer whose works would later be featured in Harper's Weekly, ventured to Sandy Ridge the day after the battle. His first-hand account paints a vivid picture of the aftermath: torn fences, artillery tracks, the occasional dead horse, and the tragic sight of soldiers' bodies, some gruesomely wounded, scattered across the battlefield.

Strother's exploration extended to the Confederate lines, where he encountered a concentrated area with forty Confederate bodies. Shockingly, most of them had been fatally shot in the head. This grim scene underscored the battle's ferocity and the high cost paid in human lives.

Meanwhile, Union Generals Shields and Banks were regrouping their forces in and around Winchester. They instructed General Alpheus Williams' Division, which had been moving east towards Berryville, to return. While two of Williams' brigades, led by Colonels Dudley Donnelly and George Gordon, rejoined Shields and Banks, the third brigade under Brigadier General John Joseph Abercrombie continued towards Manassas, eventually joining General McClellan's forces in the Tidewater region of Virginia. This brigade would be the only Union infantry from the Valley to reinforce the Army of the Potomac.

As Union forces reassembled in the Shenandoah Valley and Jackson received commendations from the Confederate Congress, the Battle of Kernstown gradually receded into the annals of history. But its impact was profound, marking the beginning of one of the most notable campaigns of the Civil War.

Jackson had laid the groundwork for what would become his most audacious and triumphant undertaking: the Shenandoah Valley Campaign of 1862. This campaign would not only demonstrate Jackson's military acumen but also significantly shape the course of the Civil War.

Battle of Shiloh

In the pivotal month of February 1862, Ulysses S. Grant, leading a determined Union army, clinched two landmark victories in the American Civil War – the Battle of Fort Henry and the Battle of Fort Donelson. These clashes, unfolding in Tennessee on the Tennessee and Cumberland Rivers, not only marked significant Union triumphs but also struck a strategic blow to the Confederacy. These rivers were not just waterways; they were lifelines, connecting Nashville's vital resources like its ironworks, agricultural heartlands, and status as a railroad hub and gunpowder production center. Grant's forces, bolstered by the formidable firepower of U.S. Navy gunboats – steam-powered, armored, and bristling with up to 13 artillery pieces – turned the tide in these battles. Grant's skill and success earned him a well-deserved promotion to major general, elevating him above most Western Theater generals, save for Major General Henry Halleck.

As spring approached, the Union's momentum surged. Troops marched into Savannah, Tennessee, on the Tennessee River, by March 11, gathering strength and numbers. Even as more Union forces, led by Don Carlos Buell, advanced from Nashville, Union strategists realized the need to consolidate their spread-out troops, choosing Pittsburg Landing as their focal point. Just nine miles upriver from Savannah, Pittsburg Landing offered a crucial route to Corinth, Mississippi. Near this strategic point lay Shiloh, a log church whose name, meaning "place of peace" in Hebrew, would ironically lend itself to one of the war's fiercest battles. The Shiloh battlefield, a triangle of woods, cotton fields, and peach orchards bordered by creeks and the river, was poised to become a historic site.

Meanwhile, the Confederate Army, reeling from their loss at Fort Henry on February 6, withdrew from Kentucky and parts of Tennessee. Nashville's last Confederate defenders retreated southward by February 23. General Albert Sidney Johnston, overseeing the Confederacy's Western Theater, made the contentious decision to abandon these areas. While Confederate politicians critiqued Johnston's actions, the troop consolidation further south, especially in Corinth, Mississippi, was a strategic necessity to counter the Union threat on the Tennessee River. Corinth, at the heart of a crucial rail network, became a rallying point for over 40,000 Confederate troops by the end of March.

The Union's strategy was clear: merge the armies of Grant and Buell and push south. Their goal was ambitious yet strategic - capture Corinth as a springboard for seizing Memphis, Vicksburg, and vast stretches of Confederate territory. Early April saw most of Grant's forces encamped near Pittsburg Landing by the river, with a division positioned downstream at Crump's Landing and the headquarters further north in Savannah. Buell's forces, on their way south from Nashville to Savannah, were instructed not to advance beyond Pittsburg Landing-Shiloh until the Union armies united.

On April 4, a brush with Confederate cavalry near Shiloh was noted by a Union patrol, but Union leaders didn't perceive it as a significant threat.

Conversely, Confederate leaders were acutely aware of their precarious position. Their forces, numbering 42,000 at Corinth with an additional 15,000 en route, were on the verge of being outnumbered by a potential Union force of 75,000. Opting for a bold move, they planned a preemptive strike on April 4, aiming to catch the Union Army off-guard before the second wave from Nashville could join. However, their 20-mile march north was marred by inexperience and adverse weather, leading to chaotic delays. By the afternoon of April 5, the Confederate Army finally took position, setting up camp on the southern side of the Union encampment.

Their tactical plan was to launch an assault on the Union's left flank, driving it towards the swampy terrain near Snake and Owl creeks. Meanwhile, Confederate forces along the Tennessee River were tasked with blocking Union reinforcements and cutting off supplies, aiming to create a decisive advantage in the impending confrontation.

On the early morning of April 6, a pivotal day in the Civil War, the Union forces under Grant were strategically positioned near Shiloh. Five of his six divisions were encamped from the Shiloh Church vicinity to the Tennessee River. Sherman's division, the first to arrive in Shiloh, was deployed near the main routes to Pittsburg Landing, with his brigades arrayed around the church. Colonel David Stuart's brigade anchored the Union's left flank near the Hamburg-Savannah Road, while Sherman's remaining brigades fortified the right near the Owl Creek Bridge and Pittsburg-Corinth Road. Between these positions lay Prentiss's division, with McClernand and Hurlbut's divisions stretched towards the river. W.H.L. Wallace's division was the closest to Pittsburg Landing. Lew Wallace's division, following a railroad raid in mid-March, was stationed at Crump's Landing, remaining vigilant due to nearby Confederate forces. Grant was further north at his headquarters in Savannah, with Nelson's division from Buell's army arriving there, though Buell's other divisions were still en route.

The Union camps at Shiloh were not set up defensively; no entrenchments were dug, as a battle was not anticipated in this area. Sherman and Prentiss's inexperienced divisions were at the forefront, nearest to Corinth. Despite a minor skirmish on April 4, only a few pickets were placed, indicating a low expectation of conflict. However, concerns grew when Confederate soldiers were reported near Shiloh. Colonel Everett Peabody, leading Prentiss's First Brigade, ordered a reconnaissance mission around midnight on April 5.

Major James E. Powell was tasked with leading three companies from the 25th Missouri Infantry and two from the 12th Michigan Infantry towards Seay Field, where the Confederate presence was noted. This decision, made without informing Prentiss, saw Powell's men advance southwest along a farm road towards the Pittsburg-Corinth Road.

In the early hours of April 6, a confrontation was brewing southwest of Powell's Union patrol, where the Confederate Third Brigade of Hardee's Third Corps, led by Brigadier General S. A. M. Wood, was positioned. Wood had deployed 280 skirmishers from Major Aaron B. Hardcastle's Third Mississippi Battalion, who were largely stationed in the southeast corner of James J. Fraley's cotton field, with additional pickets closer to Union lines. Around 5:00 am, these Confederate pickets engaged with Powell's men, retreating to their battalion after initial fire. As Powell's patrol approached within 200 yards of Hardcastle's main force, a more intense firefight erupted, marking the battle's commencement.

By 5:30 am, the noise from Fraley Field reached Confederate leaders, prompting General Johnston to order a general assault. Johnston directed Beauregard to coordinate reinforcements and supplies from the rear, while he himself moved to lead the frontline, effectively granting Beauregard battle control. On the Union side, Powell, falling back, alerted Colonel Peabody of facing a substantial Confederate force. Initially angered by Peabody's unauthorized patrol, which he saw as a breach of Grant's directives, Prentiss quickly realized the gravity of the situation and dispatched reinforcements. Despite Peabody's patrol inadvertently compromising the Confederate surprise, it crucially afforded the Union troops some preparation time.

However, not all Union commanders were immediately convinced of the attack. Sherman, for instance, remained skeptical until he was wounded and his orderly killed during a reconnaissance near Rea Field around 7:00 am.

The Confederate attack, initially planned as a surprise, was delayed. It took an hour post-Johnston's 5:30 am order for all Confederate troops to mobilize, and further time was lost in skirmishes near Seay Field, diminishing the impact of their surprise element. The Confederate line, spanning nearly three miles wide with the corps of Hardee and Bragg, faced organizational challenges. Beauregard's subsequent decision to extend the line with the corps of Polk and Breckinridge further weakened the assault's concentration. This led to a decision by corps commanders to divide battlefield control among themselves, resulting in a disjointed frontal assault. Johnston and Beauregard's failure to reinforce the east side meant they missed focusing on their primary objective of flanking the Union left.

In the early stages of the battle, Sherman and Prentiss led the first two Union divisions to face the Confederate onslaught, both of which were the least experienced in Grant's army. Sherman, despite initial lapses in preparation, rose to the occasion with remarkable composure and leadership, rallying his inexperienced troops amid intense artillery and frontal attacks by Hardee, Bragg, and Polk's corps. However, the inexperience of some units was evident, such as when a colonel from the 53rd Ohio Infantry Regiment panicked and urged a retreat, leading to a chaotic withdrawal by many in his regiment. Some soldiers from this regiment, maintaining their composure, later joined other units. Sherman eventually repositioned his division behind Shiloh Church, with support from McClernand's Third Brigade.

Prentiss, positioned northeast of Seay Field, faced severe challenges. His right flank, led by Peabody, was overwhelmed by two Confederate brigades. Peabody, despite being wounded multiple times, fought valiantly before succumbing to his injuries. By 8:30 am, the remnants of Peabody's brigade had been pushed back, and the Confederates overran his camp. On the eastern side, Prentiss's other brigade contended with brigades under Generals Gladden and Chalmers. Gladden was mortally wounded around 8:45 am, and despite heavy Confederate casualties, particularly from Union artillery, the Confederates advanced, capturing the 6th Division camp by 9:00 am. The sight of Union soldiers fleeing and the capture of Union camps emboldened the Confederates, who began looting, finding clothing, rifles, and food. This lack of discipline and looting disrupted the Confederate momentum, giving Prentiss a chance to retreat further north.

Meanwhile, Hurlbut, east of McClernand, had his brigades ready by 8:00 am. Upon learning of Sherman's dire situation, he sent his Second Brigade, led by Colonel James C. Veatch, to assist. Soon after, news of Prentiss's predicament reached him. Hurlbut advanced his remaining brigades south on the Hamburg-Savannah Road towards Wicker Field, only to encounter a wave of fleeing men from Prentiss's division. Unable to halt their retreat, Hurlbut positioned his brigades further south near a peach orchard, preparing to face the Confederate advance.

Grant was at his headquarters in Cherry Mansion, Savannah, enjoying breakfast when the distant rumble of artillery fire reached him. Nursing a leg injury from a horse fall, he was on crutches and anticipating the arrival of more of Buell's forces. Upon hearing the sounds of battle, Grant acted swiftly. He instructed Bull Nelson to march his division alongside the river to a point opposite Pittsburg Landing, preparing them for a ferry crossing to the battlefield. Grant then journeyed south on his steamboat, Tigress, first stopping at Crump's Landing to inform Lew Wallace to ready his division for movement. By around 9:00 am, Grant arrived at Pittsburg Landing, where he encountered retreating men. He promptly ordered a colonel to halt the stragglers, then rode inland, where he realized the scale of the Confederate attack was far greater than a mere skirmish. He immediately sent for Lew Wallace's division at Crump's Landing to join the fray.

On the Union side, Brigadier General W.H.L. Wallace's Second Brigade, under Brigadier General John McArthur, moved to fill a gap on the Union's left flank. This area was between Hurlbut's position near a peach orchard and Stuart's brigade at the extreme left. McArthur, with only two of his regiments and Battery A of the 1st Illinois Light Artillery, took his position. The rest of his forces were aiding Sherman and guarding the Snake River bridge.

Wallace's other brigades, led by Colonels Tuttle and Sweeny, positioned themselves near Duncan Field and the "Sunken Road," sandwiching between McClernand and Hurlbut's divisions. From 9:30 to 10:30 am, this area mainly witnessed artillery exchanges.

Meanwhile, on the Union's extreme left, Stuart's brigade initially dismissed the early morning musket fire as inconsequential until they heard distant artillery. At 9:30 am, Johnston, misinterpreting reports of Union movements on his right flank, responded by deploying two brigades from Bragg's Corps and calling up Breckinridge's Reserve Corps. They mistakenly targeted Stuart's Brigade's camp near Lick Creek. Stuart, positioned close to the Hamburg-Savannah Road, first faced artillery bombardment around 9:40 am, followed by an infantry attack twenty minutes later.

By 10:00 am, what remained of Sherman's division regrouped north of Shiloh Church, setting up near the crossroads of the Hamburg–Purdy and Pittsburg–Corinth Roads. By then, Sherman's Third Brigade, comprising three Ohio regiments, had disintegrated, with the last intact regiment fleeing the field. Colonel Jesse Hildebrand, the brigade's commander, stayed behind to assist McClernand's division as a volunteer aide. Sherman's First Brigade, under Colonel John A. McDowell, was isolated to the west on the Hamburg–Purdy Road. Colonel Ralph P. Buckland's Fourth Brigade, meanwhile, was fragmented and running low on ammunition.

Sherman consolidated his defense with the remaining forces, including Colonel Julius Raith's Third Brigade from McClernand's division, which had earlier reinforced his left flank. He also had the 6th Indiana Artillery Battery under Captain Frederick Behr and part of a battery from McClernand. For the first time, the Union army presented a continuous front, stretching from the remnants of Sherman's division, through McClernand, W.H.L. Wallace, remnants of Prentiss's division, Hurlbut, McArthur's brigade from W.H.L. Wallace's division, to Stuart's brigade from Sherman's division. Hurlbut was positioned near a peach orchard, Prentiss near the Sunken Road, and

W.H.L. Wallace adjacent to Duncan Field at the Sunken Road.

The Confederates renewed their assault on Sherman and McClernand at 11:00 am, with a force comprising parts of seven brigades. This attack proved costly for the Union: Colonel Raith was mortally wounded, and Behr's battery retreated after Captain Behr was killed. On the Confederate side, despite heavy losses, Wood's brigade managed to rout Colonel C. Carroll Marsh's brigade from McClernand's division. Wood's brigade also overcame Veatch's brigade, but in the process, Wood was thrown from his horse, rendering him temporarily incapacitated. His brigade subsequently became scattered and disorganized. By 11:20 am, the Confederates had control over the Hamburg-Purdy Road. However, the exhaustion and disarray among Confederate ranks allowed Sherman and McClernand to execute a strategic withdrawal about 200 yards north of the crossroads. Around 11:30 am, Sherman's isolated First Brigade, led by McDowell, successfully regrouped with McClernand's forces.

The Sunken Road, an old wagon track referenced as "an abandoned road" in the Official Records, stretched from Duncan Field to a peach orchard near the Hamburg-Savannah Road. Over time, erosion had created embankments along this track, varying from a few inches to reportedly as much as three feet. This natural trench, which gained the post-war moniker "Sunken Road," was a point of historical debate, with some historians questioning its extent of being sunken, as contemporary records and soldier accounts don't uniformly support this description. The area around Duncan Field, the Sunken Road, and the adjacent woods became a fiercely contested zone, later nicknamed the "Hornets Nest" by the Confederates due to the intensity of the fighting.

Prentiss began the day with 7,545 men. After sustaining casualties and desertions, his force dwindled to 600 men and parts of two batteries by the time he relocated near Barnes Field, close to the Hamburg-Purdy Road. Here, he positioned his troops alongside the divisions of W.H.L. Wallace and Hurlbut, forming a line along the Sunken Road. Grant, recognizing the critical nature of this position, bolstered Prentiss with an additional 600 soldiers from the recently arrived 23rd Missouri Infantry Regiment. During his visit to this 1,200-strong force, Grant's directive to Prentiss was clear: "hold at all hazards."

The Union troops along the Sunken Road benefited from natural cover provided by hickory and oak trees. The varied weaponry of the Union troops and the use of fences for shelter contrasted sharply with the Confederate attackers' need to cross open ground, complicating their frontal assaults. One such attack, led by Confederate division commander Benjamin F. Cheatham, was decisively repulsed. On the Union left, Stuart still maintained his position, facing attacks from the Confederate brigades of Generals James R. Chalmers and John K. Jackson. Around 11:15 am, the fighting intensified, leading to the retreat of most of the 71st Ohio Infantry Regiment. Stuart reorganized his remaining two regiments, but panic briefly set in. Despite being wounded, Stuart managed to restore order, temporarily handing command to Lieutenant Colonel Oscar Malmborg.

Lew Wallace's division, tasked with joining the battlefield following Grant's order, faced delays and confusion. Initially, his troops were dispersed up to five miles from Crump's Landing, strategically positioned to guard potential reinforcement routes against an attack on their isolated division. Despite receiving Grant's order early in the day, Wallace's division did not commence its movement until noon, following an additional message from Grant's messenger who arrived at 11:30 am. Complicating matters further, at 2:00 pm, another messenger informed Wallace that he was on the wrong route. Wallace had mistakenly assumed he was to reinforce Sherman and McClernand at their initial positions, unaware that these divisions had been forced to retreat towards Pittsburg Landing.

By noon, Sherman and McClernand had fallen back to Jones Field. Fortunately, three regiments from McDowell's First Brigade managed to rejoin

Sherman and McClernand, bolstered by three more regiments arriving as reinforcements. Seizing the moment, McClernand's troops, with support from McDowell's brigade, initiated a counterattack. This push successfully drove the Confederates back past McClernand's morning headquarters, although both sides suffered heavy casualties.

Around 1:00 pm, reinforced Confederate forces launched a bayonet charge, effectively repelling McClernand and McDowell back to their original coun-terattack position at Jones Field.

On the Union's right flank, the divisions of Sherman and McClernand, supplemented by Veatch's brigade, were in disarray. Their ranks had thinned as numerous soldiers, abandoning their equipment, retreated towards Pittsburg Landing. Despite this, Sherman and McClernand continued to fight valiantly with the fragmented remains of their divisions.

The situation at the Union center, however, was more stable. Prentiss's forces successfully repelled several attacks led by Colonel Randall L. Gibson's brigade. Captain Andrew Hickenlooper's 5th Ohio Independent Light Artillery Battery effectively used shrapnel and canister rounds to thwart the first charge, inflicting heavy losses on the Confederates. After a third attempt, Gibson's brigade, having sustained significant casualties including a colonel injured in the face, largely withdrew and remained inactive for the rest of the day. Among the Union's fallen was Major James Powell, the officer who had led the early morning patrol that first encountered the Confederate forces at Fraley Field. Simultaneously, Sweeny's division was actively defending against Confederate assaults near Duncan Field.

On the Union's left flank, the situation was more precarious than on the right. Stuart's two remaining regiments, temporarily under Lieutenant Colonel Malmborg's command in Colonel T. Kilby Smith's absence, made several defensive stands east of Bell Field against two of Bragg's brigades. In a twist of fate, Bragg's troops, exhausted and low on ammunition, chose to ransack the Union camps for food rather than continue their offensive. By 2:15 pm, Smith ordered Stuart's brigade to withdraw, effectively ending their combat activities for the day by 2:30 pm.

Concurrently, McArthur's partial brigade, positioned adjacent to Stuart, faced an attack around 2:00 pm from one of Breckinridge's brigades. Despite receiving reinforcements, McArthur was compelled to retreat about 300 yards north of the Peach Orchard. However, he managed to stabilize his line within 20 minutes. To McArthur's right, Hurlbut's division was also under pressure, gradually falling back under the assault primarily from Breckinridge's Third Brigade, led by Colonel Walter S. Statham. As the Union forces retreated, they strategically paused to fire upon their pursuers and utilized artillery to slow down the Confederate advance.

General Albert Sidney Johnston, leading from the front, was a striking figure amidst the chaos of battle, riding ahead of Breckinridge's line. His uniform bore the marks of bullet tears, and one of his boots was notably damaged. After issuing an order to Colonel Statham, Johnston was struck, visibly bleeding from his leg. Despite the injury, he initially downplayed its severity. However, he soon began to slump in his saddle, acknowledging when asked that he was seriously wounded. Tragically, Johnston succumbed to his wounds, bleeding to death from a torn popliteal artery in his right leg. His death, around 2:30 pm near the Bell Farm, marked him as the highest-ranking officer killed in combat during the American Civil War. A potentially life-saving tourniquet was not available, as his personal physician was attending to other wounded soldiers.

With Johnston's passing, command officially fell to Beauregard. Though some historians note that Beauregard had effectively been leading the army from the rear while Johnston was on the frontline, his formal assumption of command came after Johnston's death. The Confederate advance on their right flank (the Union's left) slowed considerably, partly due to the exhaustion and disarray among Confederate troops, who quenched their thirst at the "Bloody Pond" between the Peach Orchard and Wicker Field. Beauregard, responding to the situation, directed Brigadier General Daniel Ruggles to coordinate an assault on the Hornet's Nest.

In the meantime, the Union received naval support. At 2:50 pm, Lieutenant William Gwin, commanding the USS Tyler, began bombarding Confederate positions near the Union left. An hour later, the USS Lexington joined in, both gunboats positioning south of Pittsburg Landing. Their shelling, primarily psychological in impact due to the size of the gunboat shells compared to field artillery, provided crucial support.

On the ground, McArthur's beleaguered brigade faced intense pressure from Confederate brigades under Generals John K. Jackson and John S. Bowen. With Stuart's brigade withdrawn, McArthur also faced flanking threats from Chalmers's Brigade. Between 3:00 and 4:00 pm, McArthur was forced to retreat to Pittsburg Landing. Hurlbut's line, similarly pressured, began to crumble, leaving only one regiment by 4:30 pm. Recognizing the untenable situation, Hurlbut ordered this last regiment to fall back, further consolidating Union forces near the landing.

In the late afternoon, as the battle raged on, General Grant assigned Colonel Joseph Dana Webster, a seasoned officer from the Mexican-American War, the critical task of establishing a last line of defense at Pittsburg Landing. Webster, resourcefully utilizing both stragglers and noncombatants, began to gather artillery. His efforts included collecting siege guns and any available batteries or parts of batteries that had retreated to the landing. Ultimately, Webster managed to assemble an impressive array of about 50 artillery pieces, strategically positioning them on a ridge on the battlefield's east side.

The situation on the Union right, where Grant visited Sherman around 3:00 pm, was precarious. The remaining regiments were depleted, ammunition reserves were dwindling, and many soldiers had either deserted or joined other units. Some regiments, heavily diminished, were directed to Pittsburg Landing for reformation. At this juncture, the Union line had retreated to the vicinity of Jones Field. The opposing Confederate forces, meanwhile, were in the process of reorganizing, with some units being redeployed towards the Hornet's Nest. Following another Confederate assault at 4:00 pm, Sherman and McClernand were compelled to retreat further by 5:00 pm.

On the Union's left flank, Bragg attempted to chase the retreating Union troops but faced increasing difficulties due to the effective fire from Union gunboats. With the Tennessee River at high tide, Union gunboat commanders realized that by adjusting their gun elevation and using reduced charges, they could accurately target enemies near the river. This tactical change resulted in the USS Tyler achieving direct hits on Chalmers's Brigade, starting at around 5:35 pm. These gunboat assaults provided critical support, hindering the Confederate pursuit and contributing to the Union's defensive efforts.

The Confederate army, fixated on conquering the Hornet's Nest, dedicated substantial effort and resources to its assault, rather than opting to bypass this stronghold. Historians have estimated that between eight to fourteen separate infantry charges, including those from earlier in the day, were directed at this position, engaging approximately 10,000 Confederate troops.

By 3:30 pm, the Confederates started positioning all available artillery around the Hornet's Nest. This resulted in what was, at the time, the largest assembly of field artillery in North America, with over 50 pieces, an effort led by Brigadier General Ruggles and known as "Ruggles's Battery." While Ruggles claimed credit for this formation in his report, it's believed that others, including Major Francis A. Shoup (Hardee's artillery chief) and Brigadier General James Trudeau, may have also played significant roles. By 4:00 pm, this massive artillery force began bombarding Wallace and Prentiss's positions in the Hornet's Nest, with the artillery concentrated near Duncan Field and south near the Eastern Corinth Road. It wasn't until

4:30 pm that all Confederate batteries were fully engaged, though their overall effectiveness has been a topic of debate among historians.

Meanwhile, by 4:00 pm, Hurlbut had retreated from the east side of the Hornet's Nest, and McClernand had fallen back about half a mile from the west. Recognizing the imminent threat of encirclement, Brigadier General W.H.L. Wallace attempted to lead his division northward. Tragically, around 4:15 pm, Wallace was mortally wounded while part of his division managed to escape encirclement. Over 1,000 Union soldiers were captured in a ravine north of the Sunken Road near Cloud Field, an area later dubbed "Hell's Hollow." By 4:45 pm, most of Wallace's division had been removed from the battlefield, leaving Prentiss with about 2,000 men. At approximately 5:30 pm, various Union regiments, including those under Prentiss, began to surrender, resulting in the capture of around 2,200 Union soldiers.

As the Hornet's Nest was finally overrun, Grant's forces had successfully established a defensive line extending from Pittsburg Landing to the Hamburg-Savannah Road and beyond to the north. Sherman took command of the right flank of this line, with McClernand holding the center. The left was secured by the remnants of W.H.L. Wallace's division, now under Colonel Tuttle's command, and Hurlbut's division. Additionally, around 10,000 to 15,000 stragglers and noncombatants were gathered at the landing. This line was bolstered by the artillery that Colonel Webster had assembled, with the added support of two nearby gunboats. Grant and Webster actively moved along this line, encouraging the men to maintain their fire against the Confederates.

Significant reinforcements began arriving from Buell's army around 5:00 pm, starting with the 36th Indiana Infantry Regiment. This regiment was promptly positioned on the east side of Grant's Last Line, ready to assist in the defense. The Union gunboats, particularly the Lexington, played a crucial role in this defense, firing 32 rounds into the Confederate forces in just 10 minutes. This intense naval support helped repel the Confederate assault, leading Beauregard to call off further attacks shortly after 6:00 pm. There was a belief among Buell's forces and some in Grant's army that their arrival had been pivotal in saving Grant's Army of the Tennessee. Grant, however, held a different view, believing that by 6:00 pm the Confederate army was too fatigued to continue effectively.

Beauregard, halting the attacks at sunset, anticipated that Grant's army could be defeated the following day. Unaware that Grant was already receiving reinforcements, Beauregard had been misled by a telegram stating Buell's army was in Alabama. The Confederate forces, dealing with significant disorganization and having just processed prisoners from the Hornet's Nest around 5:30 pm, were not in a position to mount effective night attacks, which were rare due to the risk of friendly fire. Moreover, the Confederate army was weary and had suffered approximately 8,000 casualties.

For many years, critics argued that Beauregard missed a crucial opportunity to defeat Grant's army at Shiloh. However, modern historians like Cunningham and Daniel have challenged this view. Cunningham pointed out that critics often overlooked key factors on the Shiloh battlefield, such as the Confederate army's disorganization, the limited time before sunset, and Grant's fortified position supported by gunboats. Daniel emphasized the implausibility of the Confederates breaching or significantly damaging the Federal line with piecemeal night assaults. He noted that it had taken the Confederates six hours to overrun the Hornet's Nest, and Grant's Last Line was even stronger. Additionally, he highlighted issues like the Confederate troops' exhaustion, dwindling ammunition, and reports of a significant portion of their forces engaging in plunder rather than combat.

Beauregard spent the evening in what was previously Sherman's tent near Shiloh Church, while most of the Confederate army settled into the original Union camps. He sent a telegram to Richmond claiming a "complete victory" and stating that the enemy had been driven from every position. Many Confederate soldiers, believing the battle to be effectively over, indulged in looting the Union camps, with some even departing for Corinth with their spoils. This plundering also resulted in Confederate troops acquiring superior weaponry from Union soldiers who were dead, wounded, captured, or had fled.

The weather worsened that night, with rain starting at 10:00 pm and intensifying into a storm with thunder and lightning by midnight. This inclement weather, coupled with the continuous bombardment from Union gunboats, made it extremely difficult for the already exhausted Confederate soldiers to rest. Due to their fatigue and the prevailing belief that Grant's army was on the brink of collapse, the Confederate forces did not undergo reorganization, nor were plans or orders formulated for the next day. The expectation was that the commands would regroup for a "final mop-up action."

The Confederate strategy had originally been to push Grant's army away from Pittsburg Landing and trap it against the northern creeks, hindering its mobility and resupply. However, the outcome was quite different: Grant's forces were pushed back to a defensible position at Pittsburg Landing, where they could be reinforced and resupplied.

Grant's Army of the Tennessee faced significant losses at Shiloh: 7,000 men killed or wounded, 3,000 captured, and another 10,000 who were too frightened to engage in combat. Before receiving reinforcements, Grant had about 18,000 combat-ready troops on his Last Line. With most Union camps captured, these weary and hungry soldiers faced a night in the open without blankets, compounded by the discomfort of rain and cold weather.

Reinforcements began to arrive in the evening. At 7:15 pm, 5,800 fresh troops from Lew Wallace's division reached the battlefield, taking positions next to Sherman. By 9:00 pm, Brigadier General Thomas Crittenden's division from Buell's army started arriving, and by 11:00 pm, the entire division was assembled at the landing. Buell would eventually have nearly 18,000 men available for the battle. The Union line, extending from west to east, was formed by the divisions of Lew Wallace, Sherman, McClernand, Hurlbut, Crittenden, and Nelson. Prentiss's division was effectively decimated, and Tuttle was behind the line, attempting to reorganize W.H.L. Wallace's division.

Earlier in the day, when Colonel James B. McPherson, Grant's chief engineer, inquired about preparing for a retreat, Grant firmly rejected the idea, expressing his intention to attack at daylight. In a meeting at sunset, Buell learned of Grant's plan for a sunrise attack. Despite Grant's seniority, Buell, considering himself independent, planned his own attack on the east side of the line without consulting Grant. Late at night, Sherman found Grant resting under a tree and remarked on the challenging day they had endured. Grant confidently responded that they would defeat the Confederates the next day.

Between midnight and 4:00 am, Brigadier General Alexander M. McCook's division from Buell's Army of the Ohio arrived in Savannah, with the first unit reaching Pittsburg Landing around 4:00 am. Meanwhile, the Confederate 47th Tennessee Infantry Regiment, a poorly-armed group of 600 recruits, marched towards the battlefield, arriving only by 8:00 am. This regiment was Beauregard's sole reinforcement. After accounting for casualties and desertions, Beauregard's Confederate force was reduced to fewer than 20,000 combatants.

On the east side of the Union line, Buell's offensive commenced at 5:00 am with the deployment of Nelson's three brigades. As the morning progressed, Nelson was reinforced on his right by Crittenden's division. Together, these two divisions pushed forward, driving away Confederate skirmishers, and were gradually joined by brigades from McCook's division on Crittenden's right. However, McCook's full strength, with all three brigades, wasn't assembled until around noon.

On the Confederate side, General Hardee led the right flank opposing Nelson, with the most organized unit being the division under Brigadier General Jones M. Withers. The skirmishers that Nelson initially pushed back included Colonel Nathan Bedford Forrest's cavalry and parts of Chalmers's Brigade from Withers' division. Behind these skirmishers were Chalmers's Brigade and an ad-hoc brigade comprised of three regiments, supported by a line of mixed regiments and several artillery batteries.

In the Davis Wheat Field, a small area between Barnes Field and the Peach Orchard, Colonel William B. Hazen's brigade, part of Nelson's division, sustained over half of the day's losses for Nelson's entire division. Additional combat occurred near Sara Bell Field, leading to a three-hour stalemate, after which both sides withdrew around noon, with Nelson retreating to Wicker Field. During these engagements, Hardee sustained a slight wound but still led a counterattack. To Nelson's west, both Crittenden and McCook advanced but were eventually pushed back to Duncan Field. By noon, Buell's army had secured the Hornet's Nest.

Grant's offensive started with Lew Wallace's fresh division successfully pushing back Pond's weary brigade from Jones Field. A Confederate counterattack led by Gibson and Wood was met with resistance when Sherman brought his division into the fray, resulting in the Confederates being driven back. McClernand and Hurlbut also entered the battle, contributing to the forward movement of all four Union divisions by 10:30 am. At this point, Cleburne's brigade, numbering 800 men, suffered heavy losses during their unsuccessful assault on the Union forces.

After a brief pause, Buell's forces renewed their attack shortly after noon. Nelson and Crittenden advanced to the Hamburg-Purdy Road within about two hours, while McCook, moving westward along the Corinth-Pittsburg Landing Road, inadvertently created a gap with Crittenden. This gap was filled by Grant's reserve brigades, effectively maintaining the Union line. The Confederate army, despite a valiant six-hour resistance against Buell's fresh troops, was nearing the end of its ability to hold off the Union advance.

On Grant's side of the battlefield, around noon, Sherman and McClernand's advance was halted by an attack from Cheatham's Confederate division, forcing them back about 300 yards north. Lew Wallace, facing light opposition, assumed a defensive stance and delayed his offensive until Sherman and McClernand repelled Cheatham's forces. Bragg established another line near Water Oaks Pond, where a two-hour engagement unfolded, with Beauregard personally directing various Confederate units.

McCook's westward (instead of southward) advancement at 1:30 pm placed him on Bragg's right flank, with Wallace, Sherman, and McClernand opposing Bragg's front. Bragg eventually retreated south of the Hamburg-Purdy Road, and Beauregard launched a counterattack primarily with Wood's brigade. This force momentarily pushed McCook back until he regrouped and repelled the assault. Beauregard and Bragg were subsequently forced to fall back, with Union forces crossing the Hamburg-Purdy Road by 2:30 pm.

Beauregard, throughout the morning, had been anticipating the arrival of 20,000 troops under Brigadier General Earl Van Dorn to swing the battle in the Confederates' favor. However, upon learning of Van Dorn's continued distance, Beauregard initiated a withdrawal to Corinth around 1:00 pm. By 2:00 pm, Breckinridge began organizing a rear guard near Shiloh Church, with Confederate artillery engaging in a deceptive bombardment to mask their retreat. By 3:30 pm, the last of the Confederate artillery was withdrawn towards Corinth.

Grant and Buell faced criticism for not pursuing the retreating Confederate army, with some historians arguing that Lew Wallace's fresh division should have been utilized for this purpose. Rain began at 6:30 pm, turning to hail as temperatures dropped, marking the end of the battle with significant casualties on both sides.

On April 8 at 10:00 am, Union forces under Sherman and Wood initiated a pursuit of the Confederate army. Breckinridge's rear guard, including about 350 cavalrymen led by Colonel Forrest and comprised of various cavalry groups, was tasked with covering the retreat. They engaged in skirmishes with Union forces; on one side, Wood's brigades clashed with Wirt Adams's Cavalry and withdrew, while on the other, Forrest's group attacked Sherman's men, resulting in Union casualties of 15 killed, 25 wounded, and 53 captured. Forrest himself was wounded but managed to escape. Following this encounter, Sherman ceased the pursuit, and Breckinridge continued southward.

The Battle of Shiloh was one of the bloodiest engagements in the American Civil War, with substantial casualties on both sides. Union forces suffered a total of 13,047 casualties, which included 1,754 killed, 8,408 wounded, and 2,885 missing or captured. Of these, Grant's army accounted for 10,944 casualties, while Buell's forces incurred 2,103. The brigades commanded by Sweeny, Veatch, and Colonel Nelson G. Williams each experienced over 600 killed or wounded, not accounting for those captured or missing. The Official Records report two brigade commanders killed or mortally wounded, five wounded, and one captured. However, one historian suggests that the high officer casualties likely led to an underreporting of total casualties, estimating the actual number closer to 14,500 for the Union.

Confederate casualties amounted to 10,699, with 1,728 killed, 8,012 wounded, and 959 missing or captured. These figures, however, do not include casualties from the cavalry or the 47th Tennessee Infantry Regiment, which joined on the second day of battle. It's believed by some historians that the Confederate casualties were probably closer to 12,000. Cleburne's brigade alone suffered 790 wounded and 188 killed, the highest numbers for any brigade in the battle. In addition to the mortal wounding of Johnston and a slight injury to Hardee, Beauregard's report lists six casualties among major and brigadier generals. Notably, one of the Confederate soldiers killed was Samuel B. Todd, Mary Todd Lincoln's brother.

At the time, Shiloh was the largest battle fought in America and significantly impacted perceptions about the war's duration, especially in the Union ranks. The battle's approximately 23,746 casualties, which may be underestimated, ranked it among the top ten (6th or 7th) in terms of casualties in the American Civil War. The toll at Shiloh, which was around 20,000 men killed or wounded, was higher than the combined total of earlier major battles like Manassas (Bull Run), Wilson's Creek, Fort Donelson, and Pea Ridge, which together accounted for around 12,000 casualties.

Siege of Fort Pulaski

The majestic Savannah River, emerging from the Appalachian Mountains, carves its path eastward, defining the border between Georgia and South Carolina. A mere twelve miles from the coast, this mighty river graces the historic city of Savannah before merging with the sea. Along its course, the river is intricately sliced by numerous channels weaving through the coastal barrier islands. These islands, often tidal and blanketed in lush marsh grass, create a mesmerizing vista reminiscent of a vast savannah from afar.

Nestled close to the ocean, on the muddy banks of Cockspur Island, lies Fort Pulaski. This formidable structure was strategically built to oversee the passage of ships and shield Savannah from potential attacks. The city of Savannah, once a bustling international port in the antebellum South, thrived as a pivotal cotton hub. It was also renowned for its shipbuilding, essential marine businesses, and railroad shops - the lifelines of its military industries. Intriguingly, three railroads converged in Savannah, with two mirroring the alignment of the coastal barrier islands.

Cockspur Island holds tales of a pre-Revolutionary War stockade and a later fortification built in the 1790s, only to be claimed by a hurricane in 1804. Following the War of 1812, a strategic plan to fortify America's eastern and gulf coasts with masonry forts led to the selection of Cockspur Island once again in the early 1820s. The initial vision for a grandiose two-story pentagonal fort, similar to Fort Sumter, was soon revised due to the island's muddy terrain, resulting in a unique single-story design with casemate guns and an upper layer of parapet guns.

The construction saga of Fort Pulaski is a chronicle of resilience and innovation. Overseen initially by Major Samuel Babcock, the project saw the young Lieutenant Robert E. Lee, fresh from the United States Military Academy, play a pivotal role in locating the fort's site and supervising the construction of vital drainage systems. Although reassigned in 1831, Lee's legacy at the fort remained. Named in 1833 in honor of Count Casimir Pulaski, a hero mortally wounded in the 1779 Battle of Savannah, the fort's construction was a battle against natural adversities, including malaria and yellow fever, culminating in its completion in 1847 under Lieutenant Joseph King Fenno Mansfield.

Believed to be an invincible bastion, Fort Pulaski stood as a symbol of strength among the network of masonry forts guarding America's coasts. Deemed impervious to any ground assault and too distant for enemy artillery, it was thought to be as unassailable as the Rocky Mountains. However, the unforeseen advent of rifled artillery during the Civil War in 1862 would shatter this illusion.

The formidable Fort Pulaski, with its distinctive pentagonal shape, was a marvel of military architecture. Designed to strategically oversee the Savannah River's southern and northern channels, its walls formed a protective shield, with two faces each dedicated to these vital waterways. The western side, facing towards Savannah, was considered the least vulnerable. Intriguingly, at each of the three ocean-facing angles, a unique structure called a pancoupé was built, featuring a single casement and embrasure for a gun, specifically to eliminate any potential blind spots.

By 1840, the fort was armed with twenty 32-pounder naval guns, a number that remained unchanged until Georgia authorities seized control in 1861. The fort's brick walls, an impressive seven and a half feet thick and towering twenty-five feet above the water line, were a testament to its strength. Additionally, a demilune protected the gorge, and a moat, as wide as forty-eight feet in places, encircled the entire structure.

The tide of history turned when South Carolina declared its secession on December 20, 1860. Georgia's Governor Joseph Emerson Brown, in consultation with Colonel Alexander Robert Lawton, decided to preemptively occupy Fort Pulaski. On a dreary January 4, 1861, troops, along with artillery, embarked on the Ida steamer and landed on Cockspur Island. The fort's lone caretaker quickly surrendered, handing over the fort with its rusting artillery and limited ammunition. Just twelve days later, Georgia formally seceded from the Union.

Upon occupation, the fort was in a state of neglect, with unlivable quarters and a moat choked with silt and marsh grass. It took the labor of one hundred and twenty-five slaves several months to restore the fort to a habitable condition. During the first half of 1861, the 1st Regiment of Georgia Volunteers and other state troops not only refurbished the fort but also fortified the surrounding barrier islands.

In October 1861, Major Charles Hart Olmstead, a Savannah native and graduate of the Georgia Military Academy, took command of the fort and was soon promoted to colonel. His military background, combined with his experience as a local businessman and regimental adjutant, served him well. Under his leadership, thousands of pounds of gunpowder and ammunition were transported to the fort, and its artillery was significantly bolstered to 48 guns, including 12-inch mortars, English Blakely rifles, and 10-inch columbiads. The Ida, along with other steamers, continued to supply the fort with necessary materials such as lumber, arms, and food.

On May 27, 1861, the Union's naval blockade of the Confederacy took a significant turn with the arrival of the first Federal blockading vessel at the Savannah River's mouth. This marked the official closure of the port, although a handful of blockade runners managed daring entries in the following months. As the blockade intensified with more Union vessels joining, the Confederates constructed a sand fort near the lighthouse on Tybee Island, strategically positioned southeast across the south channel from Cockspur Island. This fortification served to keep the blockading ships at bay and deterred any land assaults by Union forces.

The strategic landscape shifted further when General Robert E. Lee assumed command of the Department of South Carolina, Georgia, and East Florida on November 7, 1861. Facing the Union's capture of Port Royal Sound and Hilton Head Island, Lee ordered the evacuation of Georgia's vulnerable coastal island defenses, redirecting their artillery resources to Savannah. His defensive strategy hinged on mobile cavalry patrols and the swift relocation of infantry and artillery via coastal railroads to counter any invasion threats.

The Union's control of Port Royal Sound and Hilton Head Island was a crucial element in their blockade strategy. These locations, along with Fernandina in Florida, were seized to serve as coaling stations for the blockading fleets. This joint operation was under the command of Brigadier General Thomas West Sherman and Commodore Samuel Francis DuPont. Key figures in Sherman's staff included Captain Quincy Adams Gillmore, the chief engineer; Lieutenant Horace Porter, the ordnance officer; and Lieutenant James Harrison Wilson, the chief topographical engineer. These three officers were destined for distinguished careers over the next four years.

Sherman swiftly secured the neighboring South Carolina coastal islands. Following the Confederate evacuation of their Tybee Island fort, the day after Hilton Head's abandonment, Federal forces quickly occupied Tybee Island. On November 25, General Sherman and Captain Gillmore, using telescopes, conducted a reconnaissance of Fort Pulaski and concluded that the fort could be subdued with a combination of mortars and breaching guns. Within a week, Gillmore requisitioned an impressive arsenal for the task:

sixteen mortars, ten heavy rifled guns, and ten columbiads, setting the stage for a significant military engagement.

According to traditional military strategy, the use of plunging mortar fire was essential to break through and damage the parapet and the casemate arches underneath, while smooth bore guns were employed to methodically break down the thick walls into fragments and dust. At this time, rifled guns were a relatively new technology. Some tests in Britain had demonstrated their effectiveness against masonry walls, and Gillmore was aware of these developments. These rifled guns were found to be more efficient than smooth bore guns of a similar caliber, especially when fired from distances exceeding a mile. Despite General Sherman's skepticism about the effectiveness of rifled guns, he permitted Gillmore to incorporate them into his bombardment strategy.

In early December, Colonel Rudolph Rosa's 46th New York took position on Tybee Island, soon to be reinforced by two companies of the 3rd Rhode Island Heavy Artillery, which occupied the abandoned Confederate sand fort. Later that month, Colonel Alfred Howe Terry's 7th Connecticut also arrived on Tybee.

Meanwhile, General Lee was actively working on reinforcing the inner coastal defenses. Along with Governor Brown, Brigadier General Lawton, and other officers, Lee visited Fort Pulaski on November 10-11. He expressed to Colonel Olmstead that while they could expect heavy shelling from Tybee Island, he doubted the possibility of the fort being breached from such a distance, citing the maximum effective range of cannonballs against masonry as 800 yards, whereas Tybee was over 1,700 yards away. Lee seemed to be unaware of the advancements in rifled gun technology. During his visit, Lee advised Olmstead to install sand bag traverses between the parapet guns for protection against shell bursts, to dig ditches in the parade ground to intercept rolling shells, and to dismantle any wooden structures along the officers' quarters to minimize fire risks. He also suggested covering the interior of the fort with blindages and several feet of earth for additional protection. Consequently, numerous barges loaded with heavy beams were transported from Savannah and floated up the irrigation ditch from the south channel into the fort's moat. By February, when the fort was effectively isolated, Olmsted had fortified it with 45 guns and three external mortars.

General Sherman then instructed Captain Gillmore to consider setting up a battery on Jones Island, located about three and a half miles upriver from Fort Pulaski on the South Carolina side of the Savannah River. Gillmore identified a dry area on the island, approximately one mile from the nearest wharf on the north shore. He described Jones Island as having a semi-fluid mud substrate that would quiver under impact, like from men jumping or ramming earth. The surface, reinforced by reed and grass roots, would allow men to walk over it sinking only a few inches. However, if this top layer was compromised, they would sink significantly deeper, in some places much more than two feet.

In early February 1862, soldiers on Daufuskie Island, located south of Hilton Head Island, undertook the massive task of cutting 10,000 pine trees. These trees, fashioned into rafts, along with sandbags, were transported to Jones Island for construction purposes. By February 8, a wharf was completed, and just two days later, a corduroy path crossed the island, laying the groundwork for a battery platform. During the following nights, amidst a relentless rainstorm, teams of 35 men each embarked on the grueling task of moving six cannon to the battery, two at a time. This process involved a meticulous method of rolling the guns over pairs of planks, continually rearranging the planks in front as the guns advanced. The men faced challenges with the sinking terrain and slippery planks, often sinking to their knees and resorting to using ropes to move the planks. Despite the guns frequently slipping off and sinking into the mud, the perseverance of these men resulted in all six guns being positioned on the platform by sunrise on February 12. This new installation, named Battery Vulcan, was just eight inches above high tide.

The next day, the steamer Ida, unaware of the new battery, made its routine journey down the river towards the fort. When Battery Vulcan opened fire, five of its guns recoiled back into the mud. Nevertheless, Ida managed to reach the fort unscathed, conducted her business, and returned to Savannah via Lazaretto Creek. Subsequently, the battery platform was expanded and the muddied guns were retrieved and cleaned.

On February 20, Union forces established Battery Hamilton on the smaller Bird Island, directly opposite Battery Vulcan, effectively shutting down river traffic. Two days later, they obstructed Lazaretto Creek by sinking an armed vessel, further isolating the fort. Aside from occasional newspaper deliveries, Fort Pulaski was now cut off from Savannah.

As early as December 1861, General Sherman had been advocating for Captain Gillmore's promotion to Brigadier General, a rank he believed befitting the engineer's responsibilities in directing the upcoming siege operations. After extensive correspondence and initial denials, Gillmore was finally promoted to acting Brigadier General in February 1862.

Now General Gillmore began preparing his siege batteries on Tybee Island's northwestern shore, which featured several patches of higher ground. The distance from Tybee Island's northeast landing to the proposed battery sites spanned two and a half miles, with the final mile being particularly challenging due to low, marshy terrain. This route required the construction of a corduroy road, made from brushwood and sticks, and was exposed to the fort's view. By late February, the Tybee Island garrison had grown significantly, comprising the 46th New York, the 7th Connecticut, two companies of the 1st New York Volunteer Engineers, five companies of the 8th Maine, two companies of the 3rd Rhode Island Artillery, and a few members of Lieutenant Wilson's company of engineers.

General Gillmore was at the helm of the extensive preparations for the bombardment of Fort Pulaski. Starting February 21, the first heavy artillery piece was brought in, and over the subsequent seven weeks, a formidable arsenal of thirty-six guns was assembled. This collection included twelve 13-inch mortars, four 10-inch mortars, six 10-inch columbiads, four 8-inch columbiads, five James rifles of various calibers, and five 30-pounder Parrott guns. Notably, the James rifles and Parrott guns, both rifled muzzle loaders, were significant advancements in artillery technology. Their innovative projectiles engaged with the rifling upon firing, enhancing both accuracy and penetrating power compared to the traditional balls used in smooth bore guns.

The logistics of handling these massive artillery pieces were daunting. A 13-inch mortar tube weighed a staggering 17,000 pounds, and a 10-inch columbiad tube was not far behind at 15,000 pounds. Tybee Island lacked proper wharf facilities for unloading such heavy artillery, necessitating the use of lighters – flat-bottomed boats – outfitted with thick planks to support the weight of the gun tubes and carriages. The challenging surf of Tybee's Atlantic beach added to the complexity. During high tide, soldiers ashore hauled the lighters toward the beach with ropes. As the lighters reached shallow waters, up to fifty men would tip them, rolling the heavy artillery into the water. At low tide, a laborious process involving up to 250 men dragging the equipment above the high tide line ensued, often taking over two hours.

Ingenious sling carts, essentially two pairs of large wheels connected by heavy beams, were prepared by the infantrymen for transporting the guns and carriages. Up to 250 men would then pull these carts in the dark, following commands given by whistles, as they could only whisper to maintain stealth. The last mile of the journey was particularly challenging due to boggy terrain, often causing the wheels to sink deep into the mud.

In total, eleven battery sites were constructed on the northwest shore of Tybee Island. The construction of gun platforms, magazines, shelters, and the mounting of the guns was carried out at night, often in rain, to avoid detection by the fort's defenders. Once a camouflaged parapet was in place, work proceeded more openly but still under the cover of darkness, with all signs of activity being concealed by dawn.

The Confederates grew increasingly suspicious of the Union activities. On the night of March 22, three Confederate soldiers managed to cross the south channel and discovered a Federal battery. Reporting back to Colonel Olmstead, he ordered the fort to fire on the western end of Tybee Island at dawn. Although he observed no apparent damage, the Confederates were now aware of the batteries. Additionally, two days prior, a group of men from the 46th New York, captured during a reconnaissance mission west of Tybee Island, confirmed the presence of these batteries, with this information reaching Colonel Olmstead by April 4.

In a significant change of command, Major General David Hunter replaced Brigadier General Thomas W. Sherman as the leader of the Department of the South on March 31. Sherman, despite securing Port Royal Sound and occupying the surrounding South Carolina islands, Tybee Island, and Fernandina in Florida, was perceived as not being aggressive enough in advancing the siege preparations on Tybee Island. Hunter, a graduate of the United States Military Academy and a known abolitionist, was also a close associate of President Abraham Lincoln. Along with Hunter came Brigadier General Henry Washington Benham, tasked with overseeing the northern sector of Hunter's Department. An engineer by training, Benham quickly inspected the Federal batteries with Gillmore and urged their rapid completion.

As April commenced, the Federal infantrymen started intensive training on their guns, guided by the Rhode Island artillerymen. They practiced all aspects except actual firing, raising concerns among some that the Union gunners might not have accurately gauged the range of their weapons before the bombardment. Additionally, there were rumors of an ironclad being built in Savannah that could potentially breach Batteries Vulcan and Hamilton, posing a threat to their operations. The Federal forces had eleven batteries, each with its specific armament and distance from Fort Pulaski.

Each gun had 900 shots or shells stored in nearby service magazines, alongside enough gunpowder for two days of firing. An extra stockpile of 3,600 barrels of gunpowder was kept near Tybee Island's lighthouse. On the night of April 9, General Gillmore issued his final orders for the attack strategy. The mortar batteries were instructed to target the parapet above the casemates to collapse the arches underneath. Columbiads in Batteries Lyon and Lincoln were to aim over the southeast wall to hit the interior of the gorge and north faces. After neutralizing the barbette guns, Batteries Scott, Sigel, and McClellan were to focus on the pancoupé between the south and southeast walls and then the adjacent casemate on the southeast wall.

On the morning of April 10, the Confederates noticed that the brush concealing the Federal batteries on Tybee Island's north side had been removed. Fort Pulaski's artillery, consisting of ten barbette guns, six casemate guns, and two mortars, had limited capability to target Tybee Island. Only a fraction of these could aim at the easternmost Federal batteries housing the rifled guns. Soon, a small boat bearing a Union officer with a white flag approached Cockspur Island's south wharf. Lieutenant Wilson delivered General Hunter's ultimatum for surrender, giving a deadline of thirty minutes. Colonel Olmstead used this time to prepare his men, distribute ammunition, and ready the hospital. His response was firm - he was there to defend, not surrender the fort.

As soon as Hunter received the refusal, he ordered the bombardment to commence at 8:15 a.m. The initial exchange of fire was erratic as both sides adjusted to the range. Within an hour, the Federal batteries were firing three rounds per minute, enveloping Tybee Island's northwest shore in smoke and flashes of fire. Colonel Rosa of the 46th New York, defying orders at Battery Sigel, led volleys of fire that were more enthusiastic than accurate. Gillmore, frustrated with Rosa's approach, eventually replaced him and his men with trained naval artillerists from the offshore Wabash.

Around noon, an incident involving the rebel flag, which was momentarily brought down, led the Federals to believe they had secured a victory, only for the Confederates to quickly hoist it again on a cannon rammer, prompting the Federal forces to resume firing.

Inside Fort Pulaski, the intensity of the bombardment quickly became apparent as an early shot dislodged a gun through a casemate opening, and the James projectiles were effective in fracturing the bricks. Colonel Olmstead described the relentless onslaught of shells and rifle shots filling the air, accompanied by deafening explosions. Within three hours, three casemate guns were dismounted, and by the end of the first day, most of the guns facing the sea were rendered inoperable. Olmstead witnessed a columbiad shot striking the fort wall, causing it to bulge inward, signaling the inevitable outcome of the bombardment. By day's end, nearly all of the wall's thickness had been eroded.

Olmstead's inspection of the fort's exterior after the first day revealed severe damage. The pancoupé at the southeast angle was completely breached, and the rampart above was shattered, leaving an 8-inch gun dangling precariously. The adjacent casemates were similarly nearing destruction, with large chunks of masonry littering the moat.

The Federal forces maintained a slow rate of fire throughout the night and intensified their efforts with the dawn of April 11. The rifled gun shells penetrated deeper into the brick wall, and the columbiad balls caused more masonry to crumble into the moat. By noon, three casemate arches were visibly open, and the focus shifted to an adjacent casemate. It became clear that the southeast wall's face was being systematically dismantled. With the moat filled with debris, General Benham planned an assault for April 12, which ultimately was not needed.

By midday, the fort was in ruins, with seven barbette guns dismounted and the west side of the wall heavily damaged. At 1:00 p.m., a shell entered an open casemate, passed across the parade ground, and exploded in a magazine, miraculously not igniting the twenty tons of powder stored there. Olmstead realized the next hit could be catastrophic and decided to cease resistance. At 2:00 p.m., Confederate fire stopped, and a white flag was raised, despite only three Confederates being seriously wounded.

During a storm on April 11, Benham and his staff struggled to find a boat to reach Pulaski. Gillmore, however, managed to find sailors from the Wabash who rowed him to the fort. He secured the gates upon entry and negotiated the surrender terms with Olmstead. When Halpine's party arrived to take charge of the surrender, they were initially kept waiting until Gillmore secured the signed surrender document. The garrison of 385 men was taken prisoner, and their flag and officers' swords were surrendered.

The 7th Connecticut and 1st New York Volunteer Engineers started repairing the breach by the end of May, and their work is still visible today. The guns from Tybee Island were relocated, some even used in the siege of Fort Sumter. Batteries Vulcan and Hamilton were also disarmed. The 48th New York eventually replaced the 7th Connecticut as the garrison, which was later reduced in 1863.

The Federal forces fired over five thousand projectiles, with the Confederates firing about a third of that number. Gillmore noted that the largest James projectiles penetrated up to twenty-six inches, with most damage being attributed to the James rifles. The Parrott rounds penetrated up to eighteen inches, while the columbiads were effective in dislodging large masses of masonry. Less than 10% of mortar rounds hit the fort, and they caused minimal damage to the casemate arches. The siege revealed that rifled artillery had revolutionized siege warfare, making future sieges and bombardments more efficient and effective, as evidenced in Gillmore's subsequent campaign against Fort Sumter.

This event marked a turning point in military engineering, with Major General David Hunter recognizing its significance akin to the impact of the Monitor and Merrimac in naval warfare. The bombardment demonstrated that traditional stone or brick fortifications could no longer withstand the force of heavy caliber rifled artillery.

Capture of New Orleans

The dramatic capture of New Orleans on April 29, 1862, marked a pivotal moment in the American Civil War, as Union forces led by Flag Officer David Glasgow Farragut and Major General Benjamin Franklin Butler seized control of the Confederacy's most vital port on the Mississippi River. This strategic victory not only wrested the Confederacy's largest and most bustling city from its grasp but also handed the Union the keys to the lower Mississippi River Valley, a move they swiftly leveraged to their advantage.

Rewind to January 26, 1861, when Louisiana's secession set the stage. New Orleans, brimming with potential for defending the Confederacy's largest port, was guarded by two stone fortresses, Forts St. Philip and Jackson, at the southern gateways of the Mississippi River. Yet, the city's naval defenses were threadbare. Enter Brigadier General P.G.T. Beauregard, who, on February 13, 1861, urgently appealed for enhanced defenses against the vulnerable Mississippi River. He envisioned a stronghold, fortified with river-blocking booms, beefed-up armaments, and clear lines of sight. But his warnings largely fell on deaf ears, with state and Confederate leaders underestimating the threat from the Gulf, focusing instead on northern defenses at locations like Island No. 10, Fort Pillow, and Vicksburg.

Meanwhile, New Orleans' local commanders grappled with reinforcing the city's immediate defenses. Brigadier General David Emanuel Twiggs, despite his efforts to fortify New Orleans and at seventy-one, struggled with the demands of leadership. His request for a replacement led to Major General Mansfield Lovell taking the reins, who faced the constant challenge of recruiting and equipping soldiers only to see them reassigned elsewhere.

On other fronts, Confederate defenses were evolving. Captain Lawrence Rousseau, for instance, acquired ships for the Confederate Navy, transforming the steamship Habana into the formidable commerce raider CSS Sumter. Under the skillful command of Raphael Semmes, the Sumter managed a daring escape from the Mississippi River on June 3, 1861, outmaneuvering Union blockades that were rapidly materializing under President Abraham Lincoln's orders. Although the Union Navy, led by Secretary Gideon Welles and Assistant Secretary Gustavus Vasa Fox, faced initial challenges in enforcing this blockade, their presence soon tightened around major Confederate ports, significantly hampering Confederate naval activities. The Sumter, under Semmes' expert navigation, stood as a notable exception, brilliantly evading capture and sailing into the Gulf.

As the Civil War intensified, the Confederates turned their attention towards locally sourced warships. John A. Stephenson, a savvy businessman, transformed the steamer Enoch Train into the ironclad ram Manassas, a vessel with limited power but significant impact. Under Commodore George Nichols Hollins, this ship became part of an emergent "mosquito fleet," which included six converted steamers on the Mississippi River – McRae, Calhoun, Ivy, Tuscarora, Pickens, and Jackson – and two others, Florida and Pamlico, stationed on Lake Pontchartrain. This makeshift navy held the fort for New Orleans until the Confederate government launched its own shipbuilding initiative.

However, the limitations of Hollins' fleet soon became evident. In October, five Union warships entered the Mississippi River delta, prompting a daring response. Lieutenant Alexander Warley, in a bold move, seized control of the Manassas from Stephenson near Fort St. Philip. Leading a flotilla of three fire rafts and six gunboats, Hollins engaged in the Battle of the Head of the

Passes. Despite limited firepower, they managed to ground Union Captain John Pope's ships temporarily, earning Hollins local acclaim.

Parallel to these events, Confederate Navy Secretary Stephen Russell Mallory was driving an ambitious shipbuilding program. By September 1861, contracts were in place to construct the ironclads Mississippi and Louisiana, vessels akin to the Merrimack in design, boasting heavy armaments and iron plating. Yet, these projects faced numerous hurdles. Overwhelmed shipbuilders and foundries, diverted to private ventures like the Pioneer submersible and other military projects, struggled to provide necessary resources. Delays in sourcing materials, coupled with labor disputes, significantly hampered these ironclads' progress, preventing them from playing a crucial role in defending New Orleans.

The strategic landscape shifted again in early 1862. Hollins' fleet left New Orleans to counter Union advances upstream, leading to a reshuffling of naval command. Commander John K. Mitchell was tasked with overseeing all naval operations, with specific focus on completing the Louisiana. Commanders Arthur Sinclair and William Conway Whittle were also appointed for overseeing the Mississippi and the New Orleans station, respectively. Concurrently, Confederate Secretary of War Judah Philip Benjamin authorized Major General Lowell to independently acquire and outfit ships, leading to the creation of a 14-ship River Defense Force under Stephenson.

The strategic importance of New Orleans quickly caught the attention of Northern military leaders. In November 1861, Secretary of the Navy Gideon Welles, along with Commander David Dixon Porter and Assistant Secretary Gustavus Vasa Fox, began serious discussions about targeting the city. A pivotal meeting on November 14, 1861, with President Abraham Lincoln, Secretary of State William Henry Seward, and Major General George Brinton McClellan, led to the proposal of a naval expedition to attack New Orleans via the Gulf of Mexico. Initially hesitant, McClellan endorsed the plan after learning it required only 10,000 soldiers.

For this critical mission, Welles appointed Captain David Farragut to lead the operation. Despite concerns about his Southern roots, Farragut's loyalty was assured by his foster brother, Porter, and his naval prowess was well recognized. Assuming command of the West Gulf Blockading Squadron on January 9, 1862, Farragut focused on capturing New Orleans, deemed "the great object in view" by Welles. Porter, instrumental in advocating for the operation, was assigned to command the mortar boat flotilla, crucial in the initial bombardment of Forts St. Philip and Jackson. Once these defenses were weakened, Farragut's frigates could then advance towards New Orleans. Major General Ben Butler's land forces significantly bolstered Farragut's naval operation.

Farragut's squadron faced numerous challenges en route to the attack. The journey from Atlantic bases around Florida to the western Gulf was just the beginning. A lack of forward bases posed a resupply problem, particularly for coal. Farragut maximized his fleet's initial load of munitions and coal for the western journey. Upon arrival, the shallow Mississippi River bar presented another obstacle, hindering the larger warships from entering the river. Sailors lightened the ships by removing cannons and other materials, either towing the vessels across the bar or seeking deeper passages for crossing.

However, the lack of forward bases, particularly for coal resupply, emerged as a critical issue. Farragut, recognizing this, noted the impracticality of relying on distant Tortugas for rapid resupply. The presence of Butler's transports, loaded with extra coal, proved essential in keeping Farragut's fleet operational.

Farragut also faced the potential threat of the formidable Confederate ironclads Louisiana and Mississippi. Their heavy armaments and armored casemates posed a serious risk to his wooden-hulled warships. Without access to similarly armored vessels, like the USS Monitor which remained engaged in the Chesapeake, Farragut had to act swiftly before the Confederate ironclads could fully leverage their advantage.

Despite the strategic position of Farragut's squadron, Confederate forces were unable to capitalize on its vulnerabilities. The Union's success in capturing Forts Henry and Donelson in February 1862 opened new avenues for offensives in Tennessee and western waters, significantly depleting New Orleans of both troops and Hollins' naval squadron. The aftermath of General Ulysses S. Grant's victory at Shiloh on April 6–7 further drained military resources from the city. Hollins, whose fleet was no match for Foote's warships, stayed upstream near Island No. 10 until he learned of Farragut's entry into the Mississippi River. Racing back to New Orleans, Hollins proposed attacking Farragut's force but was instead relieved of his command by Mallory for disobeying orders.

The construction of the Confederate ironclads was still incomplete at this crucial juncture. The Louisiana was launched on February 4 but remained unfinished by mid-April, lacking essential components like rudders to navigate the strong river currents. The Mississippi, launched in late April, was similarly under-equipped, with limited machinery and only a couple of cannons. This left Lovell and Mitchell unable to rely on these ironclads should Farragut advance. In response, Lovell declared martial law in New Orleans in mid-March.

Farragut, with his fleet refueled and over the sandbar, initiated his offensive. Porter commenced the bombardment of Fort Jackson on April 15, escalating it three days later with his sixty mortar boats. Despite being anchored in naturally covered areas, the mortar boats faced intense return fire, especially Porter's exposed second division. The bombardment inflicted significant damage, setting fires within Fort Jackson and disabling several guns.

However, Farragut quickly encountered supply shortages. By April 20, he was running out of essential munitions. Butler's timely arrival provided the needed supplies, but Farragut acknowledged his reliance on the army for resources. Faced with the dilemma of continuing the bombardment or attacking, Farragut leaned towards an offensive approach, encouraged by Porter's belief in the mortars' effectiveness.

Before the attack could proceed, they needed to clear the obstructions across the Mississippi near the forts. On the night of April 20, Captain Henry Haywood Bell led an operation with the gunboats Pinola and Itasca to breach the chain boom. Under heavy fire, both vessels encountered difficulties. The Itasca grounded near Fort St. Philip, but Lieutenant Charles H. B. Caldwell managed to ram and break the chain on the east bank. Following this, the Pinola broke the chain on the west bank, clearing a path for the Union fleet beyond the boom.

As Farragut and Porter prepared their forces south of the forts, Confederate Commander Duncan requested that Stephenson deploy fire ships against the Union fleet. However, Stephenson's initial efforts on April 15 unintentionally caused more harm to his own side, as the prematurely released fire barges drifted under the forts, causing a blaze. A second attempt on April 20, coinciding with Bell's chain-cutting operation, was only marginally successful. A fire raft caused a brief moment of chaos among Farragut's squadron, briefly setting the gunboat Sciota ablaze before the crew extinguished it. Stephenson's mismanagement of the fire rafts represented a missed chance to significantly damage Farragut's fleet before it could bypass the forts.

The Confederates faced further challenges beyond their River Defense Fleet. Tensions arose between Duncan and Mitchell, who was in charge of all naval forces, over strategies to counter Farragut's advance. On April 19, the incomplete Louisiana was towed down from New Orleans. Duncan wanted to position the ironclad near Fort Jackson to engage both Porter's mortar schooners and Farragut's approaching warships. Mitchell, however, insisted on keeping the Louisiana upstream to continue work on her machinery. This disagreement persisted until Farragut's attack, exemplifying the fractured

Confederate command structure, which hampered the defense of New Orleans.

When Farragut launched his attack at 3 a.m. on April 24, Mitchell had only a small contingent of ships at his disposal: the Louisiana, the Manassas, and the steamers McRae and Jackson, with the latter assigned to disrupt Butler's landing. Stephenson commanded six gunboats from the River Defense Force, operating independently under the War Department. Neither Duncan nor Mitchell desired Stephenson's involvement. Additionally, two state government-controlled gunboats and various other vessels were scattered in the area, further illustrating the disorganized defense.

Farragut briefed his captains on the attack plan on April 23. Porter's schooners would intensify their bombardment of Fort Jackson, supported by the sailing vessel Portsmouth. Farragut divided his fleet into three divisions, with Captain Theodorus Bailey leading the first division, followed by Farragut in the center division on his flagship Hartford, and Captain H. H. Bell commanding the rear division. Their strategy involved targeting Fort St. Philip and Fort Jackson as they passed.

The attack commenced at 3:30 a.m. on April 24, with the Cayuga leading the charge. However, delays and reduced visibility due to smoke and cannon fire created confusion and disrupted Farragut's formation. The Pensacola veered off course, and other ships in the first division followed haphazardly. Farragut didn't wait for the entire first division to reorganize before advancing in the Hartford. Amidst the chaos, the Brooklyn collided with the Kineo. Bell's division managed a smoother passage, but the Hartford faced a significant threat when a fire raft, pushed by the tugboat Mosher, set the flagship ablaze after it ran aground near a water battery.

Only a few Confederate steamers were able to directly engage Farragut's forces. The Manassas, commanded by Lieutenant Alexander Warley, used the river's current to its advantage, attempting to ram multiple Union frigates.

Though it missed the Pensacola, it managed to clash with the Mississippi, causing damage above the waterline, and successfully rammed the Brooklyn, damaging its hull.

The McRae had a fierce exchange with the Iroquois, trading heavy fire at close range, but eventually retreated towards Fort St. Philip. The Governor Moore, part of the River Defense Fleet, engaged in a notable skirmish with the Varuna near Quarantine. After ramming the Varuna and causing critical damage, the Governor Moore also suffered from the Varuna's retaliatory fire. The conflict resulted in the sinking of the Varuna, and the eventual destruction of the Governor Moore by its own captain to prevent capture.

By dawn, thirteen of Farragut's ships remained operational and had successfully passed the forts. Despite the intense engagement, casualties were relatively low, with a total of 38 fatalities and 159 wounded among Farragut's fleet. Several ships, including the Varuna, Itasca, Hartford, Brooklyn, and Mississippi, sustained notable damage.

On the Confederate side, the forts had minimal casualties, but their naval forces suffered significantly, with most of the River Defense ships either destroyed or grounded. The Louisiana remained afloat but required extensive repairs.

Farragut, seizing the momentum, paused at Quarantine for rest and repairs. The Manassas, pursued by the Mississippi and Kineo, was eventually abandoned and destroyed by Union forces. Farragut's fleet then continued upriver, passing remaining Confederate defenses and arriving in New Orleans by early afternoon the next day. As they approached, they witnessed widespread destruction caused by retreating Confederate forces, including the burning of the incomplete ironclad Mississippi, which the Tifts had unsuccessfully attempted to tow to safety. Confederate forces also began evacuating government property towards Camp Moore, in a bid to save what they could from the advancing Union forces.

The surrender of New Orleans unfolded over four days following Farragut's arrival. On April 25, Farragut dispatched Captain Bailey to demand the city's surrender, but Mayor John Monroe, citing martial law, deferred to General Lowell. Initially, Lowell refused to surrender, boasting of his fifteen thousand troops. However, he soon suggested evacuating to avoid bombardment and left for Camp Moore with his remaining forces. Farragut repeated his surrender demand on April 26, even sending sailors to hoist the US flag over the Mint building, but they were met with hostility and the flag was soon torn down.

Despite the public's defiance, Mayor Monroe acknowledged the city's vulnerable position after Lowell's departure. He informed Farragut that New Orleans was powerless and effectively conceded. However, Farragut delayed formal occupation until April 29, when he landed sailors and Marines under Captains H. H. Bell and Albert Kuntz. Bell raised the US flag at the Customs House and City Hall, marking the city's occupation.

Meanwhile, the forts downstream, Forts Jackson and St. Philip, remained in Confederate hands but were increasingly under pressure. Colonel Higgins of Fort Jackson rejected Porter's surrender demand on April 25, prompting further bombardment. Porter also suggested to Butler to land troops near Fort St. Philip. Following this, about three hundred men in Fort Jackson's garrison mutinied, spiking their guns and seeking escape from Confederate service. Most mutineers eventually swore allegiance to the Union.

Isolated and with Mitchell still attempting repairs on the ironclad Louisiana, both forts surrendered on April 28. The Navy received sole credit for capturing New Orleans and securing the forts' surrender. The surrender was not without controversy; to prevent its capture, Warley and Mitchell decided to destroy the Louisiana, an action that occurred under a flag of truce and killed one from the ensuing explosion, infuriating Porter. Following this, Mitchell surrendered his remaining ships, consolidating Union control over New Orleans and completing its capture.

Battle of Corinth

In the wake of the Union Army's decisive victory at the Battle of Shiloh on April 6–7, Major General Henry Halleck meticulously assembled a formidable force by uniting three key Union armies: the Army of the Tennessee, the Army of the Ohio, and the Army of the Mississippi. This strategic consolidation aimed at a critical offensive towards Corinth, Mississippi, a crucial hub for railroad logistics. Halleck, deeply impacted by the heavy casualties suffered at Shiloh, adopted a cautious yet relentless approach. His strategy involved a methodical campaign of offensive entrenchment, carefully fortifying positions after each progressive advance.

By May 25, 1862, Halleck's armies had made a painstakingly slow advancement, covering a mere five miles in three long weeks. Despite the slow pace, this deliberate approach positioned them ideally to initiate a siege on Corinth. The Confederate forces, led by General Beauregard, faced daunting challenges. Their morale had plummeted, and they were significantly outnumbered, with Union forces doubling their strength. Compounding their difficulties were the deplorable conditions, including contaminated water sources, which led to rampant outbreaks of typhoid and dysentery, decimating thousands of Confederate soldiers. This harrowing situation mirrored the horrific casualty rates they had previously endured at Shiloh.

Meanwhile, the Federal division under General Stanley embarked on a critical reconnaissance mission on April 29, 1862. Their objective was clear: to locate and engage the enemy forces. Brigadier General Elliot, spearheading a contingent comprising 16 cavalry companies, including the valiant 2nd Iowa Cavalry Regiment and elements of the 2nd Michigan Cavalry Regiment, encountered and swiftly engaged Confederate pickets from Forrest's 3rd Tennessee Cavalry Regiment. The Confederates, caught off-guard, hastily retreated, inadvertently leaving some of Patton Anderson's brigade's infantry exposed and vulnerable in their camp.

The 2nd Iowa Cavalry, seizing this opportunity, boldly captured 11 Confederate soldiers in a swift assault. Their momentum unbroken, they proceeded to enter Monterey, capturing additional enemy forces. The regiment's advance continued until they reached a strategically significant bridge, fiercely defended by Washington's Louisiana Battery and Colonel Kelly's 3rd Tennessee Cavalry Regiment. In a daring move, the 2nd Iowa charged headlong into a hail of canister fire, suffering casualties but demonstrating remarkable courage. Despite their bravery, they were compelled to withdraw after sustaining losses.

Major General Henry Halleck's forces were marked by the daring and aggressiveness of one commander in particular: John Pope. Commanding the Left Wing of the army, Pope distinguished himself with his bold tactics, operating at a considerable distance from Halleck's main headquarters. On May 3, Pope demonstrated his strategic acumen by capturing the town of Farmington, located mere miles from the crucial target of Corinth. This move signaled a significant advance, yet it also posed a dilemma for Halleck.

In an unexpected twist, Halleck, instead of capitalizing on Pope's momentum by advancing the Center Wing under Don Carlos Buell, ordered Pope to pull back and realign with Buell. This decision set the stage for a critical confrontation. General Pierre G. T. Beauregard of the Confederate forces, sensing an opportunity, commanded Earl Van Dorn to launch an attack on Pope's advanced position on May 9. Despite being caught in a precarious situation, Pope skillfully executed a tactical withdrawal, managing to regroup with Buell's forces.

The ensuing skirmish saw Braxton Bragg of the Confederate States Army leading a substantial force of 25,000 men. In stark contrast, the Union Army had a mere 12,000 troops on hand. Despite the disparity, the battle's outcome was not as one-sided as one might expect. Van Dorn's corps, which was barely engaged in the fight, suffered only 9 casualties. However, Daniel Ruggles's division, bearing the brunt of the battle under Bragg's command, faced heavier losses with 8 dead, 89 wounded, and two missing or captured. The Union forces, despite being outnumbered, held their ground with 16 killed, 148 wounded, and 14 missing or captured.

Amidst these clashes, the 8th Wisconsin Volunteer Infantry Regiment played a crucial role. Tasked with drawing out the enemy to gauge their strength, they strategically withdrew to a swamp north of the town after their engagement. Their brave efforts were not without cost: the regiment reported 5 killed, 14 severely wounded, and 19 slightly wounded. Notably, they were accompanied by Old Abe, the famous Screaming Eagle, a symbol of their courage and tenacity.

Meanwhile, the 5th Minnesota Infantry Regiment arrived in Corinth on May 24. Reporting directly to General John Pope, they were promptly assigned to the Second Brigade, First Division, of the Army of the Mississippi. Barely settled, the regiment was thrust into the fray. Within four days of reaching the front lines, they found themselves engaged in the latter stages of the Battle of Farmington. Their introduction to the battlefield was a baptism by fire, as they incurred several casualties in their first combat experience.

Major General William Tecumseh Sherman emerged as a pivotal figure during the Union's approach to Corinth. Sherman, keenly aware of the critical importance of breaking the Confederate defenses, devised a daring assault plan targeting the formidable position held by Brigadier General James R. Chalmers near the Russell house, a key point in the Confederate front lines.

On May 16, Sherman convened a meeting with General Henry Halleck and General George Henry Thomas to outline his audacious strategy. The plan hinged on a coordinated attack led by the brigades of Colonel Morgan L. Smith and Brigadier General James W. Denver, with Major General Stephen A. Hurlbut's division poised to lend crucial support. The attack, set in motion on May 17, saw Denver's forces on the right flank, Smith's in the center, and Hurlbut's reserves strategically positioned on the right.

Chalmers, known for his tenacity, mounted a fierce resistance. His troops, entrenched within the Russell house, unleashed a storm of fire upon the Union forces. A critical moment arrived when the Confederates nearly outflanked Smith's right, only to be valiantly repulsed by Colonel Thomas Kilby Smith and the stalwart 54th Ohio Infantry. The tide turned when a battery from the 1st Illinois Artillery swung into action, decisively tipping the scales in favor of the Union. Chalmers, recognizing the shift in momentum, executed a tactical retreat to Philips Creek, leaving the high ground—and the Russell house—to Morgan Smith's brigade.

In this intense clash, Sherman's forces incurred 10 fatalities and 31 wounded, predominantly from Smith's brigade. The Confederate losses remained uncertain, but Sherman's reports indicated at least 12 enemy soldiers dead on the field. This engagement coincided with another significant maneuver by Brigadier General Thomas W. Sherman, who successfully repelled a Confederate force defending a crossing at Bridge Creek.

Further south, on May 21, Major General William "Bull" Nelson initiated a bold move. He ordered Colonel Thomas D. Sedgwick to undertake a reconnaissance-in-force against the entrenched Confederate positions along Bridge Creek near Widow Surratt's farm. Sedgwick, advancing from Union trenches held by Brigadier General Thomas J. Wood's division, deployed the 20th Kentucky infantry at the edge of a clearing, with the 1st Kentucky infantry to the left, bracing for a confrontation in a densely wooded area. Almost immediately, the Kentuckians were engulfed in enemy fire.

The Confederate resistance was formidable, forcing Sedgwick into a strategic withdrawal. He responded by bringing forward artillery and the 2nd Kentucky infantry, while General Wood provided cavalry support from his division. A critical intervention came from Captain Alvan C. Gillem of Buell's staff, who personally supervised the Union artillery, and the 31st Indiana infantry in reserve, collectively stabilizing the Union line. Despite three additional attempts by the Confederates to flank the Union position, they ultimately retired to a creek beyond the Surratt farm. General Nelson, exhibiting strategic caution, instructed Sedgwick to maintain his position until nightfall before returning to camp.

A week later, in a continuation of these tense engagements, General Buell launched an offensive aimed at securing the high ground surrounding the Surratt farm, further escalating the chess game of military maneuvers and counter-maneuvers.

On the morning of May 27, in a crucial strategic move, Major General Henry Halleck issued orders to Major General William T. Sherman to seize control of a log house along the Corinth Road. This house, strategically located at the cusp of a cotton field and skillfully converted into a blockhouse by the Confederates, was a critical point in the Union's plan to make a significant demonstration against Corinth itself. The Confederates had fortified this log house by removing the chinking between the logs, turning it into a formidable defensive position.

Sherman, known for his tactical acumen, swiftly organized an attacking column. The formation saw Morgan L. Smith's brigade positioned on the left and James W. Denver's brigade on the right. Additional support came from John A. Logan's brigade, part of John A. McClernand's reserve corps, and James C. Veatch's brigade from Stephen A. Hurlbut's division. The attack commenced with a signal from Colonel Ezra Taylor, who fired several artillery rounds, marking the beginning of the infantry assault.

Denver and Smith, with their brigades, advanced rapidly and fiercely stormed the log house, seizing control of the critical hilltop position. The Confederates, however, were not to be easily subdued. They mounted a spirited counterattack, driving in Sherman's skirmishers. But the Union forces, bolstered by a robust line of infantry and artillery support, repulsed this counteroffensive. The next day, the rest of Sherman's division, along with additional artillery, moved forward to consolidate this new strategic position, which offered an advantageous view into Corinth. Generals Ulysses S. Grant and George H. Thomas, present on the field, approved the conduct of the operation.

Meanwhile, Confederate infantry had been utilizing a hill near the Widow Surratt farm for picket outposts. With his forces aligned, Halleck tasked General Don Carlos Buell with the mission to clear the Confederates off this strategically significant hill. Buell selected Major General Alexander M. McCook's reserve division for this task, aiming to use the hill as a staging point for a further attack against Corinth. On the same day, May 27, McCook organized his brigades for a surprise offensive, intending to overwhelm the Confederates with a combination of surprise and sheer force.

The brigades of Brigadier General Lovell H. Rousseau and Brigadier General Richard W. Johnson spearheaded the advance, moving in a coordinated manner. Colonel Frederick S. Stumbaugh's brigade followed in support of Johnson, while Colonel Robert L. McCook's brigade (from Thomas W. Sherman's division) supported Rousseau. Johnson's brigade faced heavy skirmishing, but the hill was swiftly captured. McCook's division immediately entrenched the position, deploying heavy artillery and began shelling the Confederate lines. Beauregard's artillery offered only minimal resistance in return. The seizure of the Surratt farm hill enabled Halleck to bring forward siege guns for the impending bombardment of Corinth.

On May 28, Major General William "Bull" Nelson gave orders to Colonel Sedgwick to capture a Confederate-held crossing of Bridge Creek, a minor tributary of the Tuscumbia River. Sedgwick, leading his brigade, moved out from the main Union trenches with the 2nd and 20th Kentucky infantry regiments at the forefront. After overcoming the Confederate pickets, Sedgwick encountered a larger force guarding the bridge. The Kentucky regiments managed to secure the eastern end of the bridge. With the addition of the 31st Indiana infantry and Captain John Mendenhall's artillery battery, the Union forces compelled the Confederates to completely abandon the bridge.

As the Union army readied itself for a siege on Corinth, the Confederate leadership, faced with a dire situation, convened a council of war. In a masterstroke of military deception, Confederate Commander General P. G. T. Beauregard orchestrated a retreat that would become legendary. To mask their withdrawal plans, Beauregard ingeniously ordered some of his men to be given three days' rations, hinting at an imminent attack. This ruse worked as anticipated; a few soldiers defected to the Union side, unwittingly carrying this misleading information.

Meanwhile, as the Union's preliminary bombardment echoed across the battlefield, and their forces maneuvered into position, the Confederate army commenced its nocturnal exodus on May 29. Utilizing the Mobile and Ohio Railroad, they efficiently transported their sick and wounded, heavy artillery, and copious supplies. In a display of cunning, arriving trains were greeted with cheers, feigning the arrival of reinforcements. The Confederates further bolstered their deception with "Quaker Guns"—dummy cannons—placed along their earthworks. To complete the illusion, campfires were kept ablaze, while buglers and drummers played on. Under the cover of this orchestrated chaos, the bulk of the Confederate forces silently retreated, eventually regrouping in Tupelo, Mississippi.

When Union patrols entered Corinth on the morning of May 30, they found an eerily deserted town. The Confederate troops had vanished, leaving behind their well-crafted ruse. The Union forces quickly took control of

Corinth, establishing it as a strategic base for their ensuing operations aimed at dominating the Mississippi River Valley, particularly targeting the Confederate stronghold of Vicksburg, Mississippi.

Reflecting on these events, John Pope, a Union general known for his aggressive tactics but often criticized for his strategic shortcomings, later commented in his memoirs. He lamented that Halleck's excessively cautious campaign had squandered the potential of a remarkable ensemble of Union officers. This array of military talent included illustrious names like Grant, Sherman, Sheridan, Thomas, McPherson, Logan, Buell, Rosecrans, and many others, whose combined capabilities, Pope believed, could have led to more decisive victories.

In October 1862, a Confederate army led by Major General Earl Van Dorn made a bold attempt to retake Corinth. This effort culminated in the Second Battle of Corinth, where they faced a Union army commanded by Rosecrans. Throughout this battle, Confederate forces occasionally seemed to gain the upper hand but repeatedly failed to capitalize on these moments, leading to a crushing defeat that significantly weakened Confederate presence in the region. Rosecrans, despite achieving a critical victory, missed a pivotal opportunity to decisively crush the rebel forces, allowing Major General Earl Van Dorn and his troops a narrow escape. The battles for Corinth thus became a crucial turning point in the Civil War, setting the stage for the Union's campaign to open the Mississippi River valley and further dismantle the Confederacy's strategic strongholds.

Battle of Drewry's Bluff

In the early months of 1862, as the winter thawed into spring, the situation in the Eastern Theater of the American Civil War was tenuous for the Union forces. The previous year had been marred by setbacks, with defeats at Bull Run and Ball's Bluff casting doubt on the Federal army's ability to secure a swift and decisive victory in the east. However, a transformation was underway, led by Major General George Brinton McClellan, who took command of the Military Division of the Potomac in August 1861. Under his leadership, the newly formed Army of the Potomac experienced a significant boost in both numbers and morale.

McClellan, known for his tireless dedication, had already earned a minor victory in western Virginia and had made significant contributions during his tenure in the Department of the Ohio. His political maneuvering and military acumen culminated in his appointment as general-in-chief on November 1, 1861. Despite these achievements, by January 1862, McClellan had yet to reveal his strategic plans to President Lincoln or engage his army in significant combat.

This changed in a crucial meeting with Lincoln on January 12, where McClellan outlined an ambitious amphibious operation involving the Army of the Potomac. The following months saw escalating tensions between McClellan, Lincoln, and the cabinet, exacerbated by the Confederate army's unchallenged retreat from the Manassas area to the Virginia peninsula. McClellan's initial plan to strike along the Rappahannock River evolved into a campaign targeting Richmond, the Confederate capital, via Virginia's peninsula.

The Army of the Potomac embarked on this grand campaign from Alexandria, Virginia, towards Fort Monroe on March 17, 1862. However, McClellan's delay in action inadvertently provided Confederate forces near Richmond ample opportunity to fortify their defenses, including on the James River. During this period, Major Augustus Harrison Drewry of the 2nd Regiment Virginia Artillery sought approval from Robert E. Lee to build a fort on his property, adding another defensive layer around Richmond. Drewry, drawing men from Chesterfield County, formed a company comprising individuals ranging in age and profession, from young farmers to older carpenters and cotton-mill workers.

Assigned to Battery No. 19 near Drewry's Bluff, the company initially experienced the monotony of inactivity, a stark contrast to their expectations of war. Drewry himself acknowledged the unimportance of their initial assignment and his doubts about his men's suitability for field duty.

Augustus Harrison Drewry, born in 1817, had become a distinguished figure in Virginia by the time the Civil War broke out. Residing on his grandfather's plantation, Brandywine, in King County, Virginia, in 1861, Augustus saw his wealth grow further after marrying Mary A. Harrison, a descendant of Pocahontas. Through this marriage, he acquired a tract of land along the James River, just eight miles south of Richmond.

This land included a significant bluff, towering over 100 feet above the river, presenting a strategic advantage. The location was particularly notable for its bend in the James River, allowing for effective defensive positions against ships approaching from the southeast. The possibility of placing artillery on this bluff meant that a considerable stretch of the river below could be controlled, and additional river obstructions could further hinder the movement of Federal gunboats.

As the Confederate defense of Richmond grew in importance, Drewry proposed the idea of a fort at this location. His plan included not only the strategic defense of Richmond but also the practical deployment of his command, comprising men less suited for extended field service. Lee agreed to Drewry's proposition for a fort in this area.

The process of selecting the exact location for the fort involved Drewry, Major Rives, and Lieutenant Mason from the engineers department surveying potential sites along the river. They initially considered Howlett's location but deemed it unsuitable due to the risk of the Federals bypassing it via the Dutch Gap. Eventually, they settled on Drewry's land, particularly the high bluff, for the construction of the fort and gun placements.

Upon deciding on the location, Drewry led his unit, the Southside Artillery, to the bluff. Despite the grumblings of the men about being uprooted from their comfortable quarters, they settled in and began the construction of the fort and river obstructions.

The first task involved obstructing the river, followed by the fort's construction. Drewry provided assistance to engineer Mason, using his resources and command. However, the progress of the fort was impeded by bureaucratic hurdles and a lack of enthusiasm in Richmond. Drewry faced challenges in obtaining necessary materials and labor, resulting in a slow construction process and declining morale among his men. To improve their living conditions, Drewry focused on constructing cabins for his troops.

During this period, despite facing numerous challenges, some progress was made on the fortifications at Drewry's Bluff, known as Fort Darling. Lieutenant Mason, responsible for laying out the fort, oversaw the preparation of emplacements for three heavy guns on the river-facing side of the bluff. These included a 10-inch Columbiad from Richmond, along with other significant artillery pieces such as 8-inch and 10-inch guns.

Transporting these heavy guns was a formidable task. Two additional eight-inch Columbiads were brought down the river to the fort's location. The challenging process involved transferring the guns from lighters to dry land and then moving them up a steep incline to a position over 100 feet above the river level. Mounting the guns required skilled workmanship, including building foundations for the fort, leveling gun platforms, and establishing traverse circles.

Efforts to complete the fort accelerated with the arrival of Colonel Robert Tansell, who directed the mounting of the guns using a gin and extensive manual labor. Progress, however, was initially slow and only picked up momentum following increased interest and support from Confederate authorities like General Lee.

By mid-April, roughly a month after Drewry's company arrived at the bluff, the pace of work intensified. Additional artillery and troops were sent to the bluff, although they were soon redeployed to Fredericksburg. Despite these changes, work at the fort continued steadily.

The strategic importance of Fort Darling grew as General Joseph Eggleston Johnston considered abandoning the Yorktown line on the Virginia Peninsula, a defensive position aimed at halting McClellan's advance on Richmond. This development placed greater emphasis on completing the fortifications at Drewry's Bluff. Lee and Confederate Naval Secretary Stephen Mallory began to closely monitor and expedite the work on the fort.

During this time, Captain Drewry's men underwent intensive training in heavy artillery tactics. They were instructed by Robert Stuart McFarland, a seasoned soldier with experience in both the British and United States armies. McFarland trained the Confederate artillerymen rigorously in various procedures, including loading, firing, and handling the heavy guns. Additionally, they received training from a former English army Ordnance Department officer, McMellon, who imparted knowledge on ammunition handling, gunnery drills, and basic hygiene practices.

The strategic importance of Fort Darling increasingly drew the attention of Confederate leaders like Lee and Mallory. Recognizing that the fort was the last line of defense against the powerful Federal fleet, efforts to strengthen and complete it intensified. The Confederate navy's dominance on land and sea was a concern, as any Federal gunboats bypassing the bluff could threaten the Confederate capital, its government, and its military presence.

In early May, Lee sent a company of sappers and miners to bolster the garrison at Fort Darling. Shortly after, Secretary Mallory dispatched Commander Ebenezer Farrand with additional troops, including Confederate sailors and marines who had evacuated from Norfolk. These reinforcements were initially hesitant and demoralized, surprised at the prospect of resisting the formidable Federal gunboats. However, they were eventually persuaded to stay and defend the position.

Drewry, who was less than impressed with Farrand, continued to maintain command over the fort. The defense of Darling's Bluff was enhanced with artillery from various sources, including guns from the 2nd Virginia Artillery and other Confederate gunboats like the Patrick Henry and Jamestown. Additional river obstructions were put in place to hinder the Federal navy's approach.

However, weather conditions posed challenges, and one of the guns from the Patrick Henry became inoperative due to rain damage. As McClellan's army advanced towards Richmond and the Federal navy approached down the James River, efforts to complete the fort's defenses received more support from the Confederate authorities and the Richmond City Council.

In mid-May, with the Union threat escalating, Robert E. Lee ordered further fortifications at Chaffin's Bluff, an additional defensive layer along the James River. Six companies were dispatched to construct gun emplacements, and more reinforcements followed, including the crew of the CSS Virginia and Lieutenant Catesby ap Roger Jones. As Union forces threatened Norfolk and Portsmouth, the Confederate naval yards and ships that could not be moved were destroyed to prevent them falling into Federal hands.

Despite these efforts, a nine-inch Dahlgren gun positioned by Jones was found to be out of range during the battle. The urgency to complete Fort Darling's defenses peaked on May 13, when news arrived of Federal gunboats advancing towards their position. This spurred every man and officer into a frenzy of activity to ready the fort for an impending attack.

The following days saw additional reinforcements, including Confederate marine companies and a company of the Washington Artillery at Chaffin's Bluff. Confederate Secretary of War George Wythe Randolph ordered Brigadier General William Mahone's Virginia Brigade to join the defenses, anticipating a potential infantry assault from the Federal navy transports. The presence of Mahone's brigade at Fort Darling ensured sufficient Confederate infantry support to counter any such assault.

As the Union forces approached, the situation at Fort Darling became increasingly tense. The arrival of the first shell, unexpectedly soaring over the fort, marked the onset of hostilities and left those within the defenses both startled and alert. This shell, notably large, was a jarring introduction to combat for many who had never before experienced enemy fire. In the anxious moments that followed, with no immediate subsequent attacks, the soldiers at Fort Darling remained vigilant, manning their guns while others continued fortifying the defenses. Preparations went on through the night, with some soldiers working continuously, and others resting with the understanding that they would be alerted if the enemy boats appeared.

The morning of May 15, 1862, presented challenging weather conditions. George B. McClellan, commander of the Army of the Potomac, noted in communications with Secretary of War Edwin McMasters Stanton that the weather had been consistently wet and dreary, continuing into the day of the battle. Despite the rain, the USS Galena and other Federal gunboats were advancing towards Fort Darling. At the fort, the day began with light showers, adding to the already tense atmosphere.

Sergeant Mann and his mess were up early for breakfast, unaware that the day would soon escalate into a full-scale battle. The sound of a signal musket being fired hurriedly called them to action. Upon arriving at the fort, they found themselves amidst a flurry of activity, with a working party quickly arranging sandbags to form embrasures for the guns. This urgency was due to the sighting of Federal gunboats moving closer to their position.

In the moments leading up to the battle, everyone had a role to play. Some soldiers assisted with the sandbags right up until the last possible moment, while gun crews took their positions and others handled ammunition duties. Key figures like Captain Farrand, Captain Drewry, and Lieutenant Wilson were stationed at Mann's gun, ensuring everything was in order for the impending engagement. Captain Jordan and the Bedford Artillery were responsible for another crucial gun position. As they stood ready, the anticipation and readiness were palpable, with all eyes on the river, awaiting the signal to commence firing.

The dynamics of the engagement quickly evolved with the arrival of Federal gunboats. Between 6:00 and 6:30 a.m., the Confederate forces, still waiting for the command to fire, watched as the USS Galena and USS Monitor advanced towards their position. By 7:45 a.m., the Galena, under Commander John Rodgers, anchored in the channel, positioning itself broadside to Fort Darling. Before Galena could fully settle into position, the Confederate guns from Drewry's Bluff opened fire, landing two hits on Galena's port bow, disabling an entire gun crew.

In the midst of this chaos, United States Marine Sergeant John Freeman Mackie took command of a group of Marines, leading them onto the gun deck to man the weapons and return fire. For his bravery and leadership during this battle, Mackie was later awarded the Medal of Honor.

Simultaneously, the USS Monitor was attempting to position itself within the channel, facing two significant challenges. The river obstructions required clearing, necessitating work parties to be exposed on the deck, and the Monitor's guns could not be elevated high enough to effectively target the Confederate positions from its initial placement. This dilemma forced the Monitor to reposition to a more effective firing range, a maneuver that consumed valuable time.

Meanwhile, three wooden Federal gunboats – the Aroostook, Port Royal, and Naugatuck – also entered the fray, engaging Drewry's Bluff from varying distances. Commander John Rodgers quickly recognized that the threat was not limited to the Confederate guns on the bluff, as sharpshooters along the riverbanks added another layer of defense, harassing the men on the Federal boats.

As the engagement intensified, all Confederate batteries on the bluff were actively firing upon the Federal squadron. Sergeant Mann's battery, along with others, had commenced firing under Farrand's orders. However, the Confederate forces faced their own set of challenges – Captain Jordan's ten-inch gun was rendered nearly inoperable due to recoil damage, and a naval gun brought in to reinforce the position was also put out of action when its log casemate collapsed.

With two of their main guns disabled, the Confederates were left primarily with two eight-inch guns from Captain Drewry's company. These guns, firing 64-pound shells, continued to engage the ironclads and gunboats.

Despite some of their artillery being compromised, the Confederate forces began to inflict significant damage on the Union ironclad, USS Galena. After several rounds merely left marks on the Galena's exterior, one shot finally breached its armor, causing substantial internal damage. This hit validated Commander Rodgers' subsequent acknowledgment that the Galena was not impervious to enemy fire. The intensity of the Confederate assault was evident in the damage sustained by the Galena, with numerous men injured by fragments of the ship's own iron and structural damage inflicted upon the vessel.

The Federal squadron, comprising various ships, also faced substantial challenges. On the USS Port Royal, Lieutenant George Upham Morris had to contend with sharpshooters from the shore whose bullets pierced the ship's bulwarks. While he managed to temporarily quell the riflemen with howitzer fire, the Confederate batteries continued to pose a threat, causing significant damage to his ship.

The E.A. Stevens, also known as the Naugatuck, engaged in a fierce exchange of gunfire, with both musketry and artillery fire being heavily exchanged. Lieutenant David C. Constable, leading the Naugatuck, continued the engagement until their own gun malfunctioned. Similarly, on the USS Aroostook, Lieutenant J.C Beaumont faced issues with ammunition compatibility, causing delays and leaving the ship vulnerable to Confederate gunfire. Beaumont had to reposition the Aroostook further downstream to safely continue the engagement.

On the Confederate side, casualties and close calls were mounting as well. Sergeant Mann and Lieutenant Wilson both experienced perilous moments, with Wilson injured by a bursting shell and Mann tripping over equipment. Tragically, Captain Jordan and several of his men, all Confederate navy sailors, were killed while attempting to remount their gun during the battle.

Throughout the engagement, Captain Drewry played a prominent role, actively commanding and motivating his men from a conspicuous position atop the fortifications. Despite the danger and the pleas of his men, Drewry remained steadfast, directing the fire of his guns with precision and determination. His leadership was marked by a focus on targeting the wooden boats in the Federal fleet, urging his men to drive them away with their fire.

The battle lasting close to four hours, reached its climax as Sergeant Mann observed the three wooden Federal gunboats retreating from Fort Darling, followed by the ironclads, Monitor and Galena. Commander Rodgers of the Galena reported the depletion of nearly all their ammunition, prompting the decision to withdraw from the engagement. With the Federal fleet retreating, Confederate soldiers, upon hearing the order to cease fire, celebrated their victory, but Captain Drewry, aware of the potential for a renewed assault, instructed his men to repair the damaged defenses in preparation for any future attacks.

In the aftermath of the battle, Confederate President Jefferson Davis and General Lee visited the site. They observed the damage and the ongoing repair efforts, with General Lee offering guidance on restoring the sandbag fortifications. As time passed without any signs of a Federal naval return, it became evident that the battle for Drewry's Bluff had concluded, revealing the extent of the damage and casualties.

The USS Monitor, having been struck three times by Confederate fire, sustained minimal damage. Lieutenant William Nicholson Jeffers reported that the hits caused no significant damage and there were no casualties. Despite the resilience of the Monitor, Jeffers acknowledged that the engagement had limited success and emphasized the challenges of reducing such fortified positions without land force support.

In stark contrast, the USS Galena suffered considerably more. Hit 44 times, the Galena faced a myriad of challenges: armor penetration, internal explosions, fire outbreaks, and substantial water intake. Commander Rodgers highlighted the efforts of J.W. Thomson, who managed to repair broken valve gear and extinguish a fire, all under enemy fire. The Galena's casualties were severe, with 14 dead or mortally wounded and 10 injured. Among them was Acting Master Benjamin W. Loring, who bravely managed his division despite repeated losses of his crew, and Mr. Boorom, a gunner killed by shell fragments, who Rodgers remembered as a valuable officer to the service.

The Galena, despite sustaining heavy damage during the battle at Drewry's Bluff, managed to inflict significant harm on the Confederate defenses and crew, resulting in seven fatalities and eight injuries. Commander Rodgers of the Galena commended the bravery and efficiency of his crew, highlighting the contributions of several individuals. T. Millholland, an assistant engineer, was recognized for his dual roles in managing the steam fired department and effectively engaging Confederate sharpshooters. Mr. Jenks, master's mate, was also acknowledged for his role in managing the small-arms personnel and countering enemy sharpshooters.

Among the crew, Charles Kenyon, a fireman on the Galena, was noted for his courage in addressing a technical issue with the ship's weaponry despite sustaining severe burns. Jeremiah Regan, the quartermaster and captain of one of the guns, was recommended for promotion due to his exemplary performance during the battle. The Marines on board were also commended for their efficiency, particularly when they filled in at the guns.

Sergeant John Freeman Mackie, who played a pivotal role in the battle, was not specifically mentioned in Rodgers' report but received significant recognition later. In July, President Lincoln, Secretary of the Navy Gideon Welles, and other high-ranking officials visited the Army of the Potomac and inspected the Galena. During this visit, Lincoln acknowledged the crew's bravery, and Mackie, along with others, was singled out for his actions during the battle. Mackie was later promoted and awarded the Medal of Honor, becoming the first Marine to receive this honor.

On the USS Port Royal, the captain was wounded by Confederate rifle fire, believed to be from a sharpshooter. The ship also sustained a direct hit from a shell below the water line, forcing Lieutenant Morris to withdraw for repairs due to the significant water intake.

The successful defense of Drewry's Bluff on May 15, 1862, can be attributed to the extensive preparations and reinforcements that were rapidly mobilized. It is estimated that nearly 1,800 Confederate soldiers and sailors were stationed at Drewry and Chaffin's Bluffs on the day of the battle. Additionally, around 4,000 reinforcements were en route under General Mahone's command. The fort's artillery capabilities had also significantly increased since Captain Drewry and his company's arrival in March, with twelve guns positioned in various stages of readiness.

Tactical measures like sinking the Jamestown in the channel were instrumental in securing the water approach to Richmond via the James River. However, historian Steven Newton pointed out that the Confederate forces faced challenges beyond the Federal navy, notably a chaotic and inefficient command structure at the bluff. The situation was complicated by changes in command and some disregard for Commander Tucker, who had overseen the navy's work parties.

Despite these command issues, the primary credit for the Confederate victory is often attributed to Captain Drewry and the Southside Heavy Artillery. Their resilience and effective defense were crucial in repelling the Federal navy. This sentiment is echoed in historical accounts, with one Confederate veteran from 1901 highlighting the significant contribution of local farmers who joined the fight, not for military glory but to defend their country and homes. Another Confederate, reflecting on the battle at the turn of the century, praised the Southside Heavy Artillery for their crucial role in driving back the ironclad fleet.

The battle not only reinforced Major Drewry's reputation as a courageous and resourceful leader but also highlighted the extraordinary performance of the officers and men under his command. Their collective efforts were instrumental in securing a Confederate victory, earning them a place of honor in the hearts of their countrymen.

Battle of Front Royal

I n the spring of 1862, the American Civil War was escalating into one of its most critical phases. In this period, Union Major General George B. McClellan initiated the ambitious Peninsula Campaign on the Virginia Peninsula, a strategic move aiming to capture the Confederate capital of Richmond. Parallel to this, in the western region of the Shenandoah Valley, another significant military maneuver was unfolding. Union Major General Nathaniel Banks, leading a substantial force, was advancing, exerting pressure on the Confederate troops commanded by the legendary Major General Thomas J. "Stonewall" Jackson.

Jackson, renowned for his military acumen, was tasked with a critical mission: to engage Union troops in the Valley and prevent them from reinforcing McClellan's campaign. The strategic importance of the Shenandoah Valley was immense, serving as a vital agricultural region and a transportation corridor for the Confederacy. By March 21, the Union high command, assessing the situation, concluded that a large portion of Banks's force was excessive for securing the Valley. Consequently, they redirected much of this force to Washington, D.C., significantly reducing Banks's strength in the Valley to about 9,000 men from the original 35,000.

The stage was set for the First Battle of Kernstown on March 23, where Jackson, seizing the opportunity, launched an audacious attack on the Union forces. Despite being repulsed, Jackson's bold action alarmed the Union command. The battle's outcome had far-reaching implications: it compelled the Union to reinforce Banks's diminished forces and to retain an additional corps at Manassas, Virginia. This strategic diversion effectively deprived McClellan's Peninsula Campaign of approximately 60,000 troops, a significant setback for the Union.

Following the battle, Jackson, ever the tactician, retreated southward in the Valley. He soon joined forces with Major General Richard Ewell, setting the stage for further confrontations. Leaving Ewell to engage with Banks, Jackson strategically moved his troops southwest towards McDowell, Virginia. In early May, Jackson faced a Union force under Major General John C. Frémont. A part of Frémont's command, led by Brigadier General Robert H. Milroy, engaged Jackson's men in the Battle of McDowell on May 8. The Confederates, demonstrating their military prowess, emerged victorious, forcing Frémont's withdrawal.

The chess game of war continued as Jackson then redirected his forces northward to confront Banks once again. The ever-changing dynamics of the war saw parts of Banks's force being reassigned out of the Valley. On May 12, the division under Brigadier General James Shields was ordered eastward, further weakening Banks's position. Banks, recognizing his precarious situation, withdrew his remaining forces to Strasburg, setting the stage for the next chapter in the Shenandoah Valley Campaigns.

A significant shift occurred in the Confederate command structure. General Joseph E. Johnston, leading Confederate forces against Union Major General McClellan, issued an order on May 17 (dated May 13) directing Major General Richard Ewell to move his troops from the Shenandoah Valley to support Johnston's army. This order, however, intersected with the plans of Major General Thomas J. "Stonewall" Jackson, who had a different vision for Ewell's forces.

Jackson, recognizing the potential for a decisive strike against Union Major General Nathaniel Banks, sent an urgent message to Johnston on the same day, requesting that Ewell's command remain with him. On May 18, without yet having received a response from Johnston, Jackson and Ewell made a provisional decision: Ewell would temporarily stay under Jackson's command until further notice. This was a period marked by slow communications, with messages taking several days to reach their destinations. Consequently, even by May 20, when Jackson received another order instructing Ewell to move east, there was still no word from Johnston on the earlier request.

In a move to consolidate his position, Jackson reached out to General Robert E. Lee, a key advisor to Confederate President Jefferson Davis, seeking support for retaining Ewell's men. Intriguingly, later that day, a message from Johnston arrived, granting Jackson discretionary authority over Ewell's command.

This development bolstered the Confederate forces under Jackson and Ewell to a nominal strength of 17,000 men. However, historian Gary Ecelbarger estimated that due to factors like desertion and straggling, the actual number of effective troops was likely closer to 12,000 or 14,000. With this force, the Confederates resumed their northward movement to engage Banks.

The Union forces, stationed at Strasburg, had constructed fortifications facing south, anticipating a direct confrontation. However, Jackson, ever the tactician, decided to maneuver eastward, aiming to capture the Union outpost at Front Royal. By seizing Front Royal, Jackson planned to cut off Banks's communications to the east and potentially flank the Strasburg position, compelling its capture or abandonment.

On May 21, the Confederate march commenced. They crossed the Massanutten Mountain and entered the Page Valley, stealthily approaching Front Royal. At this time, Banks's forces were dispersed: approximately 6,500 men in Strasburg, about 1,000 in Front Royal, and another 1,000 in Winchester. Jackson, not fully aware of the exact Union strengths but knowing the Front

Royal garrison was weaker, saw an opportunity. Front Royal and Strasburg, though just about 12 miles apart via the direct railroad route, were also connected by longer road paths.

On the morning of May 23, Major General Thomas J. "Stonewall" Jackson meticulously orchestrated his attack strategy. He deployed Colonel Turner Ashby's cavalry with a critical mission: sever the telegraph lines and railroad connections between Front Royal and Strasburg. This move aimed to isolate the Union forces and prevent their coordination. Despite his numerical superiority over the Union troops in Front Royal, Jackson, unaware of this advantage, chose a cautious approach rather than a direct assault via the Luray Road.

Jackson's plan involved a flanking maneuver. Major General Richard Ewell's troops were directed to advance along the Gooney Manor Road, while the Stonewall Brigade, along with some artillery units, held their position at Asbury's Chapel, situated 4.5 miles from Front Royal. This strategic positioning meant that any Union forces retreating from Front Royal would be compelled to cross both the South and North Forks of the Shenandoah River, potentially hampering their escape.

Historian Gary Ecelbarger suggested that this focus on a single road might also prevent any Union escapees from Front Royal from giving Major General Nathaniel Banks an accurate assessment of Jackson's force size.

As the Confederate forces advanced, they discovered from captured Union pickets that the opposition in Front Royal was primarily the 1st Maryland Infantry Regiment. In response, Jackson ordered the Confederate 1st Maryland Infantry Regiment to lead the assault. This regiment, recently rattled by a mutiny incident, was reinvigorated by a patriotic speech from Colonel Bradley T. Johnson. The attack commenced around 2:00 pm, spearheaded by the Marylanders and supported by Major Roberdeau Wheat's Louisiana Tigers, a notoriously unruly battalion, with the rest of Brigadier

General Richard Taylor's Louisiana brigade in reserve. These attacking forces totaled about 450 men.

Belle Boyd, a notable figure, rode from the town to provide Jackson with information about the Union force. However, historians like James I. Robertson Jr. and Peter Cozzens have downplayed Boyd's impact, noting that she provided little new information to Jackson.

The Union troops, caught off guard and without any cavalry at Front Royal, were unable to anticipate the Confederate advance. The Confederate attack swiftly overwhelmed the Union forces, compelling Colonel John Reese Kenly, the Union commander, to retreat to Richardson's Hill, strategically located between Front Royal and the South Fork. Here, Kenly deployed two 10-pounder Parrott rifles for defense. Despite some Union soldiers being captured within the town and the loss of a Union supply train, organized resistance within Front Royal was minimal, with one Confederate soldier likening it to "more like a police riot than a fight between soldiers."

Kenly's remaining force, about 700 infantrymen, took a defensive position in front of an open meadow, a challenging terrain for a frontal attack. Despite their effective use of the Parrott guns, the Union forces faced a formidable Confederate assault.

As the Union cannons pounded his lines, Confederate General Thomas "Stonewall" Jackson instructed his chief of artillery, Colonel Stapleton Crutchfield, to set up counter-artillery. However, the initial Confederate battery was inadequately equipped, its range too short to effectively counter the Union position. Crutchfield managed to deploy three longer-range cannons, leading to a fierce fifteen-minute artillery exchange.

Colonel John Reese Kenly, commanding the Union forces, attempted to bolster his defense despite his limited resources. A small unit of the 29th Pennsylvania Infantry Regiment held the ground between the Shenandoah

River's two forks, while 100 men from the 5th New York Cavalry Regiment, sent from Strasburg by Union Major General Nathaniel Banks that morning, engaged the Confederate skirmishers. In the midst of this, Confederate forces intensified their assault: Colonel Bradley T. Johnson's Maryland regiment attacked from the center, the 6th Louisiana Infantry Regiment struck the Union left flank, and additional troops from Brigadier General Richard Taylor's brigade engaged the Union right.

Simultaneously, Confederate cavalry units, including the 2nd and 6th Virginia Cavalry Regiments led by Colonel Thomas Flournoy, aimed to seize the North Fork bridge. Their control of this bridge would effectively cut off the Union's last retreat route. These cavalry forces had earlier disrupted Union communications by cutting railroad and telegraph lines before joining the main battle at Front Royal.

Faced with these developments, Kenly decided to retreat around 4:30 pm. The Union troops fell back across the South and North Fork bridges, setting them ablaze to hinder Confederate pursuit and destroying some supplies to prevent their capture. Despite these efforts, the Confederates managed to extinguish the fires at the South Fork bridge. Jackson quickly called for reinforcements, including the Stonewall Brigade, but they were too far behind to participate in the immediate action.

Kenly reorganized his forces on Guard Hill, across the North Fork, with an augmented strength of approximately 800 men, including reinforcements from the 29th Pennsylvania. Meanwhile, the Confederate forces, in their disarray, looted the abandoned Union camp. It wasn't until around 5:45 pm that Banks received word of the unfolding events at Front Royal, the news delivered by a lone messenger.

Around 6:00 pm, the Confederate forces made a pivotal move. A few of Colonel Thomas Flournoy's cavalrymen managed to ford the river, while parts of the 8th Louisiana Infantry Regiment daringly swam across. They successfully extinguished the flames on the North Fork bridge. Although part of the bridge had collapsed, it remained passable for men crossing in single file. Realizing the vulnerability of his position at Guard Hill with Confederates now across the river, Colonel John Reese Kenly ordered a withdrawal to the small community of Cedarville, Virginia.

In a decisive action, General Thomas "Stonewall" Jackson instructed Flournoy to lead 250 cavalrymen across the damaged bridge to chase the retreating Union forces. Jackson himself followed closely behind the cavalry. Kenly made a last stand approximately 1.5 miles north of Cedarville. He deployed his artillery and commanded the New York cavalry to charge. However, in a crucial moment, the cavalry commander faltered and ordered a retreat instead. The Union troops then formed a defensive line at Fairview, a local residence. Despite facing a Union volley that heavily damaged Company B of the 6th Virginia, Flournoy's cavalry charged twice, ultimately breaking through the Union line, which descended into chaos. Kenly was wounded and captured, along with most of his troops.

Simultaneously, Colonel Turner Ashby had encountered Union resistance during his mission to disrupt communications. Around 2:00 pm, his men had attacked Buckton Station, defended by elements of the 3rd Wisconsin and the 27th Indiana Infantry Regiments. Despite repelling two Confederate assaults, Ashby succeeded in severing the railroad and telegraph lines, isolating Front Royal from Banks's forces.

The casualties of the Battle of Front Royal varied according to different sources. Peter Cozzens reported Confederate losses at 36, with Union casualties at 773, including 691 prisoners. Other estimates suggested Union prisoners numbered around 700, with Confederate casualties under 100. The National Park Service and historian Robert G. Tanner estimated Union losses around 900 and Confederate losses slightly over 100. Gary Ecelbarger estimated similar Union losses. The Confederates captured significant Union equipment, including both Parrott rifles, several wagons, and supplies worth about $300,000. Ashby's raid also resulted in the capture of two locomotives.

For his bravery in the bridge-burning episode at Front Royal and later at the Battle of Weldon Railroad, Union soldier William Taylor was awarded the Medal of Honor in 1897. In response to the Confederate victory at Front Royal, Banks hastily retreated from Strasburg. Jackson then engaged Banks's forces at Middletown the next day, leading to the Confederate victory in the First Battle of Winchester on May 25.

Following this, Jackson moved towards Harpers Ferry, while Union Generals Frémont and Shields converged on Strasburg to counter him. Ashby was killed in a skirmish on June 6. Ewell, tasked with engaging Frémont, defeated his forces at the Battle of Cross Keys on June 8, subsequently destroying a bridge to prevent Frémont from joining Shields. Jackson then defeated Shields in the Battle of Port Republic on June 9. With Shields and Frémont retreating, Jackson rejoined Lee's army for the Seven Days battles. Jackson's Valley Campaign had effectively prevented Union forces from reinforcing McClellan, marking a strategic Confederate success.

Battle of Seven Pines

General Joseph E. Johnston masterfully executed a strategic retreat with his 75,000-strong Confederate army from the Virginia Peninsula. This maneuver was in response to the relentless advance of Union General George B. McClellan's formidable 105,000-man army, inching ever closer to the Confederate capital, Richmond. Johnston ingeniously established a defensive stronghold starting from Drewry's Bluff on the James River, a site already etched in history for a significant Confederate naval triumph.

This defensive line, meticulously planned by Johnston, extended in a counterclockwise formation. It was strategically positioned so that the center and left flanks of his army were shielded by the Chickahominy River. This natural barrier was particularly advantageous in spring, transforming the eastern lands of Richmond into impassable swamps. In a calculated move, Johnston's forces burned most bridges over the Chickahominy, fortifying their positions to the north and east of the city, preparing for the looming Union onslaught.

On the other side, General McClellan, with tactical acumen, placed his massive army focusing on the northeastern sector surrounding Richmond for two pivotal reasons. Firstly, the nearby Pamunkey River offered a vital line of communication, potentially allowing McClellan to outflank Johnston's left. Secondly, anticipating the reinforcement of the I Corps led by Maj. Gen. Irwin McDowell, marching south from Fredericksburg, McClellan needed to secure their route of entry.

As the Union's Army of the Potomac methodically advanced up the Pamunkey River, they established crucial supply bases at Eltham's Landing, Cumberland Landing, and White House Landing. The White House plantation, owned by W.H.F. "Rooney" Lee, son of the legendary General Robert E. Lee, became the operational epicenter for McClellan. Utilizing the Richmond and York River Railroad, McClellan was able to transport heavy siege artillery right to the outskirts of Richmond. His approach, however, was cautious and measured, influenced by flawed intelligence overestimating Confederate strength.

By the end of May, a significant development unfolded as McClellan's army managed to construct several bridges across the Chickahominy, positioning themselves formidably around Richmond. The Army was strategically distributed, with one-third south of the river and two-thirds to the north.

General Joseph E. Johnston, positioned at the fringes of Richmond, realized the untenability of withstanding a protracted siege by McClellan's forces. Initially, Johnston aimed to strike at the Union's right flank, north of the Chickahominy River, hoping to act before the arrival of McDowell's corps from Fredericksburg. However, upon learning that McDowell had been redirected to the Shenandoah Valley, thus not reinforcing the Army of the Potomac, Johnston revised his strategy. He opted not to assault across the Chickahominy, instead planning to exploit the Union army's divided position over the river by targeting the isolated III and IV Corps to the south.

Johnston's revised plan was ambitious, involving nearly three-quarters of his army—about 51,000 men from 22 infantry brigades—against the Union's 33,000 men in the III and IV Corps. The Confederate strategy was intricate: A. P. Hill and Magruder's divisions were to engage the Union forces north of the river lightly, serving as a distraction. Meanwhile, Longstreet was tasked with leading the primary assault south of the river, intending to encircle Keyes from three directions. The plan hinged on the weakness of Brig. Gen. Silas Casey's division, the least experienced segment of Keyes's corps, positioned west of Seven Pines. Overpowering Casey would potentially leave the III Corps vulnerable and trapped against the Chickahominy.

However, the execution of this complex plan was fraught with mismanagement from the onset. Johnston communicated the orders to Longstreet verbally in a protracted, unclear meeting on May 30, leaving other generals with vague and conflicting written instructions. A critical lapse in communication was the failure to inform all division commanders of Longstreet's tactical command south of the river, a significant oversight given the higher ranks of Huger and Smith.

Complicating matters, Longstreet either misunderstood or intentionally altered his orders, deviating from his intended route along the Nine Mile Road to join Hill on the Williamsburg Road. This decision not only delayed the advance but also confined the attack to a narrow front, significantly diminishing the force's potential impact. The situation was further aggravated by a severe thunderstorm on the night of May 30, which caused the Chickahominy River to flood, destroyed several Union bridges, and transformed the roads into impassable mud.

The onset of the battle on May 31 was marked by confusion and missteps. General Longstreet, deviating from the plan, chose the Williamsburg Road over the Nine Mile Road. Meanwhile, Huger, whose orders lacked a specific attack time, was caught off guard by the sound of a nearby division marching, signaling his delayed response. Amidst this disarray, Johnston and his deputy, Smith, remained at their headquarters, unaware of Longstreet's position or Huger's delay, expectantly waiting for news of the battle's commencement. It wasn't until five hours past the planned start, at 1 p.m., that D.H. Hill, driven by impatience, pushed his brigades into action against Casey's division.

Hill's division, numbering around 10,000 men, emerged forcefully from the woods, confronting the 100th and 81st New York regiments. These regiments, positioned as heavy skirmish lines, were swiftly overrun by Hill's assault. Despite being inexperienced, Casey's troops resisted valiantly, fiercely defending their earthworks, but the overwhelming force led to significant losses on both sides. The Confederates, however, underutilized their strength, engaging only four of the thirteen brigades on their right flank, thus not fully capitalizing on the Union's vulnerability.

Casey, in desperation, called for reinforcements, but received a delayed response from Keyes. The Confederate forces eventually broke through, capturing a Union redoubt and forcing Casey's men to retreat to secondary defensive positions at Seven Pines. During these critical moments, the high commanders on both sides were largely in the dark about the battle's intensity. Heintzelman, for instance, reported to an unwell McClellan at 2:30 p.m. that there was no update from Keyes. Similarly, Johnston, positioned just 2.5 miles from the frontline, was unaware of the battle's escalation until 4 p.m., due to an acoustic shadow that muffled the sounds of combat.

In the thick of the battle, Hill, who had been engaging with only four brigades for nearly four hours, requested reinforcements from Longstreet, who sent only Richard Anderson's brigade. The ferocity of the fighting was evident in the casualties sustained by Rodes's brigade, which lost over half of its strength. Brig. Gen Robert Rodes was wounded, leading Col. John B. Gordon of the 6th Alabama, a future major general, to take command. Gordon himself narrowly escaped injury, with bullets piercing his clothing and canteen. He also witnessed his brother, Captain Augustus Gordon, grievously wounded among the fallen, but the battle's intensity afforded him no opportunity for aid (Augustus ultimately survived). Additionally, Brig. Gen Gabriel Rains, nearing his 59th birthday and among the oldest officers in the Army of Northern Virginia, was wounded, passing command to Col. Alfred Colquitt of the 6th Georgia, who would later be appointed as the brigade's permanent commander.

The Union Army's advance towards Richmond was bolstered by the innovative support of the Union Army Balloon Corps, under the command of Professor Thaddeus S. C. Lowe. This aerial reconnaissance unit established two balloon camps north of the Chickahominy River, at Gaines's Farm and Mechanicsville. On May 29, Lowe observed a significant buildup of Confederate forces near New Bridge and the Fair Oaks train station, promptly reporting this vital intelligence.

However, adverse weather conditions on May 30 and strong winds on the morning of May 31 hindered the launch of the aerostats Washington and Intrepid until noon. When finally airborne, Lowe spotted Confederate troops organizing for battle. This crucial information was conveyed to General McClellan's headquarters by 2 p.m. Through the day, Lowe continued to transmit updates via telegraph from the Intrepid, including a notable observation on June 1 of smokeless Confederate barracks to the left of Richmond. Despite receiving this intelligence, McClellan did not capitalize on it with a counteroffensive.

Meanwhile, at around 1:00 p.m., Confederate General Hill, bolstered by Richard Anderson's brigade, launched an attack on the Union's secondary line near Seven Pines. This line was held by remnants of Casey's division, Brig. Gen. Darius N. Couch's IV Corps division, and Brig. Gen. Philip Kearny's division from Heintzelman's III Corps. Hill orchestrated a flanking maneuver with four regiments under Col. Micah Jenkins, part of Longstreet's command, targeting Keyes's right flank. This offensive pushed the Federal line back a mile and a half beyond Seven Pines, to the Williamsburg Road.

In a concurrent development, another of Longstreet's brigades, led by Col. James L. Kemper, charged the Union lines but was repelled by artillery fire, ceasing hostilities in that sector by 7:30 p.m. As the evening progressed, Longstreet, along with the remainder of his division and Huger's three brigades, arrived at the battlefield. On the Union side, reinforcements arrived as well, including Brig. Gen Israel Richardson's division from the II Corps and Joe Hooker's division from the III Corps, although one brigade and the division artillery remained behind to guard the bridges over White Oak Swamp.

On the afternoon of May 31, as the Battle of Seven Pines unfolded, General Joseph E. Johnston was informed of the combat for the first time around 4:00 pm through a message from Longstreet, urging him to join the battle. Responding promptly, Johnston headed towards the front along the Nine Mile Road, accompanied by a division of five brigades led by Brig. Gen. William Chase Whiting. Earlier that day, Whiting had been appointed to command Maj. Gen. Gustavus Smith's division.

As the division, spearheaded by Col. Dorsey Pender's 6th North Carolina Regiment, approached the railroad crossing, they encountered artillery fire. This confrontation marked the beginning of the Battle of Fair Oaks Station. The Union artillery, part of Brig. Gen John Abercrombie's brigade from Couch's division, offered strong resistance. Whiting attempted to flank the Union artillery with his former brigade, now under Col. Evander Law, but faced stiff opposition from Abercrombie's forces, including four artillery pieces.

Simultaneously, Brig. Gen Edwin V. Sumner of the II Corps, determined to join the fray despite the Chickahominy River's swollen state, managed to bring his command into action from the north. The first of Sumner's brigades to engage was led by Brig. Gen Willis Gorman of Brig. Gen John Sedgwick's division, which countered Law's brigade. Law's attack, initiated by Col. Pender and later reinforced by Brig. Gen. J. Johnston Pettigrew and Col. Wade Hampton III's brigades, faltered under the pressure of Sumner's additional brigades and artillery.

In the intense combat, Confederate Brig. Gen. Robert Hatton, recently promoted, was fatally shot in the head. Hampton was injured in the ankle, and Pettigrew was severely wounded and captured. Despite repeated

Confederate assaults, Sedgwick's formidable artillery and infantry defenses held firm, with Whiting's troops, lacking artillery support, suffering heavily.

A decisive counterattack by Sumner eventually forced the Confederate troops to retreat. It was during this counteroffensive that Pettigrew was discovered and taken to a Union field hospital. Johnston, wounded twice during this phase of the battle, was evacuated, passing command to Maj. Gen. Gustavus Smith. As dusk approached, Whiting, facing over 1,200 casualties and the loss of many officers, called off the attacks. Sedgwick's division, in contrast, sustained fewer than 400 casualties.

Although two of Magruder's brigades arrived as the day ended, they did not participate in the fighting. Similarly, Whiting's fifth brigade, the renowned Texas Brigade under Brig. Gen John B. Hood, remained unengaged, having been dispatched to support Longstreet and positioned in the woods west of Fair Oak Station.

Around dusk General Joseph E. Johnston suffered severe injuries. He was hit by a bullet in the right shoulder and almost immediately, a shell fragment struck his chest. The impact rendered him unconscious and caused a broken shoulder blade and two broken ribs. Johnston was promptly evacuated to Richmond for treatment. In his absence, G.W. Smith assumed temporary command of the army. However, Smith's health issues and indecisive leadership during this critical period left a poor impression on Confederate President Jefferson Davis and General Robert E. Lee, who was then serving as Davis's military adviser. Following the cessation of fighting the next day, Davis appointed Lee as the new commander of the Army of Northern Virginia.

Overnight between May 31 and June 1, scouts from Israel Richardson's division reported the proximity of two Confederate regiments, positioned merely 100 yards away. Richardson opted against a night assault, but had his troops prepare for battle. By morning, the Confederate regiments had retreated. At 6:30 am, the Confederates, led by Brig. Gens William Mahone and Lewis Armistead (with Brig. Gen Albert G. Blanchard's brigade in reserve), renewed their assault on Richardson's division. Although they initially pushed back part of Richardson's line, his forces, bolstered by Brig. Gen David B. Birney's brigade (which had been misrouted the previous day), managed to repel the attack.

Birney, who had disobeyed orders by taking a wrong turn, was arrested by Heintzelman but later cleared by a military tribunal and restored to his command. Huger's division, after intense combat, was forced to retreat. Mahone reported 338 casualties, and although Armistead did not specify his losses, they were presumed to be substantial. The Union side, including Richardson and Birney's units, suffered 948 casualties. Brig. Gen Oliver O. Howard was among the injured, losing his right arm to a Minie ball and necessitating a lengthy recovery.

Richardson's division, particularly Howard's brigade, bore the brunt of the Union casualties, accounting for approximately 60% of their losses. Nearby, Pickett's brigade suffered 350 casualties. South of their position, the brigades of Roger Pryor and Cadmus Wilcox, engaged by Hooker's division, resisted valiantly before being ordered to retreat. By mid-morning, Confederate forces withdrew to the defensive positions at Casey's earthworks west of Seven Pines, marking the end of the fighting.

In the aftermath of the Battle of Seven Pines, both the Union and Confederate sides claimed victory, despite suffering nearly equal and substantial casualties. The battle halted George B. McClellan's advance on Richmond, forcing the Army of Northern Virginia to retreat into Richmond's defensive fortifications. The Union army incurred 5,031 casualties, while the Confederate losses totaled 6,134. This made it the second largest and bloodiest battle of the Civil War at that time, surpassed only by the Battle of Shiloh.

The battle is remembered differently by the two sides: Union soldiers often referred to it as the Battle of Fair Oaks Station, highlighting the location of their most effective resistance. Conversely, Confederates called it Seven Pines, where the fiercest fighting and heaviest casualties occurred. This name, as noted by historian Stephen W. Sears, aptly reflects the battle's most intense location.

McClellan, deeply affected by the carnage, expressed his distress over the dreadful cost of victory in a letter to his wife. Consequently, he repositioned most of his army south of the river and, despite continuing siege plans, lost the strategic initiative. Casey's division was unfairly blamed for the near-defeat, leading to Casey's removal from command and the division's reassignment to guard duty, effectively sidelining them for the remainder of the campaign.

The battle marked a turning point with the appointment of Robert E. Lee as the new Confederate commander. Lee immediately began reorganizing the Confederate army, making strategic changes in brigade assignments, nominating replacements for fallen officers, and dismissing underperforming generals Albert G. Blanchard and Raleigh Colston. This shift in command dramatically altered the course of the war.

Within three months of Lee taking command, the landscape of the war had significantly changed. McClellan's once threatening position near Richmond had been reversed, with his forces driven back and Major General John Pope defeated at the Second Battle of Bull Run. The front lines were now alarmingly close to Washington D.C. It would be nearly two years before the Union Army approached Richmond again, and almost three years before its eventual capture, underscoring the profound impact of the Battle of Seven Pines and Lee's leadership on the Civil War's trajectory.

Seven Days Battles

In the spring of 1862, General McClellan launched the ambitious Peninsula Campaign, aiming to seize the Confederate stronghold of Richmond and swiftly conclude the Civil War. This bold move began with a strategic landing at Fort Monroe, as McClellan's forces embarked on a daring march up the Virginia Peninsula.

However, the campaign took an unexpected turn when Confederate Brig. Gen. John B. Magruder's formidable Warwick Line defenses caught McClellan off guard. Thwarted in his plans for a rapid advance, McClellan found himself compelled to lay siege to Yorktown. But as the Union army was gearing up for this major assault, the Confederates, now under Johnston's command, skillfully retreated towards Richmond.

The first fierce clashes erupted at the Battle of Williamsburg on May 5. Here, the Union troops claimed some tactical victories, yet the elusive Confederate forces continued their strategic withdrawal. Efforts to flank them at Eltham's Landing on May 7 proved futile in halting their retreat. Then, in a dramatic showdown at Drewry's Bluff on May 15, the Confederate forces boldly repelled an audacious attempt by the United States Navy to reach Richmond via the James River.

As the Union army neared Richmond, the skirmish at Hanover Court House on May 27 seemed a mere prelude to the larger conflict. This was followed by a surprise Confederate counterattack at the Battle of Seven Pines or Fair

Oaks. This fierce two-day battle ended inconclusively with heavy casualties on both sides, but it had profound implications. Johnston's wounding led to the ascent of the formidable Robert E. Lee, who would soon demonstrate a bold and aggressive style of leadership.

Lee, known initially for his cautious approach, lacked numerical superiority over McClellan. Yet, he meticulously planned an offensive campaign, hinting at the assertive tactics he would employ throughout the war. Meanwhile, McClellan, hindered by adverse weather and waiting for better conditions, remained inactive, allowing Lee to fortify his positions.

General Robert E. Lee, facing the might of the Union Army, devised a daring and intricate plan of attack. Unlike the conventional strategies of attrition or siege, Lee's approach, set in motion on June 23, demanded flawless coordination and execution from his commanders. His army was poised to face a divided Union force, straddling the swollen Chickahominy River. While the majority of the Union troops formed a semi-circle south of the river, a significant portion under Brig. Gen. Fitz John Porter fortified positions north of it.

Lee's strategy hinged on a bold maneuver: crossing the Chickahominy with the main force to strike the Union's vulnerable northern flank. He would leave just two divisions to maintain a defensive stance against McClellan's superior numbers, thus concentrating about 65,500 Confederate troops against a mere 30,000 Union soldiers. This left a modest force of 25,000 to defend Richmond and engage the remaining 60,000 Union troops.

Adding to the intrigue, Confederate cavalry under Brig. Gen. J.E.B. Stuart had recently completed a daring reconnaissance of Porter's position, identifying key weaknesses.

Lee envisioned a two-pronged assault beginning on June 26: Jackson would target Porter's right flank, while A.P. Hill would advance from Meadow

Bridge towards the Federal trenches at Beaver Dam Creek. Lee anticipated Porter's forces would retreat under this pressure, sparing the need for a direct assault. Longstreet and D.H. Hill would then join the fray, moving through Mechanicsville. Meanwhile, Huger and Magruder were tasked with creating diversions, masking Lee's true intentions.

The goal was clear: overwhelm Porter from two sides with a massive force, then press on to Cold Harbor, severing McClellan's communications with White House Landing.

In contrast, McClellan also had plans for an offensive, informed by intelligence of Lee's impending movements and the imminent arrival of Stonewall Jackson's reinforcements from the Shenandoah Valley. Despite knowing Jackson's proximity, McClellan refrained from reinforcing Porter's exposed corps. Instead, he planned to resume his offensive before Lee could fully mobilize. Anticipating Jackson's approach, he increased cavalry patrols and aimed to advance his siege artillery closer to Richmond by seizing high ground on Nine Mile Road near Old Tavern. To facilitate this, he planned an attack on Oak Grove, aiming to position his forces advantageously for an assault on Old Tavern from multiple directions.

Battle of Oak Grove

On the morning of June 25th, at precisely 8:30 a.m., a grand spectacle of war unfolded as three Union brigades, under the command of Brig. Gens. Daniel E. Sickles, Cuvier Grover, and John C. Robinson, commenced their advance in a formidable line of battle. Their movements, precise and coordinated, promised a show of strength that might tilt the scales in this pivotal engagement.

However, the battlefield, rife with unpredictability, soon transformed their orderly assault into a maelstrom of chaos. Sickles's New Yorkers, part of the famed Excelsior Brigade, grappled with the daunting task of navigating through dense abatis and swampy terrain. Their progress was further hindered by unexpectedly fierce resistance from Confederate forces, resulting in a disarray that threw the entire Federal line into disarray.

Seizing this moment of turmoil, Confederate General Huger launched a counterstrike with Brig. Gen. Ambrose R. Wright's brigade. The attack was notably marked by one of Wright's Georgia regiments donning striking red Zouave uniforms, a sight that sowed confusion among Grover's Union troops. Mistaking these adversaries for their own, due to the prevalent belief that Zouave units were unique to the Union Army, they hesitated to fire. This moment of recognition and realization was critical — by the time they identified the enemy and commenced firing, the battle's momentum had subtly shifted.

Amidst this chaos, the 26th North Carolina, under Brig. Gen. Robert Ransom and engaging in their first battle, executed a flawlessly timed volley of rifle fire. Their attack targeted Sickles's brigade, disrupting their already hampered assault and instigating a disorderly retreat of the 71st New York, later described by Sickles as a "disgraceful confusion."

This turn of events prompted an urgent response from corps commander Heintzelman. He immediately dispatched reinforcements and informed General McClellan, who was attempting to command the battle remotely via telegraph from three miles away. McClellan, lacking crucial details of the unfolding battle, reacted with alarm. At 10:30 a.m., he issued a perplexing order for a withdrawal back to their fortifications, leaving his on-field commanders baffled.

McClellan's decision to personally arrive at the front caused a significant pause in the hostilities, lasting about two and a half hours. Upon his arrival at 1 p.m., McClellan, realizing the situation was not as dire as he had initially feared, reversed his earlier command. He ordered his troops to advance once more, to reclaim the ground they had fought over earlier that day. The renewed engagement, fueled by determination and a desire to rectify earlier setbacks, raged on until the veil of nightfall brought a temporary halt to the hostilities. This day of battle, marked by confusion, bravery, and rapid shifts in fortune, exemplified the volatile nature of war, where plans often succumb to the unpredictability of the battlefield.

Battle of Beaver Dam Creek

General Robert E. Lee's masterfully crafted battle strategy, intricate in its design, faced immediate setbacks as the battle unfolded. At the heart of these challenges was the delayed arrival of Jackson's forces. Weary from their intense recent campaign and a grueling march, Jackson's men lagged significantly behind schedule, disrupting the synchronization crucial to Lee's plan.

By mid-afternoon, with the sun arcing high in the sky, General A.P. Hill, driven by impatience and perhaps a sense of urgency, initiated an attack without formal orders. Hill's division, with the notable exception of Brig. Gen Lawrence O'Bryan Branch's brigade, marched into Mechanicsville. There, they encountered George McCall's Union division, sparking initial skirmishes around the town. McCall, recognizing the strategic advantage of the terrain, retreated to a more defensible position across Beaver Dam Creek. The stage was set for a fierce standoff.

The Union forces, under the command of Brig. Gens John F. Reynolds, Truman Seymour, and George G. Meade, fortified their positions with meticulous care. Reynolds' and Seymour's brigades, flanked by the divisions of Brig. Gens George Morell and George Sykes, formed a formidable semicircle, braced to repel the Confederate onslaught. Supporting this robust array of 26,000 infantrymen were 32 artillery pieces, poised to unleash devastating firepower.

Meanwhile, Jackson and his troops arrived only in the waning hours of the afternoon. In a bewildering turn of events, Jackson, unable to locate A.P. Hill or D.H. Hill and seemingly oblivious to the raging battle nearby, ordered his men to set up camp, effectively removing a significant force from the day's combat.

Hill's 11,000 men, many inexperienced and untested in battle, launched a series of desperate attacks. Brigades under John R. Anderson, James Archer, and Charles W. Field spearheaded these assaults, while Maxcy Gregg's brigade remained in reserve. As the Confederates advanced, John Reynolds, overseeing the Union defense, observed their approach with a mix of grim determination and stark realism, comparing their onslaught to flies swarming over gingerbread.

The Union artillery and infantry, well-positioned and prepared, unleashed a torrent of gunfire and cannonade. The Confederate lines, bravely advancing, were decimated by this relentless barrage, their ranks torn apart by the Union's superior firepower. Despite having 24 artillery guns at his disposal, A.P. Hill refrained from employing them in a concentrated effort against the Union gunners. Instead, he deployed individual batteries to support the infantry, many of which were swiftly neutralized by the Union's counter-artillery fire.

This chaotic battle scene, marked by the relentless sound of gunfire, the cries of the wounded, and the sheer determination of both sides, exemplified the brutality and unpredictability of war. The Union defenses, like an unyielding wall, repelled each Confederate attack, inflicting severe casualties and thwarting the ambitious plans of General Lee. As nightfall approached, the battlefield, strewn with the aftermath of a day's fierce combat, stood as a testament to the courage and resolve of the soldiers and the tragic cost of war.

As the intense battle raged on, a critical moment unfolded when some of Anderson's men managed to breach the creek, momentarily posing a serious threat to Reynolds's position. However, the Union forces, bolstered by Meade's brigade and reinforcements from Morell's division, swiftly responded. This timely support played a crucial role in repelling the Confederate brigades, inflicting severe casualties and regaining control of the situation.

In the midst of this turbulent combat, General Robert E. Lee, realizing the gravity of the unfolding events, called upon the divisions of Longstreet and D.H. Hill. As he assessed the situation, President Jefferson Davis, accompanied by the Confederate cabinet, arrived on the battlefield. Davis, perplexed by the scene, questioned Lee about the army's presence and actions. Lee, in a moment of candid frustration, sarcastically remarked on the chaos and the disarray of the forces.

The battle continued with William D. Pender's brigade launching an attack on the Union's left flank at Ellerson's Mill, defended by Seymour's brigade. However, the entrenched Union infantry and their formidable artillery setup once again proved too much for the Confederate forces, compelling Pender to retreat.

The Confederate assaults persisted with Roswell Ripley's brigade of D.H. Hill's division being the next to charge. In a direct assault against the Union entrenchments, Ripley's brigade suffered devastating losses, particularly the 44th Georgia, which incurred massive casualties, including most of its officers. The encounter was so fierce that General Ripley narrowly escaped death, nearly decapitated by an artillery shell. Meanwhile, Union casualties in this sector remained relatively low, a testament to their strong defensive positioning.

Reflecting on these costly assaults years later, D.H. Hill poignantly remarked on the grand yet tragically unaffordable nature of such engagements for the South.

As the day turned to night, more Confederate reinforcements arrived, including the rest of D.H. Hill's division and Longstreet's forces. On the Union side, George Morrell's division relieved McCall's exhausted troops, who were running low on ammunition. However, the dwindling daylight prevented the full deployment of the newly arrived Confederate divisions.

Jackson, though present on the battlefield, did not engage in the attack. Yet, his proximity to Porter's flank prompted McClellan to issue a strategic withdrawal of Union forces to Boatswain's Swamp, significantly eastward. McClellan's decision was driven by concerns over the Confederate buildup threatening his supply line along the Richmond and York River Railroad. This strategic shift to the James River as a new base of supply marked a pivotal moment in the campaign. It meant abandoning the siege of Richmond, a significant turn in the course of the Civil War, as the Union army adapted to the evolving dynamics of this brutal and unpredictable conflict.

Battle of Gaines' Mill

The initial phase of the Battle of Gaines' Mill unfolded between noon and 1 p.m. on June 27, marked by strategic maneuvers and unexpected confrontations. The day's action began when D.H. Hill's division, having reached Old Cold Harbor, prepared to join forces with Stonewall Jackson. Hill, leading two brigades, pushed forward but was met with unforeseen resistance from Union infantry. In an attempt to quell this opposition, he deployed the Jeff Davis Battery from Alabama, only to find it quickly overwhelmed by two formidable six-gun batteries from Brig. Gen. George Sykes's division.

Hill, taken aback by the level of resistance and the realization that he was facing the Union's front rather than its flank, decided to hold his position, awaiting Jackson's arrival. Unbeknownst to General Lee, stationed at his headquarters at the Hogan-owned "Selwyn" house, the sounds of this skirmish never reached him, leaving him unaware of the unfolding situation.

Meanwhile, A.P. Hill's division had crossed Beaver Dam Creek early in the morning, encountering only light resistance from the previously fortified Union lines. As they moved eastward towards Gaines' Mill, coinciding with D.H. Hill's engagement, Porter sought reinforcement from McClellan, requesting Slocum's division's support.

In the thick of battle, Maxcy Gregg and Lawrence O'Bryan Branch's brigades took the lead in the assault. Having remained unengaged at Beaver Dam Creek, these brigades were fresh and ready for combat. However, they soon encountered stiff opposition from Colonel Hiram Berdan's 1st U.S. Sharpshooters and the 9th Massachusetts Infantry. Gregg's advance was significantly hampered by these skilled marksmen and the challenging swampy terrain.

A particularly intense clash occurred when the 1st South Carolina Rifles assailed a Massachusetts battery, only to be fiercely repelled by the 5th New York's Zouaves. This encounter led to staggering losses for the South Carolinians, with 57% casualties, marking the greatest regimental loss for the Confederates that day. Branch's brigade, too, faced severe losses, with 401 men falling in just two hours of combat.

Joseph R. Anderson's brigade launched multiple assaults on the Union lines but failed to make any significant impact. Field's brigade struggled amidst the swampy conditions, leading to chaotic scenes where some soldiers mistakenly fired upon their own comrades.

The fierce resistance and challenging terrain proved formidable obstacles for the Confederate forces. While some of Gregg's men managed to cross the creek, the rest faced an insurmountable barrier, marking a pivotal moment in this intense and grueling day of battle.

Confederate General A.P. Hill, diverging from his initial orders, made a bold decision to attack a well-fortified Union position. This audacious move, rather than pursuing a retreating enemy, resulted in a staggering loss of approximately 2,000 soldiers from his 13,200-strong force. This defeat was a significant blow, especially considering the heavy casualties incurred at Mechanicsville just the day before, which had already depleted over a quarter of the Light Division's men.

Meanwhile, Union General George B. McClellan, stationed a few miles away at his headquarters, was drawing encouragement from the optimistic telegrams sent by his subordinate, General Porter. In response to the news of the enemy's apparent retreat, McClellan urged Porter to aggressively engage, employing the term "chasseur" to emphasize the need for swift, hunter-like action. He also instructed General Franklin to seize the opportunity to flank the enemy by crossing the river over the Duane bridge. However, McClellan's plans were soon disrupted by the news that the VI Corps commander had, in a precautionary measure against a potential Confederate onslaught, destroyed the very bridge that was central to their flanking maneuver.

Simultaneously, Brigadier General Edwin V. Sumner of the II Corps alerted McClellan to enemy movements opposing his forces. This information, coupled with the unexpected developments at the Duane bridge, dampened McClellan's initial optimism, prompting him to order the packing of his headquarters' equipment in preparation for a potential retreat.

On the Confederate side, General Robert E. Lee was deeply involved in the day's actions, seen rallying his troops perilously close to the front lines. His presence, while morale-boosting, also brought discomfort due to the risk involved. General Longstreet, arriving to support A.P. Hill, immediately recognized the challenges posed by the terrain for an effective assault and thus held off his attack until Stonewall Jackson could join on Hill's left flank.

However, for the second time in the Seven Days, Jackson's arrival was delayed. A significant miscommunication with Pvt. John Henry Timberlake of the 4th Virginia Cavalry, who misunderstood Jackson's route, led the

Confederate force down an incorrect path. After rectifying their course, Jackson's men faced further setbacks, including road obstructions by the retreating Union army and harassment from sharpshooters, all contributing to their late arrival on the battlefield.

The first of Jackson's units to reach the scene was Major General Richard S. Ewell's division. Upon their arrival, they were immediately directed by Lee's aide, Walter Taylor, to engage in the battle without delay. With A.P. Hill's troops significantly weakened and the threat of a counterattack by Porter looming, Lee instructed Longstreet to initiate a diversionary attack. This was intended to stabilize their lines until Jackson could fully deploy his forces for a coordinated assault from the north.

In this critical juncture, Brigadier General George E. Pickett's brigade led a frontal assault under Longstreet's command. However, they were met with intense resistance and suffered severe losses, including Pickett himself, who sustained a shoulder injury, rendering him inactive for the remainder of the summer. Colonel Eppa Hunton of the 8th Virginia subsequently took over the brigade's command.

The battle raged on with fervor as General Ewell initiated his assault at approximately 3:30 p.m., making a decisive move without waiting for his full division to be properly aligned. He was acting on General Robert E. Lee's directive, which emphasized the importance of sustaining the attack momentum along the same path forged by the brigades of Gregg and Branch. Leading the charge was the Louisiana brigade, under the command of Colonel Isaac Seymour, who was filling in for Major General Richard Taylor due to medical reasons. However, Seymour, lacking extensive battle experience, found his troops disoriented in the challenging terrain of Boatswain's Swamp. This confusion escalated dramatically when Seymour fell victim to a Union rifle volley, causing disarray among his men.

In a bold move, Major Roberdeau Wheat, the charismatic leader of the

Louisiana Tigers Battalion, stepped forward to rally the brigade. His efforts, however, were cut short as he was tragically struck down by a fatal bullet. With their leaders lost, the Louisiana Brigade was compelled to withdraw from the fray. Ewell persisted in his attack with two regiments from Brigadier General Isaac R. Trimble's brigade, yet they too were hindered by the swamp's treacherous conditions, suffering heavy casualties of around 20%.

On the Union side, General Porter, bolstered by reinforcements from Slocum's division, strategically reinforced gaps in his line. Despite urgent telegrams from Porter requesting additional support, General McClellan remained hesitant to commit to a counterattack. Seeking to bolster his forces, he inquired of his corps commanders south of the river for available troops. However, with none volunteering, he directed Sumner of the II Corps to dispatch two brigades, a mere tenth of the army, across the river. Yet due to the considerable distances involved, these reinforcements would not arrive at the battlefield for another three hours.

Meanwhile, Stonewall Jackson, fatigued from the exhaustive marching and counter-marching, finally arrived at Old Cold Harbor. He began to organize his troops and those of D.H. Hill, preparing to ensnare the Federals whom he anticipated would be driven eastward by the forces of Longstreet and A.P. Hill. Receiving updates from General Lee on the evolving battle conditions, Jackson set about readying his command for an assault on the main Federal line. However, a series of miscommunications and faulty staff work delayed the movement of his troops for over an hour.

Amidst the chaos, Jackson, visibly agitated, rode back and forth. It fell to his chaplain and chief of staff, Major Robert L. Dabney, to take decisive action. Dabney managed to locate the divisions of Brigadier Generals William H.C. Whiting and Charles S. Winder, rectifying the muddled instructions they had received. In a critical meeting on Telegraph Road, Lee expressed his frustration to Jackson about the delays in reaching the battlefield. Lee's remark, "General, I am glad to see you and I only wish I could have been with you sooner," was met with an almost inaudible response from Jackson, drowned out by the battle's roar. When Lee inquired if Jackson's troops could withstand the intense enemy fire, Jackson confidently asserted, "They can stand anything, they can stand that," epitomizing the resilience and determination of his forces amidst the tumult of battle.

As the sun began its descent on the evening of June 27, General Robert E. Lee orchestrated a massive assault, unleashing 16 brigades, approximately 32,100 men, onto the Union lines. The Union, under General Porter, commanded a slightly larger force of about 34,000. However, these Union troops were weary from earlier skirmishes, and their ability to function cohesively was compromised by the piecemeal manner in which reinforcements were fed into the battle to plug gaps. Despite these challenges, the Union soldiers held the advantage of a well-defended terrain and superior artillery firepower.

The Confederate advance was not a uniform charge across the 2.25-mile front but a series of staggered, smaller-scale unit engagements. The left flank, led by D.H. Hill, faced formidable opposition from the battle-hardened regulars under George Sykes. The 20th North Carolina, part of Hill's division, managed a significant breakthrough, overrunning a Union battery. Its commander, Colonel Alfred Iverson, later notorious for his role at Gettysburg, was wounded in this assault. Meanwhile, the 5th Alabama, under Colonel Charles Peues, suffered heavy losses, including the fatal wounding of Peues and the capture of the regiment's colors by the 5th Maine.

At the center of Lee's assault were Brigadier General Alexander Lawton's five Georgia regiments, a massive brigade of nearly 4,000 men, participating in their first battle and outnumbering the rest of Jackson's division. They pushed forward, supported by the Stonewall Brigade, and the brigades of Samuel V. Fulkerson, and Arnold Elzey, and Isaac R. Trimble from Ewell's division. Interestingly, Jackson's division contained the largest and smallest

Confederate brigades on the field; his third brigade, temporarily led by Lieutenant Colonel Richard H. Cunningham in Brigadier General John R. Jones' absence due to illness, consisted of just over 1,000 men and was held in reserve, not participating in the active fighting. During the assault, Arnold Elzey was critically injured by a shot to the head, an injury that ended his active field command in the war, leading to Colonel James A. Walker of the 13th Virginia taking command of Elzey's brigade. Samuel Fulkerson was also mortally wounded, succumbing to his chest wound the next day, and Colonel Edward T.H. Warren of the 10th Virginia assumed command of the brigade.

The Confederate right flank faced the most challenging terrain, including a quarter-mile open wheat field descending into Boatswain's Swamp and then rising to meet two lines of Union defenders situated on higher ground. James Longstreet, leading this flank, ordered Pickett's brigade back into the fray, bolstered by the brigades of Roger Pryor and Cadmus Wilcox, while holding the other three brigades in reserve. Longstreet later reflected on the formidable nature of the position in his report, acknowledging the tactical disadvantage they faced.

As dusk approached, a critical breakthrough occurred on Longstreet's front. Brigadier General John Bell Hood's Texas Brigade advanced rapidly and forcefully, piercing a hole in the Union line. This fierce assault led to heavy casualties among Whiting's two brigades, including the wounding or killing of four regimental commanders and the division's chief of artillery, Captain William Balthis. Pickett's brigade also found success in its second assault of the day, contributing to the disintegration of the Union line. Unable to counter the Confederate breakthroughs on their center and right, the Union defenses collapsed. In total, nine Union regimental commanders were either killed or mortally wounded in the battle.

Amidst this chaos, the 4th New Jersey Regiment, along with its colonel, were encircled and captured by Longstreet's division. The remaining men of the regiment were led by a lieutenant colonel. Sykes's regulars executed a strategic withdrawal from the McGehee house to Grapevine Bridge. The Union brigades of Brigadier Generals Thomas F. Meagher and William H. French, arriving from the II Corps, were too late to impact the battle, serving instead as a rear guard during Porter's retreat. A battalion of the 5th U.S. Cavalry, under Captain Charles J. Whiting, launched a desperate charge against the Texas Brigade but were ultimately forced to surrender after sustaining heavy losses.

By 4 a.m. on June 28, Porter had completed his retreat across the Chicka-hominy River, burning the bridges to hinder pursuit. During the chaotic retreat from Gaines' Mill, another Union General, John F. Reynolds, was captured by Confederate forces while he was sleeping under a tree, adding to the Union's list of losses in this crucial engagement.

Union Troops Withdraw

On the historic night of June 27, in a move that has since become a subject of intense debate among military historians, General George B. McClellan made the fateful decision to order the complete withdrawal of his Union army to Harrison's Landing on the James River. This decision was perplexing on multiple levels. Firstly, the Union forces were in a strategically favorable position, having successfully repelled strong Confederate assaults. Remark-ably, they achieved this while engaging only one of their five corps in the thick of battle. Major General Fitz John Porter, in particular, had displayed commendable leadership, holding his ground against overwhelming odds.

Moreover, McClellan was privy to crucial information that should have bolstered his confidence: the War Department had recently formed the new Army of Virginia, with explicit instructions to reinforce his position on the Peninsula. Yet, despite these advantages, McClellan seemed to have been profoundly unsettled by Confederate General Robert E. Lee's tactics, leading him to relinquish his strategic initiative.

In a bold and somewhat defiant telegram to the Secretary of War, McClellan stated, "If I save this Army now I tell you plainly that I owe no thanks to you or any other persons in Washington—you have done your best to sacrifice this Army." Notably, the military telegraph department, in a telling move, chose to exclude this sentence from the version delivered to the Secretary.

In the tactical reshuffling that followed, McClellan instructed Keyes's IV Corps to secure the west of Glendale, safeguarding the army's retreat. Porter was dispatched to Malvern Hill to establish defensive positions. The army's supply trains were directed southward toward the James River. Crucially, McClellan departed for Harrison's Landing without establishing a clear route for withdrawal or appointing a second-in-command, effectively distancing himself from direct command of the battles during the remainder of the Seven Days. This retreat across the Chickahominy River, following the Battle of Gaines's Mill, represented a significant psychological triumph for the Confederacy, signaling the safety of Richmond from imminent Union capture.

Meanwhile, Lee's cavalry brought pivotal intelligence, reporting the abandonment of Union defenses along the Richmond and York River Railroad and at the White House supply depot on the York River. Observations of large dust clouds south of the Chickahominy River corroborated this information, finally convincing Lee that McClellan was indeed retreating toward the James River. Until this revelation, Lee had anticipated a different maneuver from McClellan, expecting him to withdraw eastward to secure his supply line to the York River. Consequently, Lee had positioned his forces accordingly, unable to make decisive moves without clear evidence of McClellan's intentions.

Battle of Garnett's & Golding's Farm

Nestled on the brink of the Chickahominy River's bluffs, near Old Tavern, lay the fertile lands of James M. Garnett's farm, a location that would soon become an integral part of Civil War history. Close by, Simon Gouldin's Golding's Plain stretched out, adding to the strategic landscape. Between these two pivotal farms lay a dramatic natural feature: a steep ravine, bisected by a creek, leading up to an area known as Garnett's Hill. This geographical setting was poised to witness a significant confrontation during the Battle of Gaines's Mill.

On the eve of the battle, June 26, 1862, Union soldiers from Brigadier General William T. H. Brooks's brigade of William F. "Baldy" Smith's 2nd division of the VI Corps began a crucial operation. They started positioning artillery pieces atop Garnett's Hill under the cover of darkness, a task that continued into the following morning by Brigadier General Winfield Scott Hancock's brigade of the same corps. By the morning of June 27, six formidable batteries of reserve artillery were strategically arrayed, ready for the impending conflict.

Meanwhile, Confederate forces under Major General David R. Jones began to occupy their positions in the vicinity. Brigadier General Robert Toombs's brigade established themselves west of the ravine, while Colonel George T. Anderson's brigade positioned northwest of the area, less than a mile from the Garnett residence. Both Anderson's and Toombs's artillerists received orders to engage the Union soldiers whenever feasible. The Union troops, meanwhile, were instructed to brace for a general engagement but to avoid direct confrontation with the Confederates if possible. This set the stage for a spirited artillery exchange lasting about an hour, culminating in a Confederate retreat. The Union's twenty-three well-placed cannons held firm against the Confederates' ten, which were exposed in an open field.

In the afternoon, elements of Major General Lafayette McLaws's Confederate division made a daring advance towards the Union line near the Garnett farm around 4 pm, only to retreat under intense Union artillery fire after ten minutes. The battlefield quieted for a while, but the silence was shattered by Toombs's aggressive attack on the Union line around 7 pm. Toombs, ordered to conduct reconnaissance or "feel the enemy", instead initiated a fierce and sustained engagement. The fighting continued past nightfall, with Toombs's advance eventually being repulsed by Hancock's brigade after a grueling hour and a half of combat. The Confederates endured approximately 271 casualties throughout the day's engagements, underlining the intensity and ferocity of the conflict at Garnett's farm.

The next day, June 28, the Union and Confederate forces clashed again, this time near the Golding house. Major General Jones, suspecting that the Union forces near the house were retreating, authorized Toombs to conduct a reconnaissance-in-force to verify this. However, Toombs, in a decisive move, transformed the reconnaissance into a full-scale engagement, advancing with some of Anderson's men. Before any countermand could be issued, the Confederates found themselves repelled by the VI Corps.

Battle of Savage's Station

The early hours of June 29th marked the beginning of a pivotal encounter in the American Civil War. It was around 9 a.m. when the first skirmish erupted on the farm and orchards of Mr. Allen, located approximately 2 miles west of Savage's Station. This seemingly serene landscape transformed into a battle-field as two Georgian regiments from Brigadier General George T. Anderson's brigade engaged in a fierce exchange with two Pennsylvanian regiments from Sumner's Corps. This intense battle, spanning approximately two hours, resulted in 28 casualties for the Georgians and 119 for the Pennsylvanians. Amidst the chaos, the Confederates suffered a significant loss as Brigadier General Richard Griffith was mortally wounded by a fragment from a Union shell.

Meanwhile, Confederate General John Magruder, grappling with the effects of morphine taken for indigestion, was plunged into confusion. Fearing an overpowering attack from a superior force, he urgently requested reinforcements from General Robert E. Lee. In response, Lee dispatched two brigades from Major General Benjamin Huger's division, with the stipulation that they must return by 2 p.m. if not engaged.

Concurrently, General Stonewall Jackson, a key component in Lee's strategy, was unexpectedly delayed. Tasked with rebuilding bridges over the Chickahominy River, he also received an ambiguous order from Lee's chief of staff, leading him to believe his role was to guard the river crossings north of the river. This miscommunication represented a critical failure in the Confederate strategy.

However, the Union forces were not without their strategic missteps. General Samuel P. Heintzelman, acting independently, decided that his corps was not required to defend Savage's Station, assuming that the forces of Generals Edwin V. Sumner and William B. Franklin were adequate. Heintzelman's decision to follow the main body of the Union army, without informing his fellow generals, would soon have significant implications.

As the afternoon approached, Magruder faced the dilemma of relinquishing the two brigades from Huger's division, as per Lee's order. Now, contemplating an assault on Sumner's formidable force of 26,600 men with his own 14,000, Magruder hesitated. It wasn't until 5 p.m. that he resolved to send only two and a half brigades forward. Brigadier General Joseph B. Kershaw commanded the left flank, Brigadier General Paul J. Semmes the center, and Colonel William Barksdale (leading Griffith's Brigade) the right.

At this juncture, Generals Franklin and John Sedgwick, while on reconnaissance west of Savage's Station, observed Kershaw's brigade advancing. Initially mistaking them for Heintzelman's men, they soon recognized their error. This was the first indication of Heintzelman's unannounced departure, causing considerable consternation among the Union ranks. Sumner, in particular, was incensed by this revelation, to the extent that he refused to speak to Heintzelman the following day. In response to the Confederate advance, Union artillery commenced firing, and pickets were rapidly dispatched to confront the assault.

In the heat of the battle, General John B. Magruder deployed a ground-breaking weapon, the first of its kind to be used in combat: an armored railroad battery. This inventive contraption, conceptualized earlier in June by General Robert E. Lee, was a direct response to the threat of General George B. McClellan's siege artillery. Dubbed the "Land Merrimack," this formidable weapon consisted of a 32-pounder Brooke naval rifle, ensconced within a sloping casemate made of robust railroad iron. It was propelled by a locomotive, advancing at the pace of the marching infantry alongside them. Despite the formidable firepower of this novel weapon, which indeed outclassed anything in the Federal artillery arsenal, Magruder's cautious approach in deploying only a portion of his smaller force against a vastly larger Union army foreshadowed a predictable outcome.

The battle's dynamics shifted as one of General John Sedgwick's brigades, led by Philadelphian Brigadier General William W. Burns, became the first Union unit to confront Magruder's forces. However, Burns's defensive line was stretched thin, struggling to cover the expansive front presented by Brigadier Generals Joseph B. Kershaw and Paul J. Semmes. In the midst of this, General Edwin V. Sumner's management of the battlefield was erratic at best. His approach to deploying regiments seemed almost haphazard. Initially, he sent two of Burns's regiments into the fray, followed by the 1st Minnesota Infantry from another of Sedgwick's brigades. This was succeeded by the deployment of one regiment each from two different brigades within Brigadier General Israel B. Richardson's division. By the time these units had fully engaged, the forces on both sides had reached an approximate parity, each fielding two brigades. Yet, despite Magruder's conservative tactics, Sumner was even more restrained. Of the 26 regiments at his disposal, he committed only 10 to the battle at Savage's Station.

As dusk approached, the confrontation descended into a grueling stalemate, further intensified by the onset of powerful thunderstorms. The Land Merrimack relentlessly bombarded the Union front, its shells reaching as far back as the field hospital, adding to the chaos and desperation. The closing actions of the day were marked by the valor of the Vermont Brigade, under the command of Colonel William T. H. Brooks of Brigadier General William F. "Baldy" Smith's division. This brigade, striving to secure the flank south of the Williamsburg Road, charged into the dense woods only to be met with a devastating barrage of enemy fire. The Vermonters endured severe losses, with the brigade incurring 439 casualties in total. The 5th Vermont Regiment, led by Lieutenant Colonel Lewis A. Grant, was particularly hard hit, losing nearly half of its men, 209 out of 428. This bloody and intense engagement underscored the brutal nature of Civil War battles, where innovative technology, tactical decisions, and sheer bravery collided on the fields of history.

Battle of Glendale

Tasked with a critical maneuver, Major General Benjamin Huger encountered an unexpected obstacle: a road blocked by felled trees, a defensive measure by Union forces under Brigadier General Henry W. Slocum. Rather than clearing the blockade, Huger chose a time-consuming alternative, carving a new path through dense woods. This decision led to the infamous "Battle of the Axes," a frustrating episode of mismanagement and delay. Huger's reluctance to seek alternative routes or engage in combat significantly diminished his role in the overall battle.

Meanwhile, Major General John B. Magruder found himself entangled in a series of conflicting orders from Lee. Initially directed to support Holmes on the River Road and then attack Malvern Hill, the left flank of the Union line, Magruder was later redirected to aid Longstreet. This resulted in his division spending the day in aimless countermarching, contributing little to the Confederate efforts.

Adding to the Confederate woes, General Stonewall Jackson, despite his recent successes in the Valley Campaign, displayed uncharacteristically sluggish movement and poor judgment during the Seven Days. On this occasion, he lingered north of the creek, engaging only in a limited artillery duel at the Battle of White Oak Swamp, missing the opportunity to exploit nearby fords to cross the creek and mount a more effective attack.

The Union forces, too, faced their share of challenges. In a notable incident, Brigadier General George A. McCall's Third Division of the V Corps, operating near Glendale, struggled with positioning and coordination. Tasked with securing a defensive stance at the Glendale intersection, McCall's brigades navigated poorly in the darkness, missing their target and overshooting the crucial crossroad. By the time they realized their error and backtracked, dawn was breaking. The division, halting to await further instructions, inadvertently filled a gap in the Union line, a gap that had exposed them to potential advances from Confederate divisions led by Longstreet and Hill.

In the southern sector of the battlefield, General Theophilus H. Holmes's inexperienced forces, comprising troops from the Department of North Carolina now part of the Army of Northern Virginia, struggled ineffectively against Union forces led by General Fitz John Porter. Positioned at Turkey Bridge and Malvern Hill, Holmes's men faced stiff resistance, including heavy artillery barrages and support from the Federal gunboats Galena and Aroostook on the James River.

By 2 p.m., the Confederate generals Longstreet and Hill, anticipating the start of Huger's assault, mistook distant, unidentified cannon fire as their cue to commence a coordinated attack. Longstreet's artillery opened fire on McCall's Union line, which promptly responded with counter-battery fire. Amidst this exchange, Confederate leaders including Lee, Longstreet, and visiting President Jefferson Davis found themselves unexpectedly under heavy artillery fire, likely from McCall's Pennsylvania Artillery's Parrott rifles. This onslaught resulted in two men wounded and three horses killed, prompting A.P. Hill, who was commanding that sector, to urge the senior officials to move to a safer position.

Longstreet, facing the challenge of silencing the Union's Parrott rifles, found his long-range artillery fire ineffective. He then ordered Colonel Micah Jenkins to lead a charge against these batteries. This action, soon followed by other Confederate brigades joining the fray, escalated into a general battle around 4 p.m.

Despite the delay and lack of coordination contrary to Lee's original plan, the assaults by A.P. Hill and Longstreet's divisions marked the only significant Confederate adherence to Lee's orders to attack the Union's main force. Longstreet, commanding about 20,000 men, found no support from either Huger or Jackson's divisions, despite their proximity. His troops launched an assault against the Union's much larger force of 40,000 men, who were positioned in a 2-mile arc around the Glendale intersection. The focal point of this confrontation was the position held by McCall's Pennsylvania Reserves division, consisting of about 6,000 men near Frayser's Farm and north of Willis Church.

McCall's division, also known as the Third Division of the V Corps, was strategically arranged with Brigadier General George G. Meade's Second Brigade on the right, Brigadier General Truman Seymour's Third Brigade on the left, and the First Brigade under Colonel Seneca G. Simmons (temporarily leading in place of the captured Brigadier General John F. Reynolds) held in reserve. The division was further bolstered by artillery support from Colonel Henry Hunt's Army of the Potomac's Artillery Reserve, including units such as Captain Otto Diederich's and Captain John Knieriem's New York Light Artillery batteries, as well as Lieutenant Alanson M. Randol's Battery E & G from the 1st U.S. Artillery.

Major General George B. McClellan and his subordinate commanders assigned a crucial defensive role to the V Corps of the Army of the Potomac. This decision was significant as the V Corps had already been heavily engaged in earlier battles north of the Chickahominy River at Gaines' Mill. The Pennsylvania Reserves, a part of this corps led by Brigadier General George A. McCall, were particularly chosen for this task. They had already endured intense combat at Beaver Dam Creek and Gaines' Mill, suffering around 2,000 casualties. As a result, when they entered the fray at Glendale, their capacity was severely diminished. Their depleted state was such that a historian remarked many of these soldiers were more suited for hospital beds than the battlefield.

The Confederate assault at Glendale was led by three brigades, arranged from north to south: Brigadier General Cadmus M. Wilcox, Colonel Micah Jenkins (leading Anderson's Brigade), and Brigadier General James L. Kemper. Longstreet directed these brigades in a staggered manner over several hours, their progress impeded by challenging terrain and dense forests. The 14th Alabama Infantry, one of the first units to advance, faced intense Union fire and suffered devastating losses, to the extent that they later referred to this battle as "the Slaughterhouse." Similarly, the 14th Louisiana also incurred significant casualties.

Kemper's Virginians, engaging in their first combat, launched a disorganized yet spirited attack on the Whitlock Farm, encountering McCall's artillery on the Union's extreme left flank. This sudden aggression forced McCall to reallocate his reserve brigade, commanded by Colonel Seneca G. Simmons, from the center to the left, thereby weakening his right flank. Colonel Simmons, leading this counter-charge, was mortally wounded in the process of repelling Kemper's forces.

The battle's intensity soon escalated as the Confederates, with Jenkins's support, broke through near the right center of the Union line, followed by Wilcox's Alabamians in the center and right. The fighting shifted dynamically across the battlefield, from McCall's left where Kemper initially assaulted, through the center with Jenkins's probes against Union artillery, and then to the left with combined assaults by Jenkins and Wilcox on Meade's brigade.

This brutal combat was marked by fierce hand-to-hand encounters. Soldiers resorted to using bayonets and rifles as clubs, and officers employed their typically ornamental swords in actual combat. Despite briefly capturing Captain James H. Cooper's six 10-pounder Parrott rifles, Jenkins's brigade was eventually driven back by the determined resistance of the Pennsylvania Reserves' infantrymen.

Brigadier General Cadmus M. Wilcox's assault proved notably effective around dusk. Half of his brigade, specifically the 8th and 11th Alabama Infantry Regiments, capitalized on a vulnerable point in McCall's defenses. This vulnerability arose when Lieutenant Alanson M. Randol's Battery E & G, 1st U.S. Artillery, had repositioned its guns to counter an earlier assault on McCall's center. Although Randol's six 12-pounder Napoleon guns delivered a powerful enfilading fire against Jenkins' regiments, this maneuver left his right flank exposed.

Wilcox's troops emerged from the woods, prompting Randol to redirect his fire westward, with support from Captain James Thompson's Battery G, 2nd U.S. Artillery. However, Randol's infantry support, likely from the 4th or 7th Pennsylvania Reserves, had already shifted towards the center. After initially repelling two Confederate infantry charges with canister shot, the Union infantry support faced a fresh and unexpected challenge from the 11th Alabama Regiment. Overwhelmed, they retreated through the battery, inadvertently leading the Confederate troops directly into the artillery position.

This led to fierce hand-to-hand combat around Randol's guns, described by McCall as "one of the fiercest bayonet fights that perhaps ever occurred on this continent." During this melee, General George G. Meade was severely injured, and Colonel Elisha B. Harvey of the 7th Pennsylvania Reserve Regiment was critically wounded. Wilcox's regiments were initially repulsed but quickly returned with reinforcements from Brigadier Generals Roger A. Pryor and Lawrence Branch, preventing Randol's cannoneers from removing their artillery pieces.

In a dramatic turn of events, McCall was captured after accidentally riding into the Confederate lines while searching for positions for his rallied troops. Command of his division fell to Brigadier General Truman Seymour. During the same battle, Generals Edwin V. Sumner and Samuel P. Heintzelman were struck by stray bullets; Sumner escaped serious injury, but Heintzelman's right hand was temporarily incapacitated. Captain George Hazzard, leading Battery A, 4th U.S. Artillery, was also fatally wounded.

Meanwhile, Brigadier General Philip Kearny's division, stationed on McCall's northern flank, managed to withstand repeated Confederate attacks, bolstered by reinforcements from Caldwell's brigade and two brigades from Slocum's division. On the southern flank, Brigadier General Joseph Hooker's division successfully repelled and even counterattacked against minor Confederate offensives. General John Sedgwick's division, having returned from near White Oak Swamp, filled a critical gap after a vigorous counterattack. The battle, marked by intense engagements, continued until around 8:30 p.m. On the Confederate side, Longstreet committed almost all his brigades, while Union forces responded by individually reinforcing vulnerable points in their line as needed.

Battle of White Oak Swamp

On the morning of June 30, General Stonewall Jackson led his troops south along the White Oak Road, a journey marked by a blend of military urgency and logistical encumbrance. Colonel Stapleton Crutchfield, Jackson's chief of artillery, led the column, navigating a path slowed by the presence of thousands of wounded Union prisoners and the substantial quantity of supplies captured at Savage's Station. The march was further complicated by the discovery that the only bridge over the swamp, a critical crossing point, had been destroyed mere hours before their arrival.

Upon reaching the site around noon, Jackson surveyed the scene. He promptly approved Colonel Crutchfield's strategic placement of artillery on a ridge. This emplacement was meticulously designed to launch diagonal fire across the swamp, targeting Union batteries and infantry positioned roughly 300 yards away. The Confederate artillery barrage, unleashed at 2 p.m., came as a shock to the Union forces, effectively disabling several of their cannons in a sudden and fierce onset.

Meanwhile, Jackson instructed his engineers to commence the reconstruction of the bridge. Concurrently, he ordered Colonel Thomas T. Munford's 2nd Virginia Cavalry to traverse the swamp's challenging terrain—navigating water that reached the bellies of their horses—to seize Union artillery pieces abandoned amidst the bombardment. During this daring maneuver, Jackson and Major General D.H. Hill crossed the river for a closer examination of the situation. They narrowly escaped harm when a Union artillery shell exploded just feet away, leaving them unscathed but starkly aware of the dangers they faced.

As Jackson observed the strengthening Union forces and the threat posed by their sharpshooters to his engineers at the bridge, he concluded that a direct, opposed crossing at this point was untenable. His assessment was soon supplemented by Munford's discovery of a suitable ford (Fisher's Ford) downstream, and Brigadier General Wade Hampton's identification of a nearby site for constructing a simple infantry bridge. Despite these developments and Jackson's order to Hampton to build the bridge, he refrained from any immediate action to cross the swamp. His decision was influenced by the impracticality of moving his artillery across under such conditions.

The artillery duel across the swamp intensified, eventually involving over 40 guns. Simultaneously, the Battle of Glendale raged less than three miles away. Amidst this chaos and the sound of distant gunfire, Jackson found respite under a large oak tree. There, in an almost surreal contrast to the surrounding turmoil, he succumbed to exhaustion and slept for over an hour.

Battle of Malvern Hill

Under the hazy light of dawn, General Robert E. Lee meticulously inspected the left flank of the battlefield, searching for ideal artillery positions that could turn the tide of battle. Meanwhile, his trusted lieutenant, James Longstreet, embarked on a similar mission along the right flank. Upon Longstreet's return, the two military minds engaged in a strategic discussion, weighing their observations. Their conclusion was bold: they would establish two grand battery positions, mirroring each other on the left and right sides of Malvern Hill. The plan was ambitious — the converging artillery fire from these positions was designed to severely weaken the Union line, creating a vulnerable point for a decisive Confederate infantry attack.

If this daring strategy failed, Lee and Longstreet believed the artillery barrage would at least grant them precious time to devise alternative tactics. With the battle plan crystallizing, Lee entrusted the drafting of the orders to his chief of staff, Colonel Robert Chilton. However, the orders that emerged were flawed and ambiguous. They hinged the entire attack plan on the singular signal of a charging brigade's yell — a precarious cue amidst the chaos and noise of battle that risked muddying the coordination among the fifteen brigades. This critical oversight was compounded by the appointment of Lewis Armistead to spearhead the attack. Armistead, though brave, had never commanded a brigade in battle before, adding a layer of uncertainty to the already tenuous plan. Furthermore, Chilton's orders lacked a crucial detail — the time of their issue — which later sowed seeds of confusion in the ranks, particularly affecting General Magruder's actions.

At 1 pm, the Union artillery initiated the assault, targeting initially Confederate infantry concealed in the woods and then shifting to any Confederate artillery positioning for attack. On the Confederate left, two batteries from Whiting's division and one from Jackson's commenced a vigorous artillery duel with Darius Couch's division at the Union center. This intense exchange pitted eight Union batteries with 37 guns against three Confederate batteries with 16 guns. The Union's superior firepower silenced the Rowan Artillery and rendered their position untenable. Although two Confederate batteries, strategically placed by Jackson, managed to continue firing, their impact was limited. Over the next three hours, six to eight Confederate batteries intermittently engaged the Union forces from the left flank, but their efforts were disjointed, typically engaging one at a time.

The scenario was similar on the Confederate right flank. Six batteries engaged the Union forces, but like their counterparts on the left, they operated sequentially rather than in unison. This piecemeal approach led to each being decimated by the Union's concentrated artillery fire. Furthermore, their engagement commenced later than those on the left, thwarting any chance of achieving a coordinated crossfire bombardment.

Overall, the Confederate artillery on both flanks failed to meet its objectives. Despite causing casualties, including the death of Captain John E. Beam of the 1st New Jersey Artillery, and forcing some Union batteries to reposition, the Confederate barrage was largely ineffective. In one instance, Union Army Lieutenant Charles B. Haydon reportedly slept through the artillery exchange. Batteries that did engage often lasted only minutes before losing their operational capacity.

This disarray in the Confederate ranks, according to historian Thomas M. Settles, was ultimately a failure of command on General Lee's part, as the movements on both flanks were never synchronized. D. H. Hill, disheartened by the ineffectiveness of the Confederate artillery, later termed the barrage as "most farcical."

In stark contrast, the Union artillery, under the expert direction of Colonel Hunt, McClellan's chief of artillery, executed their plan near flawlessly. Hunt adeptly redirected Union fire across various fronts, unleashing over 50 superior artillery pieces. This relentless assault disabled four of Huger's and several of Jackson's batteries almost immediately as they entered the fray. The Union artillery's dominance effectively neutralized the Confederate response, leaving their few remaining batteries to attack in a disjointed manner, achieving negligible results.

The battlefield was ablaze with artillery fire from both sides, particularly intense from the Union forces. This bombardment continued relentlessly for about an hour, only beginning to wane around 2:30 pm. As the clock struck 3:30 pm, Lewis Armistead observed Union skirmishers stealthily approaching his position near the Confederate right flank's grand battery. Reacting swiftly, Armistead dispatched half of his brigade, comprising three regiments, to repel the advancing skirmishers. While they successfully drove the Union skirmishers back, Armistead's men soon found themselves trapped under a heavy barrage from Union artillery. Seeking refuge, they took cover in a nearby ravine, which, while offering protection from the onslaught, effectively immobilized them on Malvern Hill's slopes, isolated and without support from other infantry or artillery units.

Meanwhile, John Magruder and his men, hindered by confusion over local road names, arrived at the battlefield around 4 pm, significantly delayed. Earlier in the day, Magruder had been instructed to position his forces to the right of Huger, but without knowledge of Huger's exact location, he dispatched Major Joseph L. Brent to find Huger's flank. Brent's search led to Huger, who was in disarray, unclear about the whereabouts of his own brigades. This confusion was compounded by the fact that two of Huger's brigades, under the command of Armistead and Ambrose Wright, had been redirected by Lee without Huger's knowledge. Magruder, upon learning of this, sent Captain A. G. Dickinson to report to Lee about Armistead's supposed success and to seek further instructions. Contrary to Dickinson's report,

Armistead's forces were actually pinned down on the hill, not advancing.

In a further twist, Whiting mistakenly informed Lee that the Union forces were retreating, based on his misinterpretation of Edwin Sumner's troop movements and a decrease in Union artillery fire, which was actually a strategic shift in focus to another front. These misreports led to Lee urgently instructing Magruder to advance rapidly, under the false impression that the Union was retreating and to capitalize on Armistead's non-existent success. Before Dickinson could return with these directives, Magruder received the orders originally issued by Chilton at 1:30 pm, which, unbeknownst to him, were outdated due to the earlier failure of the Confederate artillery. Misinterpreting these as a reinforcement of Lee's call to attack, Magruder was left with the erroneous belief that he had received two consecutive orders from Lee to engage in an offensive.

Compelled by what he believed were General Lee's orders to engage, yet with his own brigades not fully prepared for an attack, General John Magruder rapidly assembled a force of approximately 5,000 men. This contingent included units from Huger's brigades, notably those led by Ambrose Wright and Major General William Mahone, along with half of Armistead's brigade, who found themselves exposed on the battlefield. Magruder also sought assistance from Brigadier General Robert Ransom, Jr., another of Huger's commanders, but Ransom declined, citing strict orders to follow only Huger's direct commands.

Magruder further called upon troops under his direct command, including three regiments from Brigadier General Howell Cobb's brigade and Colonel William Barksdale's entire brigade. However, due to earlier confusion concerning the Quaker Road, these units were not in a position to immediately engage but could only move to a supporting role. Despite this limitation, Magruder, intent on immediate action, ordered an assault around 5:30 pm. Wright's brigade, accompanied by elements of Armistead's, followed by Mahone's brigade, emerged from the woods, advancing toward the Union line. Concurrently, Confederate artillery on the left flank, directed by Jackson, intensified their bombardment, aided by the late arrival of two batteries from Richard Ewell's division.

Initially, the Confederate advance was countered only by Union sharpshooters, who quickly retreated to allow their artillery a clear line of fire. The Union artillery then unleashed devastating antipersonnel canister shot. Wright's troops were pinned down in a depression on the hillside, near Armistead's position, while Mahone's brigade was forced into retreat in the same vicinity. During this initial assault, Cobb's forces moved into a close supporting position behind Armistead, and Barksdale's men provided support to Armistead's left.

The intense firefight also drew the attention of three Union naval vessels on the James River: the ironclad USS Galena, and the gunboats USS Jacob Bell and USS Aroostook. These ships began firing large missiles, each twenty inches long and eight inches in diameter, onto the battlefield. While the appearance and impact of these gunboat missiles made a considerable impression on the Confederate troops, their accuracy was poor, resulting in less damage than anticipated. The large shells, although imposing, ultimately inflicted less harm than might have been expected under the circumstances.

Dismayed by the ineffectiveness of the Confederate artillery, D. H. Hill sought guidance from Stonewall Jackson, proposing to amend Chilton's original orders. Jackson, however, insisted that Hill adhere to the initial plan: to charge following the yell from Armistead's brigade. As hours passed without any signal, Hill's troops started constructing makeshift shelters, preparing to settle in for the night. Around 6 pm, Hill and his brigade commanders, under the assumption that the absence of a signal indicated no assault would be undertaken, were discussing Chilton's order when suddenly, they heard the distinct sound of yells and the tumult of a charge from their right — seemingly from the direction of Armistead's position. Interpreting this as the awaited signal, Hill rallied his commanders, urging them to quickly join the advancing troops with their brigades.

The five brigades under Hill's command, totaling some 8,200 men, struggled through dense woods and rough terrain near Quaker Road and Western Run, losing any semblance of formation in the process. Emerging from the woods in disjointed groups, they faced the Union line in a series of uncoordinated, solitary charges. William Calder of the 2nd Regiment, North Carolina Infantry, recounted their gallant but devastating advance: "We crossed one fence, went through another piece of woods, then over another fence [and] into an open field on the other side of which was a long line of Yankees... The enemy mowed us down by fifties." Despite some brigades engaging in close-range musket fire and hand-to-hand combat, they were ultimately repelled by the Union forces. The Federal artillery response to Hill's charge was overwhelming, leaving Hill's men struggling to even maintain their ground. Brian K. Burton, in his book "Extraordinary Circumstances: The Seven Days Battles," described Hill's charge as both "unnecessary and costly," achieving little against the entrenched Union forces.

Simultaneously, General Magruder, undeterred by the limited success of previous Confederate attacks, actively mobilized reinforcements across the battlefield. He personally led various units in a series of charges against the Union line. Among these were units from Brigadier General Robert Toombs's dispersed brigade, led into a brief and chaotic charge by Magruder himself, followed by a disorganized retreat. Other units under Toombs's nominal command sporadically charged and retreated, lacking coordination.

Colonel George T. Anderson and Colonel William Barksdale's brigades also joined the fray. As Anderson's men emerged from the woods, they became separated, resulting in a disjointed advance with two regiments on the far left, Barksdale's in the middle, and three more Anderson regiments on the right. While Anderson's right flank charged and quickly retreated under intense artillery fire, his left flank never initiated their charge. Barksdale's brigade, however, managed a more substantial advance, engaging in a prolonged firefight with Brigadier General Daniel Butterfield's Union infantry, lasting over an hour.

In response to Magruder's urgent calls for reinforcements, General Lee took action. He directed Huger to release Ransom's unit to support the beleaguered troops on the battlefield. Additionally, he issued orders to the brigades commanded by Brigadier Generals Joseph B. Kershaw and Paul Jones Semmes, both part of Major General Lafayette McLaws's division, which operated under Magruder's command.

Upon their arrival, Ransom's unit initially attempted a direct uphill charge, mirroring the earlier Confederate brigades' efforts to assist Magruder. However, this proved futile, prompting Ransom to regroup his men in the woods to the Confederate right. He then ordered them to double-time, covering half a mile in a sweeping maneuver around other Confederate units, aiming to strike the far Union western flank. As the darkness descended, Ransom's troops, guided by the intermittent flashes of artillery fire, advanced closer to the Union line. Despite their determined effort, they were ultimately repelled by the artillery fire commanded by George Sykes.

Meanwhile, the brigades of Kershaw and Semmes, dispatched by Lee earlier, arrived on the scene. Semmes and Kershaw were swiftly committed to the battle, but like their predecessors, they faced staunch resistance and were eventually driven back.

Semmes found himself positioned west of the junction of Carter's Mill Road and Willis Church Road, near the vicinity of Barksdale, Mahone, and Wright. He initiated the final charge of the day west of these roads, but it too met with limited success.

Kershaw's brigade angled east, targeting the area where Toombs, Anderson, and Cobb had previously launched their attacks. The situation in this region was characterized by confusion, as Kershaw's troops arrived ahead of the reinforcements sent by Jackson. They found themselves caught in a crossfire, with friendly forces firing indiscriminately behind them and effective fire from the Federals in front. In this chaotic environment, Kershaw's troops were forced into a disorderly retreat.

Following Kershaw's charge, the subsequent Confederate brigades launched disjointed attacks, with some units pushing forward while others became separated or disoriented when encountering retreating Confederate forces. The disarray was so extensive that it slowed down Jackson's advancing troops to a near standstill. Despite attempts by unit commanders to organize regiments and rally the retreating soldiers, the effectiveness of these efforts was limited.

A few Confederate units engaged in fierce combat with Union infantry and artillery. Notably, three regiments of Barlow's brigade managed to approach the Union lines closely enough to engage in hand-to-hand combat with the troops under Brigadier General Daniel Sickles before eventually being repelled.

As night descended, orders were issued for these troops to hold their positions without further charges. Semmes and Kershaw's assaults marked the final coordinated Confederate actions, both ending without significant success.

General Porter, reflecting on the Confederate infantry charges at Malvern Hill, noted the reckless determination displayed by the Confederate forces, similar to their actions at Gaines' Mill. He highlighted the devastating effectiveness of Union artillery, which mowed down the advancing Confederate brigades, while Union infantry waited until the enemy was within close range before opening fire, further contributing to Confederate losses.

With the infantry phase of the battle concluded, Union artillery continued to fire until 8:30 pm, casting a wreath of smoke along the crest's edge and bringing the action at Malvern Hill to an end.

Battle of Cedar Mountain

The silence of guns at Malvern Hill marked a somber moment, with a staggering number of Confederate young soldiers either dead or wounded. This grim picture was the aftermath of a month-long brutal conflict. The Confederate army, now under the command of General Robert E. Lee, had managed to give the capital, Richmond, a brief respite, yet the danger lingered, exacting a heavy toll.

During the sweltering summer of 1862, the Union forces, looming large in Virginia, posed a three-pronged threat. The formidable Army of the Potomac, led by Major General George Brinton McClellan and comprising nearly 90,000 men, remained a force to reckon with on the Virginia peninsula, though now further from Richmond. In the Fredericksburg region, along the Rappahannock River, Major General Ambrose Everett Burnside's 4,000 troops were making their presence felt. Adding to the Confederate worries, the Army of Virginia, freshly formed with 50,000 soldiers under the leadership of Major General John Pope, a recent arrival from the Western theater, was advancing from the north of the state.

General Robert Edward Lee, steering the Army of Northern Virginia, faced the daunting task of rebuilding his forces after suffering significant losses in the recent Peninsula campaign. With battlefield casualties and missing soldiers, Lee's army dwindled to around 56,000 by mid-July, outnumbered by the looming Union threats. He urgently appealed to Confederate President Jefferson Davis for reinforcements.

As July wore on, Lee discerned a weakening threat from one of the Union armies. He believed General McClellan's inactivity on the Peninsula indicated a diminished risk to Richmond. In his report dated April 18, 1863, Lee recalled monitoring McClellan's front and preparing for any renewed assault on Richmond. With no imminent threat from McClellan's side, Lee shifted his focus to the Virginia Piedmont to confront another challenge.

While McClellan's forces remained dormant, Pope's army was on the offensive, crossing the Rappahannock and heading towards Gordonsville. Lee aimed to intercept this advance, protecting both Richmond and Gordonsville - a crucial railway junction vital for supplying the Confederate war effort. He dispatched General Jackson, with around 12,000 troops, towards Gordonsville on July 13. Jackson's force would later be reinforced by Lee, growing to about 25,000 soldiers.

Jackson's troops reached Gordonsville by July 19, effectively countering some of Pope's initial moves against the Virginia Central. Pope, spurred by these setbacks, intensified his reconnaissance efforts from his headquarters in Washington, DC, not joining his army in the field until July 29. Meanwhile, Jackson also sought to better understand his new adversary.

The onset of Lee's first independent campaign signaled a shift towards an offensive approach, reflecting the strategy favored by both Lee and Confederate President Jefferson Davis during the summer of 1862. The Confederate grand strategy, as envisioned by Davis, emphasized an "offensive-defensive" approach, with a strong preference for the offensive. This approach was evident from the earliest days of the conflict at Fort Sumter in April 1861, continuing through to the final battles around Richmond. Despite occasional defensive stances, Davis believed that achieving Confederate goals hinged on strategic and tactical offensives.

Lee shared this belief, especially after assuming command following General Joseph Eggleston Johnston's injury at the Battle of Seven Pines. He saw the strategic offensive as the key to lifting the siege of Richmond and regaining control of Virginia. Post-Malvern Hill, Lee's focus was divided between General McClellan's formidable army on the Peninsula and the emerging threat from John Pope's Army of Virginia.

While monitoring McClellan with a cavalry brigade, Lee's attention shifted to Pope, whose advance southward and probing actions against Confederate supply lines presented a new challenge. This movement threatened Richmond from another angle. By July 25, having already dispatched Jackson with two divisions to Gordonsville, Lee started considering a new strategy, expressing his eagerness to send reinforcements to counter Pope.

In a decisive move, Lee sent Major General Ambrose Powell Hill's division and Brigadier General William Edwin Starke's Louisiana brigade to join Jackson, advising him to strike swiftly against Pope's larger force, secure the vital supply line, and then quickly rejoin the main army. However, Jackson's cautious and deliberate approach contrasted with Lee's desire for rapid action. Jackson, wary of Federal forces near Fredericksburg and hesitant to engage Pope in a frontal assault, moved slowly, seeking more advantageous positions.

Despite Lee's initial plans to significantly reinforce Jackson, McClellan's inactivity on the Peninsula constrained his ability to further weaken Richmond's defenses. Thus, Lee had to inform Jackson that the promised reinforcements could not be sent, leaving Jackson to rely on his judgment and resources.

On August 8, a significant development unfolded when Lee received word from Jackson, who believed he had found a strategy to confront Pope. Jackson's plan involved attacking Pope's vanguard as they gathered at Culpeper, seizing an opportunity to engage Major General Nathaniel Prentice Banks' Second Corps of the Army of Virginia. Jackson hoped to replicate his earlier successes in the Valley by dividing and conquering the enemy forces.

Lee, in response, gave his approval and committed to providing support from Richmond, sending additional wagons, artillery, and positioning Brigadier General John Bell Hood's division strategically to safeguard Jackson's flank. This preparation laid the groundwork for an impending battle in Virginia, yet Jackson's forces faced challenges in mobilizing for the fight.

Jackson, known for his victories but also for his communication issues with his staff, kept critical operation details to himself. This tendency led to confusion on August 8, as he altered the marching order without informing his generals. This miscommunication caused a mix-up between Major General Richard Stoddert Ewell's and Brigadier General Charles Sidney Winder's divisions, with General Hill's troops caught in the uncertainty. This resulted in a delay and frustration, as the intended rapid movement was hindered by the logistical snarl.

The following day, August 9, was marked by oppressive heat. As the sun rose, the temperature soared to 84 degrees, challenging Jackson's men who marched in heavy wool uniforms, burdened with equipment and weapons. Yet, they pressed on, embodying the spirit of Jackson's renowned foot cavalry. Their advance led them to Cedar Mountain, eight miles from Culpeper, where they encountered the Federal Second Corps.

The battle at Cedar Mountain commenced early that day with initial skirmishes involving Federal cavalry from Maine, Pennsylvania, and New Jersey, supported by infantry, clashing with Confederate forces led by Major Richard Snowden Andrews. The conflict quickly escalated as reinforcements poured in for both sides. By early afternoon, Brigadier General Jubal Anderson Early, leading a brigade of Virginians in Ewell's division, propelled the engagement further by sending in an infantry regiment against the bolstered Federal cavalry, backed by more Confederate artillery strategically positioned on Cedar Mountain.

As the morning of August 9 unfolded, Jackson's forces were on the move, and the Battle of Cedar Mountain began to escalate. Initially, a skirmish broke out involving Federal cavalry from Maine, Pennsylvania, and New Jersey, supported by infantry, clashing with Confederate forces led by Major Richard Snowden Andrews. This initial encounter quickly grew as additional units from both sides arrived at the scene.

By early afternoon, the battle intensified. Brigadier General Jubal Anderson Early, leading a brigade of Virginians from Ewell's division, advanced an infantry regiment to engage the Federal cavalry, now reinforced with more units from New Jersey and Rhode Island. Confederate artillery was strategically placed on Cedar Mountain to support these Virginian troops.

Meanwhile, the divisions of Brigadier General Charles Sidney Winder and Major General A. P. Hill were approaching the battlefield. Upon arrival, Ewell positioned his forces strategically over Crittenden Lane, utilizing a slight elevation near the road for advantage. A formidable array of Confederate artillery was set up, ranging from Parrott rifles to Howitzers and field guns, extending from Cedar Mountain to the area near Crittenden Lane and the nearby Crittenden house. In response, Federal artillery positioned themselves along Mitchell's Station Road, with their forces lining up both north and south of the Culpeper Road. By 3:30 p.m., with significant reinforcements from both sides present, the stage was set for a much larger confrontation than the earlier skirmishes of the day.

The intensity of the battle quickly escalated as Confederate forces advanced towards the Crittenden Gate. The narrow Crittenden Lane created a bottle-neck, impeding the movement of troops and equipment. General Winder, in an attempt to manage the situation, pushed forward as much artillery as possible to counter the Federal fire. Tragically, Winder was mortally wounded during this effort. For the next hour and a half, the two armies engaged in a fierce artillery duel.

General Nathaniel Prentice Banks, leading the Federal forces, mistakenly believed he held a numerical advantage over the Confederates. Despite explicit instructions from General Pope to hold his position and defend if attacked, Banks chose to initiate an attack. This decision later sparked considerable debate among Union commanders. General Pope had intended to delay any major engagement until his forces were fully consolidated, ensuring a stronger position against the Confederates. He had even sent General B.S. Roberts to reiterate these orders to Banks, but to no avail.

Banks' decision not only defied orders but also significantly weakened his corps, rendering it less effective in subsequent battles. This misstep was seen as a pivotal factor that could lead to Union disadvantages in future engagements due to reduced troop strength. Nonetheless, Banks proceeded to order an advance of three of his brigades across an exposed landscape towards a formidable Confederate force, consisting of six infantry brigades and seven artillery batteries, with additional reinforcements en route.

The initial phase of the Federal attack started at 5:00 p.m. with skirmishers, followed half an hour later by two brigades from Brigadier General Christopher Columbus Augur's division. Brigadier General Henry Prince's brigade, part of this attack, faced a setback due to a friendly-fire incident, causing some regiments to retreat temporarily. Prince was captured by the day's end. Despite these challenges, the Federal forces made some impact on the Confederate line, prompting Jubal Early to seek reinforcements from Jackson.

As Confederate reinforcements shifted to support Early, a significant gap emerged on their left near the Crittenden Gate. Spotting this vulnerability, Brigadier Generals Samuel Wylie Crawford and John White Geary led their brigades in an attack around 6:00 p.m., with Crawford's forces successfully pushing Lieutenant Colonel Thomas Stuart Garnett's Virginians out of their position. By 6:30 p.m., Crawford's men had exploited the gap in the Confederate line.

The intense battle on the Confederate left drew Jackson's attention. Amidst the chaos, he lost his hat to a tree branch while rushing to the faltering line. On arrival, he quickly directed the artillery to pull back to prevent capture. At this critical juncture, Charles Blackford witnessed Jackson's dramatic efforts to rally his troops. Jackson, finding his sword rusted in its scabbard, detached it from his belt and, waving the battle flag over his head, fervently called on his men to rally, invoking the memory of Winder and summoning the Stonewall Brigade to push forward.

Teinforcements from Georgia and North Carolina, alongside rallied Virginians and Alabamians responding to Jackson's call, filled the gap created in the Confederate line. This swift response presented a formidable challenge to the remnants of Crawford's Federal brigade. General Crawford, reflecting on this moment in his official report, lamented the overwhelming opposition his brigade faced, leading to a retreat with significant casualties.

Crawford desperately sought reinforcement, but it was delayed. When George Gordon's Federal brigade attempted to advance in support, they encountered the weary but persistent Confederate forces, including fresh troops from General Hill's division. This resulted in both Crawford's and Gordon's forces retreating, prompting a general Confederate advance.

As the Confederate line surged forward, the Federal troops, faced with capture or defeat, retreated towards their artillery positions along Mitchell's Station Road. Concurrently, Confederate infantry, initially positioned to support their artillery, rapidly advanced to capitalize on the Federal retreat.

With the sun setting, General Banks endeavored to conduct an orderly withdrawal of his artillery and infantry towards Culpeper. To cover this retreat, he ordered a battalion of Pennsylvania cavalry to charge the Confederate line. This bold move, while costly, bought the needed time for Banks' forces to withdraw.

Meanwhile, General Pope and reinforcements were arriving at the battlefield. However, the situation quickly deteriorated for the Union forces. Amidst the chaos and darkness, and under continuous Confederate fire, Pope and his staff, including Banks, who suffered an injury, hastily departed the battlefield.

The battle continued into the night, with Confederate forces persisting in their pursuit. However, the pursuit eventually ceased due to darkness, disorganization, and exhaustion among the troops. The battle had concluded with a tactical victory for Jackson and his command, but it was a costly one. Jackson's forces suffered over 1,300 casualties, with a significant number wounded. The Union forces under General Banks endured even heavier losses, totaling around 2,353, including missing, dead, and wounded soldiers.

Despite this victory, Jackson had not achieved the complete suppression of Pope's army as directed by General Lee. In the aftermath, both Lee and Pope ordered retreats. Lee, however, was quick to resume offensive operations. By August 14, 1862, he confidently left the Richmond front, moving the rest of the Army of Northern Virginia northward to confront General Pope and the Army of Virginia again, setting the stage for the upcoming Battle of Second Manassas.

Second Battle of Bull Run

In the late August days of 1862, the Rappahannock River became a dramatic backdrop for a series of skirmishes between two formidable armies. Swollen by relentless rains, the river turned into an insurmountable barrier for Lee's forces, thwarting their attempts to cross. Meanwhile, the Army of the Potomac, swelling in numbers, began pouring in reinforcements from the Peninsula, tipping the scales further.

Lee, faced with overwhelming odds, devised a daring strategy. He dispatched Jackson and Stuart, leading half of his army, on a covert flanking maneuver. Their mission was audacious: cut through Pope's communication lines, specifically targeting the vital Orange & Alexandria Railroad. This move aimed to force Pope into a retreat, turning his army vulnerable and ripe for defeat.

On the night of August 25, Jackson embarked on this critical mission, arriving at Salem, now known as Marshall, under the cover of darkness. The plot thickened on the evening of August 26. Jackson's troops, having stealthily bypassed Pope's right flank through Thoroughfare Gap, struck a decisive blow at Bristoe Station, disrupting the Orange & Alexandria Railroad. By dawn on August 27, they had seized and devastated the immense Union supply depot at Manassas Junction. This bold and unexpected maneuver sent Pope reeling, hastily retreating from his defensive stance along the Rappahannock.

Jackson didn't stop there. During the night of August 27-28, he led his divisions northward, positioning them strategically at the First Bull Run (Manassas) battlefield. Here, they nestled behind an unfinished railroad grade beneath Stony Ridge. This location offered numerous tactical advantages – concealment amidst dense woods, prime observation points overlooking the Warrenton Turnpike, and easy access roads for reinforcements or retreat. The unfinished railroad provided an added boon, serving as natural trenches.

The Battle of Thoroughfare Gap on August 28 was a turning point. Longstreet's wing, overcoming light Union resistance, surged through the gap to join forces with Jackson. This victory, seemingly minor at first, was a crucial link in the chain of events that led to Pope's impending defeat. It symbolized the unification of Lee's army on the Manassas battlefield, setting the stage for what was to come.

The Second Battle of Bull Run, unfolded dramatically on August 28. It all began when a Union column, under the watchful eyes of Jackson near Gainesville and the Brawner family farm, marched along the Warrenton Turnpike. This column, part of Brig. Gen. Rufus King's division, included brigades led by Brig. Gens. John P. Hatch, John Gibbon, Abner Doubleday, and Marsena R. Patrick. They were moving east to join Pope's main force at Centreville. King, however, was absent due to a severe epileptic seizure earlier that day.

In a bold move, Jackson, having learned of Longstreet's impending reinforcement, daringly rode alongside the Union troops disguised as a farmer, much to the dismay of his aides. His disguise was so effective that the Union soldiers paid him no heed, mistaking him for a harmless local.

Jackson, concerned about Pope possibly pulling back to unite with McClellan's incoming forces, decided on an aggressive strategy. Returning to his concealed position, he gave the order to his commanders: "Bring out your men, gentlemen." By 6:30 p.m., Confederate artillery launched a fierce assault on the Union column, targeting particularly John Gibbon's Black Hat Brigade, which would later be renowned as the Iron Brigade.

Gibbon, an ex-artillery officer, quickly responded with fire from Battery B, 4th U.S. Artillery. This artillery duel stopped King's column in its tracks. Hatch's brigade had already passed, and Patrick's troops sought cover, leaving Gibbon and Doubleday to face Jackson's onslaught. Gibbon, under the impression that Jackson was far away in Centreville, mistook the Confederate artillery for Jeb Stuart's cavalry units. He swiftly dispatched aides to call for reinforcements and sent staff officer Frank A. Haskell to rally the 2nd Wisconsin Infantry.

The 2nd Wisconsin, commanded by Col. Edgar O'Connor, maneuvered skillfully through the woods, emerging silently on John Brawner's farm. Forming up quietly, they advanced and dispatched skirmishers who pushed back their Confederate counterparts. But as they reached the open ground, they were met by a fierce volley from the 800-strong Stonewall Brigade, led by Col. William S. Baylor. Despite being hit hard from 150 yards away, the 2nd Wisconsin stood firm, returning fire with equal ferocity.

As more units joined the fray, the battle lines remained alarmingly close, with both sides engaged in a relentless, brutal exchange of volleys. Jackson personally directed his regiments in this intense combat, bolstering his forces with three Georgian regiments from Brig. Gen. Alexander R. Lawton's brigade. Gibbon responded by bringing in the 7th Wisconsin. The battle intensified as Jackson also deployed Brig. Gen. Isaac R. Trimble's brigade to support Lawton, clashing fiercely with Gibbon's last regiment, the 6th Wisconsin. This battle, described by Jackson as "fierce and sanguinary," exemplified the intense and brutal nature of Civil War combat, with both sides demonstrating remarkable valor and resilience.

The battle reached a critical point when Trimble's brigade joined the fray.

Gibbon, to close a gap between the 6th Wisconsin and the rest of the Iron Brigade, received reinforcements from Doubleday: the 56th Pennsylvania and the 76th New York. These fresh troops, arriving after nightfall, valiantly held back the new Confederate onslaught. Amidst the chaos, Jackson ordered Captain John Pelham's horse artillery to advance, engaging the 19th Indiana at an alarmingly close range of less than 100 yards.

The conflict raged until around 9 p.m., concluding with Gibbon's forces executing a tactical withdrawal, still engaged in combat, falling back to the forest's edge. Meanwhile, Doubleday's regiments retreated in an orderly fashion to the turnpike. The confrontation, though not decisive, was costly: the Union and Confederate forces suffered over 1,150 and 1,250 casualties, respectively. The 2nd Wisconsin bore the brunt of the Union losses, with 276 casualties out of 430 soldiers. The Stonewall Brigade faced similar devastation, losing 340 out of 800. Trimble's 21st and Lawton's 26th Georgian regiments each suffered over 70% casualties. This brutal encounter saw one in every three men engaged getting shot. Confederate Brig. Gen. William B. Taliaferro reflected, "In this fight there was no maneuvering and very little tactics. It was a question of endurance and both endured." Both Taliaferro and Ewell sustained injuries, with Ewell's leg amputation sidelining him for ten months.

Despite his numerical advantage (around 6,200 to Gibbon's 2,100), Jackson didn't secure a decisive victory. Hindered by the darkness, a fragmented deployment of forces, loss of division commanders, and the Union's resilience, his strategic goal was nonetheless met: drawing John Pope's attention. Pope, misinterpreting the situation at Brawner Farm as Jackson's retreat, was convinced he had Jackson cornered, ready to be captured with Longstreet's reinforcements seemingly out of the picture.

Gibbon, along with King, Patrick, and Doubleday, deliberated their next move, especially since McDowell was "lost in the woods". Their division, weakened and facing Jackson's entire corps, was in a precarious position.

Confederate prisoners claimed Jackson's force numbered between 60,000 to 70,000, poised for an imminent strike. Given this, staying at Groveton was untenable. They contemplated retreat to either Manassas Junction or Centreville. Gibbon advised moving to Manassas Junction, given the uncertainty of enemy positions. King concurred, and the division moved south to Manassas Junction. Ricketts, in a similar predicament, also retreated south towards Bristoe Station.

Pope, planning a counterattack the next morning, was unaware of the true positions of both his and Jackson's forces. He believed McDowell and Sigel were blocking Jackson to the west, while King and Ricketts had actually retreated south. Sigel and Reynolds, positioned south and east of Jackson, were also out of the assumed configuration. Unbeknownst to Pope, Jackson had no intentions of retreating and was securely entrenched, awaiting Longstreet's arrival, a possibility Pope dismissed.

Jackson's strategy at Brawner's Farm was to engage Pope's forces and keep them occupied until Longstreet could arrive with the rest of the Army of Northern Virginia. On the morning of August 29, Longstreet, commanding 25,000 men, commenced his march from Thoroughfare Gap. Jackson, anticipating their arrival, dispatched Stuart to lead Longstreet's vanguard to strategically chosen positions. Meanwhile, Jackson reorganized his defenses, anticipating a potential morning assault by Pope. He arrayed his 20,000 men along a 3,000-yard line south of Stony Ridge, preparing for the confrontation.

Observing the accumulation of I Corps (under Sigel) near the Manassas-Sudley Road, Jackson directed A.P. Hill's brigades to fortify positions near Sudley Church on his left flank. The dense woods in the area posed a challenge for effective artillery deployment, compelling Hill to arrange his brigades in two lines, with Brig. Gen. Maxcy Gregg's and Brig. Gen. Edward L. Thomas's brigades in front. In the central segment of the line, Jackson placed two brigades from Ewell's division, now under Brig. Gen. Alexander Lawton, and on the right, he positioned Brig. Gen. William E. Starke, succeeding Taliaferro's division.

The Confederate line was bisected by an abandoned railroad grade, a remnant of the Manassas Gap Railroad Company's work from the 1850s. While parts of this grade offered a solid defensive position, others were less advantageous, and the heavy woods limited artillery use, especially along the right flank which opened to clear fields. To safeguard the left flank, Fitz Lee's cavalry and a horse artillery battery were deployed, guarding against potential Union movements across Sudley Ford. On the vulnerable right flank, previously weakened at Brawner's Farm, Jackson reinforced Starke's division with Early and Forno's brigades, both fresh and unengaged the previous evening.

At dawn on August 29, Pope was both surprised and frustrated to discover that Ricketts and King had withdrawn south. Further complicating matters, John Gibbon, who had initially recommended the retreat from Groveton, reported to Pope at Centreville without knowledge of McDowell's where-abouts, prompting an exasperated response from Pope. Meanwhile, Porter's troops were resting at Manassas, where Gibbon encountered them. King, debilitated by his epilepsy, had relinquished his command to John Hatch. McDowell, who had spent the previous day lost in Prince William County, was dismayed by Pope's orders. Consequently, King joined Porter, Reynolds temporarily aligned with Sigel's corps, and Ricketts remained distant at Bristoe Station, effectively leaving McDowell without a command. Pope, still convinced of Jackson's precarious position, failed to recognize the actual situation. His plan, predicated on the coordinated actions of all his corps and divisions, was undermined by their unexpected locations and movements.

Pope's complex attack plans for August 29 devolved into a straightforward frontal assault by Sigel's corps, the only unit ready that morning. This corps was often viewed as the army's weakest, primarily composed of German immigrants with limited English proficiency. Sigel, a German-born trained officer, was regarded more as a political general appointed by Lincoln for his ability to recruit and inspire these German-speaking Unionists, many of whom enlisted specifically to serve under him. Their prior underperformance against Jackson in the Shenandoah Valley and low morale further strained their effectiveness.

Pope's strategy was to flank Jackson on both sides. He instructed Fitz John Porter to target what he believed was the Confederate right near Gainesville, while Sigel was to confront Jackson's left at dawn. Sigel, cautious of Jackson's setup, opted for a wide-front advance. His formation included Brig. Gen. Robert C. Schenck's division, supported by Brig. Gen. John F. Reynolds's division on the left, Brig. Gen. Robert H. Milroy's brigade in the center, and Brig. Gen. Carl Schurz's division on the right. Schurz's brigades, led by Brig. Gen. Alexander Schimmelfennig and Col. Włodzimierz Krzyżanowski, initiated contact with Jackson's forces around 7 a.m.

Sigel's attack on A.P. Hill's division epitomized the day's battles near Stony Ridge. The unfinished railroad offered some natural defense, but largely, the Confederates absorbed the Union onslaught and countered fiercely. This approach foreshadowed Jackson's tactics at the upcoming Battle of Antietam. Schurz's brigades engaged in intense skirmishes with Gregg and Thomas, leading to close-quarters combat. As Milroy responded to the combat sounds, his brigade faced a barrage of Confederate gunfire. Amidst the chaos, the 82nd Ohio stumbled upon an unguarded ravine, flanking Isaac Trimble's brigade, but were soon repelled by reinforcements and retreated in disarray, causing further panic and disorder.

Schenck and Reynolds, facing severe artillery fire, responded but held back from a full infantry advance, engaging only in minor skirmishes with Jubal Early's brigade. During this, Meade's brigade encountered abandoned wounded soldiers from King's division, leading to a desperate medical evacuation under fire. Milroy, trying to regroup his battered brigade, coordinated with Brig. Gen Julius Stahel to prepare for a possible Confederate counterattack. A brief Confederate pursuit was swiftly countered by artillery, forcing Stahel to return to his initial position near the turnpike.

Believing that Kearny's division of the III Corps would back him up, Schurz initiated a renewed assault against Hill around 10 a.m. This time, Schimmelfennig's brigade was reinforced by the 1st New York from Kearny's division, bolstering Krzyzanowski's efforts. The battle in the woods west of Sudley Road intensified, reaching a stalemate until the 14th Georgia arrived to support the South Carolinians. Their volleys of musket fire overwhelmed Krzyzanowski's troops, causing them to retreat in disarray. The Confederates pursued aggressively, engaging in brutal close-quarters combat. However, as they emerged into the open, Union artillery from Dogan's Ridge opened fire, forcing them to fall back.

To the north, Schimmelfennig's units, including the 61st Ohio, 74th Pennsylvania, and 8th West Virginia, clashed with parts of Gregg and Branch's brigades but were eventually compelled to retreat. Kearny, however, remained stationary, directing his brigades towards Bull Run Creek where Orlando Poe's brigade forded the creek. Poe's advance caused alarm at Jackson's headquarters, prompting a quick evacuation of wagons and positioning of Maj. John Pelham's horse artillery. A brief firefight ensued between Poe's brigade and Confederate forces, but the sight of Confederate infantry deterred further advancement by Poe, leading him to withdraw.

Meanwhile, Robinson's brigade held positions along Bull Run Creek, and Birney's regiments were dispersed, with some supporting artillery on Matthews Hill, others in reserve, and the rest skirmishing with A.P. Hill's troops after retreating from Confederate artillery fire.

Sigel, content with the battle's progress and assuming he was engaged in a holding action until Pope's arrival, welcomed reinforcements from Hooker's division (III Corps) and Stevens's brigade (IX Corps) by 1 p.m. When Pope arrived and took command, he found Sigel's attack had failed, with Schurz and Milroy's units battered and disorganized. Although Reynolds and Schenck's divisions were fresh, they were committed to protecting the army's left flank. Pope, hoping for support from McDowell and McClellan, was dismayed to find neither on the field. Contemplating a withdrawal to Centreville but concerned about the political implications, he hesitated. However, news of McDowell's imminent arrival prompted him to plan an attack on Jackson's center.

By this time, Longstreet's forces had positioned themselves to Jackson's right, with Brig. Gen. John Bell Hood's division straddling the turnpike, loosely connected to Jackson's right. Surrounding Hood were the divisions of Brig. Gens. James L. Kemper and David R. "Neighbor" Jones, with Brig. Gen. Cadmus M. Wilcox's division in reserve.

Stuart's cavalry ran into Porter, Hatch, and McDowell as they advanced along the Manassas–Gainesville Road, leading to a brief but intense firefight that stalled the Union column. During this encounter, Porter and McDowell received a perplexing directive from Pope, later known as the "Joint Order." Historian John J. Hennessy critiqued this order as being notably contradictory and unclear, causing much debate over the years. It mentioned ongoing attacks on Jackson's left but was vague regarding Porter and McDowell's roles. Instead of explicitly instructing them to attack Jackson's right flank near Gainesville, the order ambiguously directed a move "toward" Gainesville, with a stipulation to halt upon establishing communication with other divisions. The possibility of retreating to Centreville that night was also mentioned. The order concluded with a clause allowing deviation from these instructions if advantageous, leaving it largely ineffective as a military directive.

Complicating matters, Stuart's cavalry, led by Col. Thomas Rosser, executed a deceptive maneuver by dragging tree branches behind horses to create the illusion of a large, approaching force. Concurrently, McDowell received an update from Brig. Gen. John Buford, his cavalry commander, reporting significant Confederate movement through Gainesville at 8:15 a.m., indicating

Longstreet's approach from Thoroughfare Gap. This information, crucially warning of the impending Confederate presence, caused the Union advance to halt. Strangely, McDowell delayed relaying Buford's report to Pope until around 7 p.m., leading to Pope operating under two major misapprehensions: that Longstreet was not near the battlefield and that Porter and McDowell were advancing to confront Jackson's right flank.

As Longstreet positioned his forces, General Lee contemplated an offensive against the Union left. Longstreet recalled Lee's eagerness to engage but noted that he did not explicitly order an immediate attack. Observing that Reynolds and Schenck's divisions extended south of the Warrenton Turnpike, overlapping half of his line, Longstreet advised against launching an attack at that moment. Lee conceded, especially after Jeb Stuart reported the considerable strength of the Union forces on the Gainesville–Manassas Road, indicating Porter and McDowell's formidable presence.

Pope, operating under the belief that his instructions for an attack on Jackson's right flank were being executed, initiated four separate assaults against Jackson's front. His intention was to distract Confederate forces until Porter could deliver a decisive strike. One of these attacks, led by Brig. Gen. Cuvier Grover at 3 p.m., was supposed to be supported by Kearny's division. With Isaac Stevens's division as backup, Grover advanced his brigade into the woods, launching a direct assault on Edward Thomas's Georgia brigade. Reaching the railroad embankment, Grover's men delivered a volley of fire at close range, followed by a bayonet charge. Caught off guard, the Georgians initially fell back, leading to intense close combat. However, reinforcements from Maxcy Gregg's South Carolinians and Dorsey Pender's North Carolinans turned the tide. Pender's flank attack sent Grover's brigade retreating in disarray, suffering over 350 casualties. When Pender's brigade pursued, they were halted by heavy Union artillery fire from Dogan Ridge.

Elsewhere, Joseph Carr's brigade engaged in a firefight with Confederate forces, during which Isaac Trimble, a key Confederate brigadier, was wounded. James Nagle's brigade from Reno's division, supported by Nelson Taylor's brigade, then attacked the now-leaderless Trimble's brigade, forcing them into a retreat. But like previous Union assaults that day, Nagle was outnumbered and eventually repelled by a counterattack from Henry Forno's Louisiana brigade and reinforcements including Bradley Johnson and Col. Leroy Stafford's 9th Louisiana. John Hood's division also arrived, pushing back Milroy and Nagle. Milroy's weary brigade broke and fled. Pope, in response, reallocated Schenck from south of the turnpike and, with artillery support, managed to push the Confederates back towards the railroad embankment. Amidst all this, Kearny remained inactive.

Reynolds, tasked with a diversionary attack south of the turnpike, encountered Longstreet's forces. This unexpected engagement led him to abort his mission. Pope, however, dismissed Reynolds's reports of encountering Longstreet, mistakenly assuming Reynolds had found Porter's V Corps ready to strike at Jackson's flank. Jesse Reno subsequently ordered another IX Corps assault under Col. James Nagle against Jackson's center. Nagle initially drove back Trimble's brigade from the railroad embankment, but subsequent Confederate counterattacks reclaimed their positions, pushing Nagle's forces back into open fields. They were only halted by Union artillery, continuing the pattern of intense, back-and-forth combat with neither side able to secure a decisive advantage.

At 4:30 p.m., Pope issued a clear order for Porter to attack, but due to a misadventure of his aide (Pope's nephew), the message wasn't delivered until 6:30 p.m. By then, Porter's situation hadn't improved, and he was still not in a favorable position to launch an attack. Anticipating an assault from Porter that would never materialize, Pope ordered Kearny to strike at Jackson's far left flank, hoping to pressure both ends of the Confederate line. Kearny responded at 5 p.m., sending Robinson and Birney's brigades into A.P. Hill's already weary division. The attack primarily impacted Maxcy Gregg's brigade, which was nearly depleted of ammunition and officers after resisting two major assaults throughout the day. As they retreated,

Gregg, wielding an old Revolutionary War scimitar, heroically encouraged his men, "Let us die here my men, let us die here." With Thomas's and Gregg's brigades nearing collapse, A.P. Hill urgently requested Jackson's aid. Simultaneously, Daniel Leasure's brigade managed to push back James Archer's Tennessee brigade. However, counterattacks from Jubal Early and Lawrence O'Bryan Branch's brigades repelled Kearny's division. During this conflict, Hill's brigadier Charles W. Field was severely wounded, leaving Col. John M. Brockenbrough in command.

On the Confederate right, Longstreet noted McDowell's I Corps shifting divisions towards Henry House Hill to back Reynolds, leading Lee to reconsider an offensive in that area. Longstreet, cautious of the limited daylight, proposed a preparatory reconnaissance to position troops for battle the next morning, to which Lee agreed, and Hood's division advanced. Concurrently, McDowell reported to Pope that King was ill and the division was now under Brig. Gen John P. Hatch, whom Pope disliked. Hatch, initially assigned a cavalry brigade and later reassigned to infantry for failing to execute Pope's orders, was instructed by Pope to attack along the Sudley Road. Hatch protested the impracticality due to Kearny's troops blocking the way and the approaching nightfall. Nevertheless, Pope insisted on the assault. Hood's division, having arrived on Jackson's right, forced Hatch and Reynolds to retreat to Bald Hill, capturing Chinn Ridge in the process. As night fell, Hood withdrew from the exposed position. Longstreet and his officers, wary of attacking a well-defended Union force, persuaded Lee to cancel the planned assault for the third time.

Pope, misinterpreting Hood's withdrawal as a sign of Confederate retreat, remained unaware of the full situation. Learning about Buford's earlier report from McDowell, Pope recognized Longstreet's presence but optimistically assumed he was there merely to cover a Confederate withdrawal. Pope then ordered Porter's corps to regroup with the main army, planning another offensive for August 30. Historian A. Wilson Greene criticized this decision, noting that Pope lacked numerical superiority and a strategic advantage. He argued that a more prudent action would have been to retreat across Bull Run and unite with McClellan's nearby Army of the Potomac, which had 25,000 men at its disposal.

That evening, Pope communicated with General Halleck, providing an overview of the day's combat. He characterized the fighting as "severe" and estimated Union casualties at around 7,000 to 8,000. His assessment of Confederate losses, however, was significantly exaggerated, suggesting they were double that of the Union's. This was a considerable overestimation, especially since Jackson's forces had largely been engaged in defensive tactics. Nevertheless, the Confederates had suffered notable losses among their officers, including two division commanders on August 28 and three brigade commanders—Trimble, Field, and Col. Henry Forno—who were wounded. In contrast, the Union had only one wounded brigade commander, Col. Daniel Leasure, and no general officers injured.

A contentious aspect of the Second Battle of Bull Run concerns George B. McClellan's cooperation with John Pope. As the battle unfolded, two corps of the Army of the Potomac, under William B. Franklin and Edwin V. Sumner, arrived in Alexandria. However, McClellan, citing concerns about insufficient artillery, cavalry, and transport support, refrained from advancing them to Manassas. His political adversaries accused him of deliberately undermining Pope. McClellan's own communications at the time did little to dispel these accusations. On August 10, he wrote to his wife, expressing a belief that Pope would suffer a defeat and that the responsibility for salvaging the situation would fall to him, but he insisted on having full control. To President Lincoln, he suggested on August 29 that it might be prudent to let Pope resolve his difficulties independently while focusing on securing the capital.

Longstreet's final division, led by Maj. Gen. Richard H. Anderson, arrived on the battlefield around 3 a.m. on August 30 after a 17-mile march. Exhausted and unfamiliar with the terrain, they initially stopped on a ridge east of

Groveton. At dawn, realizing their vulnerable position close to Union lines, they retreated, inadvertently reinforcing Pope's belief that the Confederate army was in retreat, a notion already shaped by Hood's withdrawal the previous night.

Pope directed McDowell to advance his corps up the Sudley Road to strike the Confederate right flank. McDowell, however, voiced reservations, unsure of the situation on the Confederate left and expressing a preference for positioning his troops on Chinn Ridge. He suggested that Heintzelman's corps, being closer, should attack the Confederate right instead. Pope eventually agreed but decided to detach King's division to support Heintzelman in this maneuver.

At Pope's 8 a.m. council of war, his generals urged a cautious approach. Reconnaissance around 10 a.m. on Stony Ridge confirmed Stonewall Jackson's men were still entrenched in their defensive positions. John F. Reynolds reported substantial Confederate strength south of the turnpike, and Fitz John Porter later corroborated this intelligence. Despite this, a reconnaissance by Heintzelman and McDowell inexplicably failed to detect Jackson's line, leading Pope to conclude that the Confederates were retreating.

During this period, a miscommunication resulted in two of Porter's brigades, Abram Sanders Piatt's and Charles Griffin's, being misrouted. Believing Pope to be at Centreville based on outdated orders, Morell directed these brigades away from the main column. Piatt eventually realized the error and turned back, reaching Henry House Hill around 4 p.m. Griffin and Morell, however, remained at Centreville, unable to return to the battlefield due to a blocked road and a broken bridge over Cub Run.

As Ricketts's division neared the Confederate lines, it became evident that the enemy was not retreating. Pope, worried about McClellan potentially claiming credit for any victory, decided to attack immediately, foregoing the option to wait for reinforcements. Around noon, he ordered Porter's corps, supported by Hatch and Reynolds, to advance along the turnpike, while Ricketts, Kearny, and Hooker were to engage the Confederate left. This plan aimed to encircle the supposedly retreating Confederates. However, the Confederates were prepared for battle and Lee, with Longstreet's force at the ready, awaited an opportunity for a counterattack. Lee had strategically placed artillery under Col. Stephen D. Lee to bombard the fields in front of Jackson's position.

Porter's corps, positioned in the woods north of the turnpike near Groveton, took approximately two hours to organize the assault on Jackson's line. The assault consisted of ten brigades, about 10,000 men, with artillery support from Dogan Ridge. Ricketts's division was to support Heintzelman, with Sigel's corps in reserve. Reynolds and King's divisions were near Henry House Hill, with Porter aiming to strike Jackson's right flank. In Morell's absence, Brig. Gen Daniel Butterfield took command, while George Sykes's division of regular troops remained in reserve. By noon, with temperatures soaring above 90 °F, the battlefield conditions were intense.

The Confederates, led by elements of Hill's and Ewell's divisions, launched an initial attack, surprising some of Ricketts's men. However, the powerful Union artillery on Dogan Ridge repelled this advance, forcing the Confederates back to their positions along the unfinished railroad.

The Union forces were up against a daunting challenge. Butterfield's division had to cover 600 yards of open pasture on Lucinda Dogan's land, with the final 150 yards steeply uphill, to reach a strong Confederate position behind the unfinished railroad. Porter then directed John Hatch's division to support Butterfield on the right. Hatch arranged his four brigades in battle formation, leading the charge with Col. Timothy Sullivan's brigade, as Hatch had taken over division command the previous day. Hatch's division had a shorter distance of 300 yards to cover but had to execute a complicated right-wheel maneuver under enemy fire to directly engage the Confederate line. They faced fierce resistance from Stephen Lee's artillery and intense volleys from Confederate infantry. Amidst the chaos, Hatch was injured by an artillery shell, rendering him unconscious and out of the battle. Despite this, his men briefly penetrated the Confederate line, causing the 48th Virginia Infantry to retreat. The Stonewall Brigade, led by Col. Baylor, quickly intervened to stabilize their line but suffered heavy losses.

In a notable moment of the battle, when Confederates from Col. Bradley T. Johnson's and Col. Leroy A. Stafford's brigades exhausted their ammunition, they resorted to throwing rocks at the 24th New York, leading to an unusual exchange of projectiles. Longstreet's artillery compounded the Union's difficulties, bombarding the reinforcements and causing severe disruptions. Hatch's brigade retreated in disarray, impacting Patrick's brigade and triggering further panic. Gibbon's brigade, positioned further back, remained untouched, while Doubleday's brigade had inexplicably left the area of engagement. Butterfield's division, under heavy Confederate fire, was on the brink of collapse.

As Porter attempted to reinforce Butterfield's weakening attack, he sent Lt. Col Robert C. Buchanan's brigade of regulars into the fray. However, this effort was disrupted by Longstreet's assault on the Union left. The Confederate advance was jubilant, with some in Starke's brigade attempting a pursuit, but they were repelled by Union reserves along the Groveton-Sudley Road. Jackson's forces, despite holding their position, were too depleted to launch a counterattack, enabling Porter to stabilize the northern section near the turnpike. However, McDowell's decision to redirect Reynolds's division from Chinn Ridge to assist Porter critically weakened the Union's southern flank. This left only 2,200 Union troops to confront a Confederate force nearly ten times their size, marking a significant tactical error in the day's unfolding battle.

Lee and Longstreet, recognizing a strategic opportunity, decided to launch their long-awaited assault aimed at Henry House Hill. This key position had been crucial in the First Battle of Bull Run and, if captured, would dominate the Union's potential line of retreat. Longstreet's force of 25,000 men in five divisions extended nearly a mile and a half, from the Brawner Farm to the Manassas Gap Railroad. The challenging terrain, including ridges, streams, and wooded areas, meant that Longstreet had to depend on the initiative of his division commanders to navigate the 1.5 to 2-mile stretch towards the hill. The attack was led by John Bell Hood's Texans and Brig. Gen. Nathan G. "Shanks" Evans's South Carolinians, followed by Kemper's and Jones's divisions, with Anderson's division in reserve. Lee signaled to Jackson as the assault began, instructing him to protect Longstreet's left flank.

Porter, realizing the gravity of the situation on the left, redirected Buchanan's brigade to counter the Confederate advance and sent for Col. Charles W. Roberts's brigade to join the action. The Union defense south of the turnpike was perilously thin, held only by McLean's and Warren's brigades. McLean was positioned on Chinn Ridge, while Warren was near Groveton. Hood's assault commenced at 4 p.m., swiftly overwhelming Warren's regiments, including the 5th New York (Duryée's Zouaves) and 10th New York (National Zouaves). The 5th New York suffered devastating losses, with nearly 300 casualties within the first 10 minutes, marking the highest single-battle fatality rate for an infantry regiment in the war. The striking red and blue uniforms of the Zouaves made a poignant scene on the battlefield, likened by one of Hood's officers to Texas wildflowers in bloom.

Meanwhile, Pope remained at his headquarters, unaware of the unfolding disaster. His attention was on a message from Henry Halleck, informing him of reinforcements on the way, including the II and VI Corps and Brig. Gen Darius Couch's division of the IV Corps. Additionally, McClellan was ordered to remain in Washington, D.C., giving Pope complete command over the incoming 41 brigades without McClellan's interference. It was only after Warren's position collapsed and McLean began to retreat that Pope grasped the severity of the situation on the battlefield.

In a rapidly evolving battlefield, McDowell directed Ricketts' division to break off its unsuccessful attack on the Confederate left and reinforce the Union left instead. McDowell, accompanied by Reynolds, set out to establish a new defensive line on Chinn Ridge, encountering Porter's retreating troops fleeing from the woods to the west. Reynolds was hesitant to move to Chinn Ridge, believing his division crucial to thwart a Confederate push from the woods. However, McDowell insisted that the imminent Confederate threat was from the south, urging immediate relocation.

Before McDowell's orders could take full effect, Col. Martin Hardin, leading Brig. Gen Conrad F. Jackson's brigade (with Jackson absent due to illness), independently moved to confront the Confederate advance. Hardin's brigade, along with Battery G of the 1st Pennsylvania Artillery, delivered a strong volley against the 1st and 4th Texas regiments, momentarily halting their progress. However, the 5th Texas regiment continued its advance, quickly overpowering the Union gunners. Nathan Evans's South Carolina brigade then outflanked Hardin's position. Hardin was wounded, and command shifted to Col. James Kirk of the 10th Pennsylvania Reserves, who was soon incapacitated. The disintegrating brigade fell back, sporadically engaging the advancing Confederates.

Nathaniel McLean's Ohio brigade soon entered the fray but was quickly surrounded on three sides by the brigades of Law, Wilcox, and Evans, leading to a retreat alongside the remnants of Hardin's brigade towards Henry House Hill.

The first of Ricketts's brigades to arrive were led by Brig. Gen. Zealous B. Tower and Col. Fletcher Webster. Tower's brigade initially succeeded in repelling Wilcox's Alabamians but then encountered the fresh forces of David R. Jones's Confederate division. Webster's regimental lineup faltered after he was killed by artillery fire, prompting a retreat. Simultaneously, Tower was incapacitated and removed from the field.

Schenck then deployed Col. John Koltes's fresh brigade, supported by Wlodz-imierz Krzyzanowski's wearied brigade. However, Koltes was soon killed, and command fell to Col. Richard Coulter, a Mexican War veteran. Despite their efforts, Koltes's and Krzyzanowski's brigades were overwhelmed by fresh Confederate brigades under Lewis Armistead, Montgomery Corse, and Eppa Hunton, leading to a chaotic Union retreat.

In the initial stages of the Confederate assault, McDowell swiftly established a new defensive line comprising Reynolds' and Sykes' divisions. As Longstreet's final reserve, Richard Anderson's division, launched their offensive, the regulars of George Sykes's division, bolstered by Meade and Seymour's brigades, as well as Piatt's brigade, formed a formidable line on Henry House Hill. This robust defense held off the Confederate attack long enough to enable the rest of the Union army to retreat across Bull Run Creek towards Centreville.

Stonewall Jackson, following somewhat vague instructions from Lee to support Longstreet, initiated an attack north of the turnpike around 6 p.m. This delay in Jackson's advance has been noted by historian John J. Hennessy as one of the significant Confederate shortcomings of the battle, potentially diminishing the impact of his forces' contribution. Jackson's assault occurred as Pope was redirecting units north of the turnpike to reinforce the defense at Henry House Hill. The Confederates managed to overrun several Union artillery and infantry units during their vigorous attack. However, by 7 p.m., Pope had successfully established a solid defensive line aligned with the forces on Henry House Hill. At 8 p.m., Pope commanded a general withdrawal along the turnpike to Centreville. This retreat, unlike the chaotic one at the First Battle of Bull Run, was executed quietly and in good order. The Confederates, exhausted and low on ammunition, did not pursue in the dark. Lee's victory was significant, but he fell short of his goal to annihilate Pope's army.

The battle's last notable engagement occurred around 7:00 PM. Lee instructed J.E.B. Stuart's cavalry to flank the Union forces and cut off their retreat. Brig. Gen Beverly Robertson's brigade, including Col. Thomas Rosser's 5th Virginia Cavalry, aimed for Lewis Ford, a crossing point on Bull Run Creek, intending to encircle the Union army. However, they encountered John Buford's Union cavalry at the crossing. After a brief but intense skirmish, Buford's superior numbers prevailed, forcing the Confederate cavalry to retreat. This encounter, lasting only about ten minutes, saw injuries on both sides, including wounds to Col. Thomas Munford of the 2nd Virginia Cavalry and John Buford, as well as the death of Col. Thornton Brodhead of the 1st Michigan Cavalry. This clash effectively safeguarded the Union army's retreat.

Battle of Harpers Ferry

On the fateful day of September 12, General Miles orchestrated a masterful distribution of his 10,400 troops into four dynamic brigades. With a keen strategic eye, he ingeniously mixed the green, unseasoned recruits with battle-hardened veterans, creating a robust and balanced fighting force. On the imposing Bolivar Heights, he positioned a formidable force of about 7,000 men. This line, a solid wall of determination, extended from the rolling Potomac River to the majestic Shenandoah, ready to confront any challenge.

Nearby, on the strategic vantage point of Camp Hill, Miles astutely placed a brigade of 1,000, a mix of heavy artillery and steadfast infantry. Their crucial role was to defend Bolivar Heights, a key position in the looming battle. Interestingly, Miles overlooked Loudoun Heights, dismissing it as a less critical location. He believed that the rough terrain would deter Confederate artillery placement, and any enemy presence there could be swiftly dealt with by the artillery on Maryland Heights.

Meanwhile, the defenses of Maryland Heights, the linchpin of the area, were primed more for repelling raiders than for an all-out defense. Halfway up the heights, a potent artillery battery stood ready: two massive 9-inch Dahlgren naval rifles, a formidable 50-pounder Parrott rifle, and four reliable 12-pounder smoothbores. These guns were strategically placed to shield both Camp Hill and Bolivar Heights.

At the crest of Maryland Heights, Colonel Thomas H. Ford, a leader of unwavering resolve from the 32nd Ohio Infantry, took command of parts of four regiments, totaling 1,600 men. Among them were the fresh recruits of the 126th New York, mere novices in the art of war, having been in the Army for only 21 days. Despite their inexperience, they constructed rudimentary breastworks and sent skirmishers ahead, a quarter-mile into the unknown, towards the Confederate threat.

On that same September 12, they first clashed with the advancing men from Kershaw's South Carolina brigade, a formidable enemy moving slowly through the challenging terrain of Elk Ridge. The Union riflemen, sheltered behind their abatis, unleashed volleys that halted the Confederates, setting the stage for a tense night before the battle.

On the morning of September 13, as the first light of dawn broke, General Kershaw initiated his bold attack. His strategy was straightforward yet daring: his brigade would launch a direct assault on the Union breastworks, while Barksdale's Mississippi troops attempted a flanking maneuver on the Federal right. Despite their inexperience, the New York troops, led by Col. Ford, displayed unexpected resilience. However, Col. Ford, feeling unwell, stayed behind the lines, leaving Col. Sherrill in charge. The battle intensified, and Sherrill, rallying his men bravely, was struck by a minié ball, causing panic among the green troops.

As Barksdale's forces closed in, the New Yorkers' lines crumbled, and a retreat ensued. Major Hewitt tried to reorganize the troops, but an order from Col. Ford to retreat sealed their fate. In a hasty withdrawal, they destroyed their artillery and retreated across a pontoon bridge to Harpers Ferry. Col. Ford's decision to retreat, later scrutinized, was deemed unjustified, leading to recommendations for his dismissal from the Army.

Simultaneously, other Confederate columns converged around Harpers Ferry. Walker reached Loudoun Heights, and Jackson's divisions positioned themselves to the west of Bolivar Heights. Astonishingly, they found these strategic positions undefended. Inside Harpers Ferry, Union officers, realizing their dire situation, urged Miles to recapture Maryland Heights. However, Miles, resolute in his command to hold his position, refused, underestimating the looming threat of Confederate artillery.

In a desperate move, Miles dispatched Capt. Russell and nine cavalrymen to seek help from General McClellan. Navigating enemy lines and treacherous terrain, they reached McClellan, who was taken aback by the dire news. He immediately dispatched a message and relief forces, urging Miles to hold his position at all costs and, if possible, retake Maryland Heights. Unfortunately, despite these efforts, the crucial message of relief never reached Harpers Ferry in time.

As the intense conflicts unfolded at South Mountain, General Jackson meticulously arranged his artillery around Harpers Ferry, showcasing his strategic acumen. This operation was no small feat: it involved hauling four Parrott rifles to the summit of Maryland Heights, a task demanding the Herculean effort of 200 men per gun, battling against gravity and terrain. Jackson, a master of coordination, intended for a synchronized artillery assault. However, Walker, positioned on Loudoun Heights, prematurely and ineffectively commenced bombardment with five guns, disrupting Jackson's plan.

Meanwhile, Jackson instructed A.P. Hill to advance along the Shenandoah's west bank, setting the stage for a potential flank attack on the Federal left the following morning.

As night fell, the Union officers in Harpers Ferry faced a grim realization: time was running out, with less than a day's window to act. Unbeknownst to them, the Confederate presence on Maryland Heights had significantly diminished, leaving a single regiment after McLaws redirected most forces to counter the Union push at Crampton's Gap.

In this desperate situation, Col. Benjamin F. "Grimes" Davis of the Union Army saw an opportunity. He suggested a bold cavalry breakout, arguing that cavalry units were virtually redundant in the town's defense. Initially, Miles dismissed this daring plan as overly ambitious. However, Davis, a figure of resolve and determination, was set to proceed regardless. Recognizing Davis' unwavering intent, Miles gave in.

Under the leadership of Davis and Col. Arno Voss, 1,400 cavalrymen embarked on a daring escape from Harpers Ferry. They traversed a pontoon bridge over the Potomac, then stealthily navigated a narrow road around Maryland Heights, moving north towards Sharpsburg. Miraculously avoiding conflicts with returning Confederate forces from South Mountain, they stumbled upon a game-changing opportunity: a wagon train carrying Longstreet's reserve ammunition from Hagerstown.

With a combination of cunning and bravery, Davis's men deceived the Confederate wagoneers, leading them astray. They then skillfully repelled a Confederate cavalry escort, capturing over 40 enemy ordnance wagons. Remarkably, this audacious operation was executed without losing a single soldier in combat, marking it as one of the first significant cavalry feats for the Army of the Potomac during the war.

As the first light of dawn broke, the strategic maneuver of Confederate General McLaws became apparent. He had skillfully positioned his 8,000 troops across Pleasant Valley in a formidable two-line formation. General Franklin, assigned by McClellan to neutralize McLaws and rescue Colonel Miles, was thoroughly deceived by this show of force. Believing he was significantly outnumbered, Franklin concluded that an attack would be a fatal error. Consequently, he halted merely six miles from Harpers Ferry, leaving Miles and his garrison without the much-needed relief.

By September 15, Jackson had masterfully arranged nearly 50 guns on Maryland Heights and at the base of Loudoun Heights, ready to unleash a devastating barrage on the Federal line at Bolivar Heights. The artillery onslaught commenced, accompanied by orders for an infantry assault. Realizing the bleakness of their situation – dwindling artillery ammunition, no sign of relief from McClellan, and overwhelming Confederate forces – Miles convened with his commanders and resignedly agreed to surrender. However, a captain's plea to resist, citing nearby Union forces, was dismissed by Miles as futile.

Tragically, as the captain withdrew, a shell struck Miles, severely injuring his leg. His behavior, which some claimed included inebriation, had so alienated his men that few were willing to assist him. Mortally wounded, he died the following day, amid rumors that he might have been deliberately targeted by his own troops.

With Miles incapacitated, the surrender formalities were conducted by Brigadier General Julius White. Jackson's victory was achieved with minimal Confederate casualties, while the Union Army faced a staggering surrender of over 12,000 men, along with a significant loss of arms and equipment. This defeat marked the largest surrender of Federal forces during the Civil War and remained so until World War II.

In the aftermath, Confederate soldiers indulged in Union provisions and appropriated Federal uniforms, leading to potential future confusion. The only discontent within Jackson's ranks stemmed from the cavalry, who were unable to replenish their mounts due to Colonel Davis' earlier breakout.

Jackson promptly dispatched news of the victory to General Lee, attributing it to divine intervention. As he entered the town, Union prisoners lined the streets, curious to glimpse the renowned Stonewall Jackson. Despite his unimposing appearance, one prisoner noted that with a leader like Jackson, they might have avoided capture.

However, the triumph at Harpers Ferry was short-lived for Jackson. He soon received an urgent summons from General Lee, directing him to quickly join the Battle of Antietam. Leaving A.P. Hill to oversee the parole of Federal prisoners, Jackson promptly set off to partake in one of the Civil War's most pivotal battles.

Battle of South Mountain

In September 1862, a pivotal moment unfolded in the American Civil War, set against the rugged backdrop of Maryland's South Mountain. This mountain, an extension of the majestic Blue Ridge Mountains, stood as a formidable barrier between the Hagerstown and Cumberland Valleys to the west and the rest of Maryland to the east.

The drama began with a twist of fate. Confederate General Robert E. Lee, leading an audacious invasion into Union territory, had meticulously crafted Special Order 191, a detailed plan for his troops' movements. However, in an extraordinary turn of events, this secret document fell into Union hands, giving General George B. McClellan a golden opportunity to strike.

Lee had divided his army, sending the fearsome Maj. Gen. Thomas J. "Stonewall" Jackson to besiege Harper's Ferry. Meanwhile, the rest of his forces, under the skilled command of Maj. Gen. James Longstreet, were stationed near Boonsboro. Lee's grand strategy was to secure Harper's Ferry, disrupt Union infrastructure, and then possibly march towards major cities like Baltimore, Philadelphia, or even Washington, D.C.

In response, McClellan, leading the formidable Army of the Potomac, moved swiftly to exploit the division in Lee's ranks. He reorganized his forces into three wings to assault the mountain passes where Lee's troops were spread thin. The Right Wing, led by the dynamic Maj. Gen. Ambrose Burnside, comprised the I Corps under Maj. Gen. Joseph Hooker and the IX Corps under Maj. Gen. Jesse L. Reno, tasked with advancing through Turner's and Fox's Gaps. Maj. Gen. William B. Franklin's Left Wing, consisting of the VI Corps and a division from the IV Corps, aimed for Crampton's Gap. The Center Wing, a reserve force under Maj. Gen. Edwin V. Sumner, stood ready to support.

Alerted to McClellan's approach, Lee hastily ordered Longstreet to reinforce the mountain passes. On the day of the impending clash, Confederate forces around Boonsboro were primarily the division of Maj. Gen. D.H. Hill, poised to confront the Union advance.

Battle of Crampton's Gap

The Confederate forces, though outnumbered, ingeniously used the mountain's rugged terrain to their advantage. At the mountain's eastern base, three regiments from Mahone's brigade and Munford's cavalry took position, while their artillery was strategically placed halfway up the slope. General Cobb's brigade, entrenched at the summit, overlooked the advancing Union forces.

As the morning sun rose, the Confederates watched General Franklin's VI Corps march through the Middletown Valley towards their stronghold. By noon, as the Union soldiers reached Burkittsville, the Confederate artillery roared to life. Under the relentless bombardment, Franklin hastily organized his troops into three columns amidst the chaos and thunder of artillery.

The VI Corps' assault commenced at 3 p.m., after an unexplained and costly delay of nearly three hours. Advancing slowly but with determination, supported by their own artillery, the Union troops began to overpower Mahone's regiments and the cavalry, along with the Confederate artillery positions on the mountain slopes. A brief rally led by General Cobb at the summit proved futile against the ferocious charge of the First New Jersey Brigade. In just fifteen minutes of fierce combat, the Union forces captured the summit, inflicting heavy casualties on the Confederates, including the loss of John Basil Lamar and Jefferson M. Lamar, both kin to Cobb's wife.

The shattered Confederate line disintegrated, with soldiers scattering in every direction into Pleasant Valley. Their spirited resistance had lasted three hours, buying precious time. Yet, the delay in the VI Corps' attack meant that by the time Franklin regrouped his men in Pleasant Valley, it was too late in the day to mount another attack against McLaws' forces on Maryland Heights.

The day after, Harper's Ferry fell to the Confederates. Meanwhile, Franklin, encamped in Pleasant Valley and mistakenly believing he was vastly out-numbered by McLaws, made no further moves.

Battle of Turner's Gap

On a sprawling battlefield extending over two miles, that Confederate Major General D.H. Hill made his stand. With a force of just 5,000 men, Hill faced the daunting task of defending both critical gaps against a surging Union army.

On the Union side, Major General Ambrose Burnside, a figure of determina-tion and tactical acumen, directed the movements of Hooker's I Corps. His orders were clear: seize control of Turner's Gap and outflank the Confederate positions. In a bold move, the famed Union Iron Brigade, known for their steadfast courage and distinctive black hats, charged at Colonel Alfred H. Colquitt's brigade along the National Road. The battle was fierce, with the Confederates doggedly holding their ground, refusing to relinquish the pass despite being driven back up the mountain.

Hooker, a general known for his aggressive tactics, strategically positioned three divisions to face two peaks just a mile north of the gap. This maneuver put immense pressure on the Confederate lines, particularly on the Alabama

Brigade under the command of Brigadier General Robert E. Rodes. Isolated and facing overwhelming odds, Rodes' brigade was compelled to withdraw, even as reinforcements from Brigadier General David R. Jones's division and Brigadier General Nathan G. Evans's brigade rushed to their aid.

As dusk fell, the rugged terrain and the cloak of darkness prevented a total collapse of Lee's line. The Union forces, persistent and relentless, had managed to secure the high ground. Yet, the Confederates, in a display of resilience and tactical grit, still clung to the gap, their line bending but not breaking under the Union onslaught.

Years later, in the 1890s, a nation looking to remember and understand this pivotal chapter in its history erected six markers at the summit of Turner's Pass, also known as Turner's Gap. These markers stand as silent sentinels across from the Old South Mountain Inn, located on the north side of Alternate U.S. 40, the historic National Pike. This road was a vital artery during the Civil War, a main highway stretching from the Chesapeake Bay to the Ohio Valley.

Battle of Fox's Gap

Drayton's Brigade and other elements of Hill's division held the line against Reno's IX Corps, in a conflict marked by strategy, bravery, and unforeseen twists of fate.

At Fox's Gap, the morning air was shattered by the roar of Union Brigadier General Jacob D. Cox's Kanawha Division as they launched their attack at 9 a.m. The Union forces made significant headway, capturing much of the land south of the gap. In a pivotal moment, Lieutenant Colonel Rutherford B. Hayes of the 23rd Ohio, leading a daring flank attack, was gravely wounded, foreshadowing his future prominence in American history.

Cox's men valiantly pushed the North Carolinian defenders, entrenched behind a stone wall at the crest of the gap. Yet, despite their early success, exhaustion set in among the Union troops, stalling their advance and leaving an opening for Confederate reinforcements to fortify their positions around the Daniel Wise farm.

General Reno, recognizing the need for decisive action, committed the rest of his corps to the battle. However, the timely arrival of Southern reinforcements under the command of Brigadier General John Bell Hood stymied the Union advance. The fighting was fierce and unyielding, with both sides demonstrating exceptional courage under fire.

In the midst of this brutal engagement, tragedy struck. Both General Jesse Reno of the Union and Confederate Brigadier General Samuel Garland, Jr., met their end at Fox's Gap, adding their names to the growing list of casualties in this grueling conflict.

In a poignant postscript to the battle, Farmer Wise, whose property had become an unwitting focal point of the fight, was paid a mere dollar for each Confederate soldier to be buried. In a grim testament to the battle's toll, over sixty bodies were interred in a dry well on his land.

As dusk fell, the situation for the Confederates at Fox's and Turner's Gaps became untenable. With Crampton's Gap lost, General Lee faced the stark reality of his outnumbered forces and ordered a strategic withdrawal from South Mountain. This move placed McClellan in an advantageous position to potentially crush Lee's army before it could regroup.

The casualties reflected the battle's ferocity: of the 28,000 Union troops engaged, 2,325 were casualties, including 443 killed, 1,807 wounded, and 75 missing. The Confederates, with 18,000 troops, suffered 2,685 casualties, with 325 killed, 1,560 wounded, and 800 missing.

The Battle of South Mountain, beyond its immediate tactical implications, served as a crucial morale booster for the previously beleaguered Army of the Potomac. The New York World captured the sentiment, proclaiming the battle a turning point that "broke the strength of the rebels." Lee, in the aftermath, pondered the viability of his Maryland campaign.

However, the aftermath of South Mountain also highlighted a critical missed opportunity for the Union. McClellan's limited actions on September 15, following his victory, inadvertently led to the capture of the garrison at Harpers Ferry. This hesitation allowed Lee precious time to unite his scattered divisions at Sharpsburg, setting the stage for the impending and monumental Battle of Antietam on September 17.

Battle of Antietam

On the eve of the Battle of Antietam, the strategic chess game between the Union and Confederate forces reached a critical juncture near the town of Sharpsburg. General Robert E. Lee, seizing the initiative, deployed his troops along a low ridge behind Antietam Creek starting September 15. This position, while not impregnable, offered a formidable defensive stance. The landscape, dotted with rail and stone fences, limestone outcroppings, and undulating terrain, provided excellent cover for infantry. The creek itself, varying between 60 to 100 feet in width, presented a minor obstacle, fordable in places and spanned by three stone bridges, each a strategic point in the looming battle.

However, Lee's position was fraught with risk. The Confederate rear was perilously blocked by the Potomac River, leaving only Boteler's Ford at Shepherdstown for a potential retreat. The situation was further complicated by the fact that Lee's immediate command barely numbered 18,000 men, a stark contrast to the massive Union army gathering nearby.

The Union forces, led by General George B. McClellan, began arriving on the afternoon of September 15. By evening, the bulk of his army had assembled. McClellan, ever cautious and mistakenly believing Lee commanded a force of 100,000, hesitated to attack immediately. This delay inadvertently allowed the Confederates crucial time to fortify their positions and for reinforcements to arrive, including Longstreet's corps from Hagerstown and Jackson's corps from Harpers Ferry.

As the sun set on September 16, McClellan ordered Hooker's I Corps to cross Antietam Creek and engage the enemy. Meade's division cautiously clashed with Hood's troops near the East Woods. The night resounded with intermittent artillery fire as McClellan positioned his troops for the decisive battle he planned for the next day. His strategy was to assault the Confederate left flank, a decision influenced by the layout of the bridges over Antietam Creek. The upper bridge, east of the Confederate guns, offered a safe crossing point for a major offensive.

McClellan's battle plan, however, suffered from poor coordination and execution. He communicated orders only to individual corps commanders, without conveying a cohesive battle strategy. The battlefield's challenging terrain compounded the difficulties, limiting commanders' awareness of the broader conflict. McClellan's own command post, located over a mile away at the Philip Pry house, further hindered effective control of his forces.

The ensuing battle on September 17 unfolded as three distinct and largely uncoordinated engagements: morning in the north, midday in the center, and afternoon in the south. This disjointed approach diluted the Union's numerical advantage and allowed Lee to adeptly shift his defenses in response to each separate Union offensive.

As the first light of dawn crept over the horizon on September 17, the Battle of Antietam commenced with a fierce offensive by the Union I Corps, commanded by Joseph Hooker. Their target was a strategic plateau, home to the unassuming Dunker Church, a simple whitewashed building belonging to a local German Baptist sect. With approximately 8,600 men, Hooker's forces were only slightly larger than the 7,700 Confederates under the legendary Stonewall Jackson. However, the Confederates' advantage lay in their robust defensive positions.

On Hooker's flanks, Abner Doubleday's division advanced on the right, while James Ricketts's division moved to the left, edging into the East

Woods. George Meade's Pennsylvania Reserves took position in the center, slightly behind the front lines. Jackson's defense was a formidable array: Alexander Lawton and John R. Jones's divisions stretched from the West Woods, across the Hagerstown Turnpike, extending to the southern edge of Miller's Cornfield, with four additional brigades poised in the West Woods as reserves.

The battle escalated rapidly as Union forces emerged into the open expanse of the Cornfield. An intense artillery duel broke out, shaking the early morning calm. Confederate batteries under Jeb Stuart to the west and Colonel Stephen D. Lee on the high ground south of the Dunker Church unleashed a storm of fire. In retaliation, Union forces responded with their own formidable artillery, including nine batteries behind the North Woods and an array of twenty 20-pounder Parrott rifles positioned 2 miles east of Antietam Creek. The ensuing barrage resulted in staggering casualties on both sides, a horrific scene Col. Lee later termed "artillery Hell."

The battle intensified when Hooker, noticing the reflection of Confederate bayonets hidden within the Cornfield, called a halt to his infantry advance. In a swift response, he deployed four artillery batteries, unleashing a relentless barrage of shell and canister fire over the heads of Union soldiers and into the dense corn. The ensuing combat was chaotic and brutal, often descending into hand-to-hand melee with rifle butts and bayonets, as visibility was obscured by the tall cornstalks. The battlefield was a cacophony of curses, shouted orders lost in the din of battle, and the incessant noise of rifles overheating and jamming from relentless firing. Soldiers were engulfed in a terrifying storm of bullets and artillery shells, marking one of the most intense and blood-soaked moments of the Civil War.

In the East Woods, Brigadier General Truman Seymour's 1st Brigade of Pennsylvanians clashed violently with Colonel James Walker's brigade, comprised of Alabama, Georgia, and North Carolina troops. The Southern forces, bolstered by the deadly accuracy of Lee's artillery, pushed Seymour's men back, setting the stage for further bloodshed.

As Ricketts's division entered the fray in the Cornfield, they too were savaged by the relentless Confederate artillery. The situation escalated when Brigadier General Abram Duryée's brigade marched directly into withering volleys from Colonel Marcellus Douglass's Georgia brigade. Despite enduring a hail of fire from just 250 yards away, Duryée's men found themselves without the crucial reinforcements needed to gain an advantage, leading to a grim and inevitable withdrawal.

The awaited reinforcements — brigades under Brigadier General George L. Hartsuff and Colonel William A. Christian — faced their own trials in reaching the heated battlefield. Hartsuff was gravely wounded by artillery, while Christian, overwhelmed by fear, fled. Eventually rallied, these men advanced into the Cornfield, only to be greeted by the same deadly artillery and infantry fire that had repelled their predecessors.

The tide momentarily turned when the Louisiana "Tiger" Brigade, led by Harry Hays, plunged into the battle. Their ferocious assault pushed the Union soldiers back towards the East Woods. The 12th Massachusetts Infantry, suffering an appalling 67% casualty rate, bore the brunt of this onslaught. However, the Tigers' initial success was short-lived. The Union forces, deploying a battery of 3-inch ordnance rifles, delivered point-blank fire that decimated the Tiger Brigade, inflicting staggering losses.

While the Cornfield became a gruesome stalemate, the Union forces made significant headway to the west. Brigadier General John Gibbon's 4th Brigade, part of Doubleday's division and renowned as the Iron Brigade, advanced decisively down the turnpike, cutting through the Cornfield and pushing into the West Woods, steadily driving back Jackson's Confederates.

A countercharge by Starke's brigade of 1,150 men briefly halted the Iron Brigade, unleashing heavy fire from a mere 30 yards away. Despite their initial success, Starke's brigade was forced to withdraw under the withering return fire from the Iron Brigade, and Starke himself was mortally wounded. This push by the Union forces created a significant breach in Jackson's line, threatening a complete collapse of the Confederate defense. Despite the harrowing cost, Hooker's corps was inching forward, making tangible albeit costly progress towards the Dunker Church.

As the sun rose higher on the morning of September 17, the battle intensified with the arrival of crucial Confederate reinforcements. Divisions under McLaws and Richard H. Anderson, weary from a night march from Harpers Ferry, joined the fray just after 7 a.m. In a strategic move, General Lee redeployed George T. Anderson's Georgia brigade from the army's right flank to bolster Stonewall Jackson's beleaguered forces.

At the same time, Hood's division, numbering about 2,300 men, surged forward from the West Woods. Their attack was driven by a mix of determination and frustration; they had been roused from the first hot breakfast they'd enjoyed in days to join the battle. Assisting Hood's advance were three brigades from D.H. Hill's division, emerging from the Mumma Farm southeast of the Cornfield, and Jubal Early's brigade, pushing through from the Nicodemus Farm to support Jeb Stuart's horse artillery.

In the midst of this, some officers of the Iron Brigade heroically rallied their men around the artillery of Battery B, 4th U.S. Artillery. General Gibbon, mindful of his former unit's valor, ensured not a single caisson was lost. Hood's men, though vastly outnumbered, fought with desperate courage, sustaining a staggering 60% casualty rate. Yet, their tenacious defense was pivotal in preventing the collapse of the Confederate line, stalling the advance of Hooker's I Corps. When queried about the whereabouts of his division, Hood grimly responded, "Dead on the field."

The toll on Hooker's forces was equally severe. After two grueling hours and suffering 2,500 casualties, they found themselves back at their starting point. The Cornfield, an area roughly 250 yards deep and 400 yards wide, was transformed into a landscape of unspeakable carnage, changing hands as many as 15 times over the course of the morning. Major Rufus Dawes of the Iron Brigade's 6th Wisconsin Regiment later described the battle near the Hagerstown Turnpike as surpassing even the notorious engagements at Fredericksburg, Spotsylvania's "Bloody Angle", and Cold Harbor in terms of sheer devastation.

In response, Hooker called for reinforcement from Mansfield's XII Corps, comprising 7,200 men. However, Mansfield's troops were mostly inexperienced, and Mansfield himself, despite four decades of military service, was new to commanding large bodies of men in combat. To prevent his untested soldiers from breaking under fire, he led them in a densely packed formation, making them an easy target for Confederate artillery. Tragically, Mansfield was mortally wounded during the advance, leaving Alpheus Williams to take temporary command of the XII Corps.

The unfolding drama witnessed the XII Corps, led by Mansfield, plunging into the fray with mixed results. The Corps' 1st Division, filled with green recruits, struggled to make headway against Hood's line, now bolstered by brigades from D. H. Hill's division under Colquitt and McRae. However, a stroke of fortune came with the 2nd Division under George Sears Greene. Greene's men managed to break through, exploiting a critical moment of confusion in McRae's ranks, who mistakenly believed they were about to be flanked. This crucial breach forced Hood and his outnumbered men to fall back to their starting position in the West Woods.

Greene, seizing the opportunity, pushed forward to the Dunker Church, achieving what had been Hooker's initial objective. His success drove off Stephen Lee's Confederate batteries, securing a significant portion of ground east of the turnpike for the Federal forces.

Meanwhile, Hooker, in an attempt to rally his scattered I Corps, became a casualty himself when a sharpshooter's bullet struck him in the foot, incapacitating the general. The reins of the I Corps briefly passed to General Meade, as Hooker's senior subordinate, James B. Ricketts, was also wounded. However, with Hooker off the field, there was a void in leadership, leaving the I and XII Corps without a central figure to rally them. Under heavy Confederate fire from the West Woods, Greene's troops were eventually compelled to withdraw from their hard-won position at the Dunker Church.

Simultaneously, General Sumner's II Corps was tasked with a critical mission at 7:20 a.m.: to flank the Confederate left and alleviate the pressure on Mansfield's forces. The plan, however, quickly unraveled. Sedgwick's division, comprising 5,400 men, forded the Antietam and entered the East Woods. Their objective was to turn left and press the Confederates southward, aligning with Ambrose Burnside's IX Corps assault. Yet, coordination faltered. They lost connection with William H. French's division, and at 9 a.m., Sumner, accompanying Sedgwick, initiated an attack in a risky formation—three brigades in long, closely spaced lines.

This formation proved disastrous. The division was soon engulfed by Confederate artillery and attacked from three sides by divisions under Early, Walker, and McLaws. In less than thirty minutes, Sedgwick's division retreated chaotically, suffering over 2,200 casualties, including Sedgwick himself, who was wounded and sidelined for several months. Historians have critiqued Sumner for his impulsive attack and lack of coordination, though recent scholarship by M. V. Armstrong suggests that Sumner's decisions were grounded in the reconnaissance available to him.

As the morning phase of the battle drew to a close around 10 a.m., two regiments from the XII Corps advanced, only to encounter John G. Walker's division, freshly arrived from the Confederate right. The ensuing clash, fought between the Cornfield and the West Woods, eventually saw Walker's forces pushed back by Greene's brigades, allowing the Federal troops to gain ground in the West Woods.

This brutal morning phase ended with staggering casualties on both sides, totaling nearly 13,000, including two Union corps commanders. The Battle of Antietam, already one of the bloodiest single days in American history.

The focus of the conflict shifted towards the center of the Confederate line by midday. In a sequence of events marked by both chance and chaos, General Sumner, having already engaged with Sedgwick's division in the morning's brutal fight, inadvertently lost contact with another of his divisions led by William H. French. French, eager for action and somewhat directionless, happened upon skirmishers and, seizing the opportunity, propelled his men forward. Amidst this confusion, Sumner's aide (and son) managed to locate French, briefing him on the dire situation in the West Woods and instructing him to draw Confederate attention by launching an attack on their center.

French soon found himself up against D.H. Hill's division. Although Hill's forces were diminished — numbering about 2,500, less than half of French's men — and his brigades had been heavily battered during the morning's confrontations, they held a robust defensive position. Perched atop a gradual ridge and entrenched within a sunken road, worn down by years of wagon traffic, Hill's men were well-prepared for defense.

French initiated a series of determined brigade-sized assaults against Hill's formidable position around 9:30 a.m. The first brigade, led by Brigadier General Max Weber and largely comprising inexperienced troops, faced a devastating onslaught of rifle fire, suffering heavy casualties. The following attack, led by Colonel Dwight Morris with more raw recruits, also encountered intense fire but managed to repulse a counterattack by Robert Rodes's Alabama Brigade. The third assault, under Brigadier General Nathan Kimball, included three seasoned regiments but similarly faltered under the relentless fire from the sunken road. French's division, in less than an hour, endured staggering losses, with 1,750 of its 5,700 men becoming casualties.

Meanwhile, reinforcements were arriving for both sides. By 10:30 a.m.,

Robert E. Lee deployed his last reserve division, around 3,400 men under Major General Richard H. Anderson, to reinforce Hill's line and extend it rightwards, aiming to outflank French. Concurrently, Major General Israel B. Richardson's division, the last of Sumner's three divisions and previously delayed by McClellan's reserve organization, arrived with 4,000 fresh troops on French's left.

Richardson's division, stepping into the fray, was poised to deliver a significant blow. The battle, already marked by intense fighting and high casualties, braced for yet another wave of fierce combat as these fresh Union forces engaged with the weary but resolute Confederates.

The Irish Brigade, led by Brigadier General Thomas F. Meagher, initiated the fourth assault against the entrenched Confederate position in the sunken road. Their advance was a striking sight, marked by the fluttering emerald green flags and the fervent presence of Father William Corby, a regimental chaplain. Father Corby, riding back and forth in front of the troops, offered words of conditional absolution, a Roman Catholic rite for those facing imminent death — a ritual he would famously repeat at Gettysburg in 1863. The brigade, predominantly composed of Irish immigrants, bravely faced a storm of enemy fire, ultimately losing 540 men before receiving the order to withdraw.

Around noon, the battle's momentum began to shift. General Richardson, upon learning that Brigadier General John C. Caldwell was lingering behind a haystack, personally sent Caldwell's brigade into the fray. By this time, Anderson's Confederate division was floundering, largely due to General Anderson being wounded early in the combat. The Confederates also suffered significant losses in leadership, including George B. Anderson (unrelated to General Anderson), whose successor, Colonel Charles C. Tew of the 2nd North Carolina, was killed shortly after taking command. Additionally, Colonel John B. Gordon of the 6th Alabama was incapacitated, though Rodes, despite his injury, remained in action. These losses sowed confusion within the

Confederate ranks, contributing to the subsequent chaos.

Caldwell's brigade, seizing the opportunity, maneuvered around the Confederate right flank. It was then that Colonel Francis C. Barlow, with 350 men from the 61st and 64th New York, identified and exploited a vulnerable point in the Confederate line. They took control of a knoll overlooking the sunken road, enabling them to fire down its length, effectively transforming the Confederate position into a deadly trap.

In a fateful moment, a command from Rodes was misinterpreted by Lieutenant Colonel James N. Lightfoot, who had replaced the incapacitated Gordon. Lightfoot mistakenly ordered his men to about-face and march away, a directive that, in the heat of battle, was assumed to apply to all five regiments in the brigade. This resulted in a mass withdrawal of Confederate troops towards Sharpsburg, leading to the collapse of their line and a significant turning point in the battle.

As Richardson's men eagerly pursued the Confederates, General Longstreet's hastily assembled artillery barrages forced them into a retreat. Amidst this tumult, D.H. Hill led a daring counterattack with 200 men, targeting the Federal left flank near the sunken road. Although Hill's forces were repelled by a fierce charge from the 5th New Hampshire, their action crucially stemmed the disintegration of the Confederate center. In the aftermath, Richardson, recognizing the untenable situation, ordered his division to withdraw north of the ridge overlooking the sunken road. This phase of the battle proved costly for his division, incurring about 1,000 casualties. Both Colonel Barlow and General Richardson were severely wounded, with Richardson's injuries proving fatal. Command of the division passed to Winfield S. Hancock, whose future reputation as a vigorous leader was yet to be established. The sudden change in command blunted the momentum of the Federal advance.

The intense fighting along the sunken road, from 9:30 a.m. to 1:00 p.m., earned it the grim moniker of Bloody Lane. The engagement left approximately 5,600 casualties (3,000 Union and 2,600 Confederate) along the 800-yard stretch of road. Despite the heavy toll, the Union forces faced a golden opportunity: exploiting the breach in the Confederate line could potentially split Lee's army and lead to a decisive victory. Ample Union forces were at hand, including a 3,500-strong cavalry reserve and the 10,300 infantrymen of General Porter's V Corps, positioned near the middle bridge, about a mile away. Additionally, Major General William B. Franklin's VI Corps had just arrived with 12,000 men, ready to capitalize on the breakthrough.

However, this critical moment was met with hesitation. Despite Franklin's readiness to advance, Sumner, the senior corps commander, restrained him. Franklin appealed to General McClellan, who, after considering both sides, sided with Sumner, instructing Franklin and Hancock to maintain their positions.

Later in the day, Major General Fitz John Porter, commander of the nearby V Corps reserve, entertained suggestions from Major General George Sykes, leader of his 2nd Division, to launch another central assault. This proposal piqued McClellan's interest, but Porter cautioned him, saying, "Remember, General, I command the last reserve of the last Army of the Republic." McClellan, weighing the gravity of Porter's words, ultimately decided against the attack.

The focus shifted to its southern end. Major General Ambrose Burnside, commanding the IX Corps, was tasked with launching a diversionary attack to support Hooker's I Corps in the north. This move was intended to draw Confederate attention away from the main offensive. However, due to a delay in receiving explicit orders, Burnside didn't initiate his attack until 10 a.m.

Burnside's approach to battle preparation was marked by a certain passivity, partly stemming from his dissatisfaction with the command structure. He had previously overseen a wing that included both the I and IX Corps, but now his authority was reduced to just the IX Corps. Despite this, Burnside continued to exert influence over the corps through Brigadier General Jacob D. Cox of the Kanawha Division, effectively using him as an intermediary.

Facing Burnside were significantly weakened Confederate forces, as General Lee had redeployed units to strengthen the left flank. At the onset of battle, Brigadier Generals David R. Jones and John G. Walker defended the area, but by 10 a.m., Walker's men and Colonel George T. Anderson's Georgia brigade had been redeployed. Jones was left with about 3,000 men and 12 guns to counter Burnside's 12,500 troops and 50 guns.

The Confederate defense was centered around a series of ridges near Sharpsburg, particularly a low plateau known as Cemetery Hill. A critical point was Rohrbach's Bridge, a 125-foot stone structure over Antietam Creek, defended by around 400 men from the 2nd and 20th Georgia regiments, led by Brigadier General Robert Toombs, along with two artillery batteries. This bridge, later famously known as Burnside's Bridge, presented a challenging objective. The approach was exposed to enemy fire, and the bridge itself was overlooked by a high, wooded bluff, offering Confederate sharpshooters excellent cover.

Despite Antietam Creek being fordable in places, Burnside has been criticized for not exploiting these shallower sections. However, the tactical advantage lay with the Confederates due to their commanding position. Burnside planned to storm the bridge while also attempting to cross at a ford identified by McClellan's engineers, located a half mile downstream. However, this effort was thwarted by unexpectedly high banks. Meanwhile, Colonel George Crook's Ohio brigade, supported by Brigadier General Samuel Sturgis's division, prepared to assault the bridge. At the same time, other elements of the Kanawha Division and Brigadier General Isaac Rodman's division struggled through dense undergrowth, aiming to locate Snavely's Ford, two miles downstream, in a bid to outflank the Confederate defenders.

The battle for control of Burnside's Bridge unfolded with intense and tragic efforts. Leading the initial assault was the 11th Connecticut, tasked with clearing the bridge for Crook's Ohio brigade. They bravely advanced under a hail of Confederate fire, sustaining heavy losses, including a third of their number and their commander, Colonel Henry W. Kingsbury, who was fatally wounded.

Crook's main assault, however, was derailed due to a miscalculation in navigating the terrain, leading his men to a point a quarter mile upstream from the bridge. Here, they engaged in a prolonged exchange with Confederate skirmishers, unable to make significant progress.

As Rodman's division struggled towards Snavely's Ford, Burnside and Cox coordinated a second attempt to seize the bridge. This effort, spearheaded by the 2nd Maryland and 6th New Hampshire of Sturgis's brigade, was met with the same lethal resistance from Confederate sharpshooters and artillery, ultimately disintegrating under the pressure.

By noon, General McClellan's patience with Burnside was wearing thin. He sent a series of urgent messages, emphasizing the necessity of taking the bridge even at a high cost. Burnside, feeling the weight of these repeated directives, responded with frustration to Colonel Delos B. Sackett, McClellan's inspector general, who had been sent to convey the urgency of the situation.

The third and decisive attempt to capture the bridge commenced at 12:30 p.m., led by another of Sturgis's brigades under Brigadier General Edward Ferrero. The 51st New York and 51st Pennsylvania, motivated by the reinstatement of a canceled whiskey ration and supported by effective artillery, charged with renewed vigor. They managed to maneuver a captured light howitzer into a strategic position and unleashed a barrage of double canister shots down the bridge, closing in to within 25 yards of the Confederate line.

By 1 p.m., the Confederate defenders, now low on ammunition and informed of Rodman's flanking maneuver at Snavely's Ford, began to withdraw under the command of Brigadier General Robert Toombs. His Georgians had inflicted over 500 casualties on the Federal forces, losing less than 160 themselves, and successfully delayed Burnside's assault on the southern flank for more than three hours.

Burnside's advance ground to a halt due to logistical oversights and tactical bottlenecks. Crucially, ammunition had not been transported across the bridge, and the bridge itself became congested with soldiers, artillery, and wagons, causing a significant two-hour delay. During this time, General Lee reinforced his right flank with additional artillery units but did not send infantry reinforcements to bolster D.R. Jones's outnumbered division. Instead, Lee awaited the arrival of A.P. Hill's Light Division, which was rapidly approaching after a grueling 17-mile march from Harpers Ferry. By 2 p.m., Hill's men reached Boteler's Ford, and at 2:30, he met with Lee, who ordered him to position his division on the right of Jones.

Unbeknownst to the Union forces, 3,000 fresh Confederate troops were about to enter the fray. Burnside's strategy was to outflank the Confederate right, move towards Sharpsburg, and cut off Lee's army from their only escape route at Boteler's Ford. By 3 p.m., Burnside advanced with over 8,000 troops, most of whom were fresh, along with 22 supporting guns.

The initial Union assault, led by the 79th New York "Cameron Highlanders," successfully pushed back Jones's division, nearing Sharpsburg. Concurrently, Rodman's division moved towards the Harpers Ferry Road. Despite heavy Confederate artillery fire, they pressed on, causing chaos in the streets of Sharpsburg, filled with retreating Confederate soldiers. Only Toombs's brigade remained intact in Jones's division, though significantly diminished.

A.P. Hill's division arrived at 3:30 p.m., splitting his forces to protect his flank and prepare for a counterattack. At 3:40 p.m., a brigade led by Brigadier

General Maxcy Gregg launched an attack on the 16th Connecticut, part of Rodman's left flank, resulting in the inexperienced Connecticut troops suffering heavy casualties. Confusion intensified as the Union soldiers mistook some Confederates, dressed in captured Union uniforms, for their own men. This led to further disarray and retreat among Union ranks.

Despite the IX Corps sustaining about 20% casualties, they still outnumbered the Confederate forces. However, the collapse of his flank unnerved Burnside, leading him to pull back his forces to the west bank of the Antietam and request reinforcements. McClellan, despite having fresh corps at his disposal, declined substantial assistance, citing concerns about being outnumbered and anticipating a major Confederate counterstrike. Consequently, Burnside's forces spent the remainder of the day defending the hard-won bridge, marking the end of their offensive operations for the day.

The Battle of Antietam concluded by 5:30 p.m., marking one of the most intense and bloody single days of combat in American history. On the morning of September 18, General Lee's Confederate army braced for a renewed Federal assault that never materialized. A temporary truce allowed both sides to tend to and exchange their wounded, after which Lee began his withdrawal across the Potomac River that evening, retreating back to Virginia.

The casualties from the battle were staggering for both sides. The Union forces suffered 12,410 casualties, including 2,108 deaths. The Confederates incurred 10,316 casualties with 1,547 fatalities. This represented a loss of 25% of the Union force and 31% of the Confederate troops engaged in the battle. The total casualties from this single day of fighting, 22,727, were nearly equal to the losses at the two-day Battle of Shiloh earlier that year. The aftermath saw additional deaths due to wounds, with 1,910 Union and 1,550 Confederate soldiers dying soon after the battle. The number of missing, later confirmed dead, included 225 Union and 306 Confederate troops. The battle also claimed the lives of several generals, including Union Maj. Gens. Joseph K. Mansfield and Israel B. Richardson, and Brig. Gen. Isaac P. Rodman, as well as Confederate Brig. Gens. Lawrence O. Branch and William E. Starke. Confederate Brig. Gen. George B. Anderson, wounded during the battle, later died from complications after an amputation.

September 17, 1862, marked the deadliest single day in American military history, with 7,650 soldiers killed. Antietam is often recognized as the bloodiest day in American history and ranks fifth in total casualties among all Civil War battles, behind Gettysburg, Chickamauga, Chancellorsville, and Spotsylvania Court House.

President Lincoln was profoundly disappointed with General McClellan's performance. He viewed McClellan's cautious tactics and poor coordination as factors that led to a stalemate rather than a decisive defeat of the Confederate forces. Lincoln's frustration was compounded by McClellan's reluctance to pursue Lee's army across the Potomac in the subsequent weeks, despite requests from both the War Department and the president. General-in-Chief Henry W. Halleck expressed regret over the inactivity of such a large Union army during a crucial period. Consequently, Lincoln relieved McClellan of his command on November 5, effectively ending his military career, and appointed General Burnside as his successor on November 9.

Battle of Shepherdstown

In the sweltering summer of 1862, the American Civil War's tides turned dramatically with General Robert E. Lee's rise to command the Confederate Army of Northern Virginia. This strategic shift came after General Joseph E. Johnston's injury at the fierce Battle of Seven Pines. Lee, a master tactician, soon faced the formidable Union Army of the Potomac, under the stern leadership of Major General George B. McClellan. In a series of intense encounters known as the Seven Days Battles, Lee boldly pushed McClellan's forces away from Richmond, the heart of the Confederacy.

However, the challenges were far from over. Lee next confronted a new Union threat from Major General John Pope's Army of Virginia. In a remarkable display of military prowess, Lee triumphantly defeated Pope at the Second Battle of Manassas in late August, despite his army reeling from heavy losses in the previous confrontations.

Undeterred, Lee audaciously led his battle-hardened troops into Union territory, crossing into Maryland. In an unexpected twist, McClellan reemerged as the Union commander, relentlessly pursuing Lee. The stakes heightened when Union soldiers stumbled upon Lee's detailed military plans, exposing the Confederate strategy to McClellan.

As September rolled in, the armies converged around Sharpsburg, Maryland, leading to the epic Battle of Antietam. Here, Lee's outnumbered forces valiantly held off Union assaults in what would become the bloodiest single day in American history, with nearly 23,000 casualties.

Despite the staggering losses, Lee's army bravely maintained its position on September 18, with McClellan hesitating to unleash his fresh troops. Under the cover of darkness, the Confederate army commenced a strategic retreat towards Martinsburg, Virginia.

At Boteler's Ford, the plot thickened with Brigadier General William N. Pendleton, a former clergyman with a controversial military reputation, tasked with covering the retreat. Pendleton, inexperienced in commanding infantry, faced the daunting challenge of securing multiple fords with limited forces and artillery.

At Boteler's Ford, General William N. Pendleton found himself in a strategically advantageous position. The Virginia side's high cliffs provided a natural defense, making it a formidable spot to hold off any assault. Pendleton deployed his 600 men, part of the brigades led by Alexander R. Lawton and Lewis A. Armistead, directly at the ford. These troops, now under the command of replacement officers due to Lawton and Armistead's injuries at Antietam, were bolstered by a carefully arranged artillery lineup of 33 cannons, with shorter-range guns near the river and longer-range ones further back. However, he couldn't find suitable positions for 11 of his cannons, leaving them unused. There was also a potential small reserve force.

General Lee's instructions to Pendleton were clear: if the Union only engaged in artillery fire, Pendleton was to retreat on September 20th. However, if faced with a significant Union attack, the retreat was to be on the evening of September 19th.

On the morning of September 19th, Union forces led by Alfred Pleasonton approached Boteler's Ford, igniting an artillery duel. As the day progressed, the Union V Corps under Fitz John Porter arrived, deploying 15 cannons with superior range and ammunition. These effectively silenced the Confederate artillery. Meanwhile, the Union 1st United States Sharpshooters took positions along the Chesapeake and Ohio Canal, harassing Confederate gunners. However, the Confederate infantry at the ford had orders to conserve ammunition and fire only if the Union attempted a significant crossing.

Pendleton, facing mounting pressure, sent reinforcements to support his artillery and cavalry, but this drastically reduced his infantry presence at the ford to just 300 men. His lack of coordination between the artillery and infantry, combined with his limited awareness of his available forces, compounded the challenges.

As dusk fell, a daring raid by the Union's 1st United States Sharpshooters, supported by the 4th Michigan Infantry, resulted in a successful crossing. The Confederate troops, already demoralized and weakened from Antietam, quickly retreated. In the ensuing chaos, and with Pendleton's staff absent, the Confederate defense at the ford collapsed.

Despite only a modest advance beyond the ford by about 2,000 Union troops, they managed to capture four guns and some prisoners. The Confederate line, led by an overwhelmed Pendleton, was effectively routed. During this retreat, Pendleton encountered the forces of Roger A. Pryor but failed to rally them for a counterattack.

Pendleton, later meeting with General Lee, mistakenly reported that all his cannons were lost. Lee spent that night trying to gauge the situation, while Pendleton rested. A counterattack was postponed until morning. The losses for Lawton's command were seven wounded, while Armistead's losses were light but unspecified.

As dawn broke on September 20, the atmosphere was thick with anticipation and the impending clash of arms. Major General Fitz John Porter, sensing the strategic importance of the moment, dispatched three brigades across the Potomac River. Leading this daring move was Charles S. Lovell's brigade, swiftly followed by the forces of James Barnes and Gouverneur K. Warren. Their mission was clear: secure a foothold and press the advantage against the Confederates.

Meanwhile, the Confederate side, under the legendary Stonewall Jackson, was not idle. Jackson, known for his tactical acumen, decided to confront the Union advance head-on. He chose the formidable A.P. Hill's Light Division for this critical task. Hill, a commander of proven mettle, swiftly organized his 2,000 men into a formidable fighting force. Arranged in two lines, each comprising three brigades, they were a sight to behold.

As the clock struck 09:00, Hill's division launched a vigorous assault. The Union forces, led by Lovell, were barely a mile from the river when they detected the Confederate movement. George Sykes, commanding the division, quickly realized the gravity of the situation and ordered a strategic withdrawal.

Amidst this chaos, a dramatic scene unfolded. The 118th Pennsylvania Infantry Regiment, a unit green with inexperience and plagued by defective weapons, found itself at a crossroads. When the withdrawal order came, the regiment's commander, distrustful of its authenticity, hesitated. This decision stemmed from the order being relayed through a staff officer to a lieutenant, bypassing the usual chain of command. The regiment, caught in a dire situation, bravely fought for about 30 minutes before being overwhelmed and put to a disorderly retreat.

The retreat was harrowing. Union soldiers, under relentless fire, struggled to cross back over the river. Tragically, some fell to enemy bullets while others met their end in the treacherous waters. The 118th Pennsylvania, already reeling, suffered additional casualties from friendly artillery fire in its desperate attempt to withdraw.

Despite the Union artillery's efforts to halt the Confederate advance, the fighting gradually subsided by mid-morning. In a late afternoon venture, a small detachment from Warren's brigade daringly recrossed the river to reclaim an abandoned cannon, a small but symbolic victory amidst the chaos.

The aftermath was a tale of exaggerated claims and harsh realities. Hill reported an improbable 3,000 Union casualties, but the actual toll was 71 dead, 161 wounded, and 131 missing. The Confederates, while victorious, suffered 30 killed and 161 wounded, mostly from the Union's artillery barrage. The 118th Pennsylvania bore a significant part of the Union's losses, with 269 casualties.

In a poignant footnote to the battle, Union Private Daniel W. Burke, a member of the heroic 118th Pennsylvania, was later awarded the Medal of Honor in 1892 for his extraordinary bravery at Shepherdstown.

The Confederates, though victorious, were not without their losses in artillery: one 10-pounder Parrott rifle, two 12-pounder howitzers, and one 6-pounder field gun from their various batteries were lost in the fray.

This encounter at Shepherdstown was not just a battle; it was a testament to the valor, the chaos, and the unpredictability of war. It underscored the human cost of conflict and the unyielding spirit of those who fought in the American Civil War.

Battle of Perryville

I n the summer of 1862, the Confederate strategic landscape was set ablaze with ambitious plans and daring maneuvers. At the heart of this intrigue was Maj. Gen. Edmund Kirby Smith, the visionary commander of the Department of East Tennessee. Smith, driven by a combination of strategic insight and bold ambition, proposed a daring campaign to claim Kentucky for the Confederacy. His plan was multifaceted: acquire vital supplies, bolster ranks with fresh recruits, divert Union forces from Tennessee, and ultimately sway the balance of the war in favor of the South.

July witnessed the audacious cavalry raid of Col. John Hunt Morgan, a foray deep into Union territory that rattled the Northern command and Washington, D.C. itself. Morgan's cavalry, welcomed and aided by many Kentucky residents, swelled in numbers, adding 300 volunteers to its original 900-strong force. Morgan's brash assurance to Kirby Smith resonated with confidence: Kentucky was ripe for the taking, potentially contributing tens of thousands to the Confederate cause.

Bragg, another key Confederate general, weighed his options. He could either attempt to recapture Corinth, Mississippi, or confront Union General Buell's forces in Middle Tennessee. Ultimately, swayed by Kirby Smith's persuasive arguments and strategic needs, he decided to reinforce Smith's campaign. Bragg undertook a grueling and complex journey, moving 30,000 infantry via a convoluted railroad route and coordinating the overland movement of supply wagons, cavalry, and artillery.

In Chattanooga, plans were laid. Smith and Bragg, combining their military acumen, crafted a campaign blueprint. The newly formed Army of Kentucky, a 21,000-strong force, would spearhead the movement into Kentucky under Smith's command. Their immediate objective: dislodge Union defenders at Cumberland Gap. Bragg's army, wearied by its arduous journey, would soon follow. Together, they aimed to outmaneuver Buell and force a decisive confrontation.

The first hints of this grand Confederate movement surfaced in late June. Col. Phil Sheridan, leading a Union cavalry reconnaissance, uncovered the abandonment of the Confederate camp at Tupelo, indicating a significant shift in Confederate strategy. Captured letters boasted of eluding the Union forces, a sentiment that impressed Maj. Gen William Rosecrans enough to recommend Sheridan for promotion.

The campaign, while bold and potentially game-changing, hinged on perfect coordination between multiple armies initially lacking a unified command. Bragg, despite being the senior general, began to harbor doubts. Smith, envisioning a path to personal glory, quickly deviated from their agreed strategy, secretly planning a solo venture into Kentucky.

The drama of the campaign unfolded rapidly. Smith, with his 21,000 men, marched from Knoxville on August 13, while Bragg left Chattanooga later on August 27. Their actions coincided with Gen. Robert E. Lee's northern Virginia campaign and operations by Confederate generals Price and Van Dorn against Grant, marking a period of intense Confederate offensives.

Meanwhile, Union General Buell, alerted to the Confederate maneuvers, was compelled to abandon his advance towards Chattanooga. He rapidly repositioned his Army of the Ohio around Nashville, preparing to defend the critical Union cities of Louisville and Cincinnati against the Confederate thrust.

The campaign's crescendo came with Bragg's capture of a Union fort at Munfordville. Faced with a strategic dilemma, he chose to reunite with Smith, who had already seized control of central Kentucky. The two Confederate armies, now in a potent alliance, poised themselves for a grand confrontation with Buell's forces.

As General Bragg set off for Frankfort on September 28, he entrusted his army to the command of General Polk. Within a week, the advancing Union forces compelled the Confederates to retreat eastward, leading to their occupation of Bardstown on October 4. Faced with the pressing need for reinforcement, Hardee, stationed at Perryville, urgently called for Bragg's support. Bragg, initially planning to gather his forces at Versailles, was forced by the rapid approach of the Federal III Corps to instead concentrate his troops at Perryville and Harrodsburg.

Perryville, a small village of about 300 inhabitants, was strategically chosen by Hardee for several reasons. Its extensive road network, linking to numerous nearby towns, provided significant strategic flexibility. Moreover, its location was crucial to protect the Confederate supply depot at Bryantsville. Additionally, amidst the scorching heat and drought conditions of the summer and early fall—a result of climatic changes possibly influenced by the distant eruption of Mt. Dubbi in East Africa—the village's potential as a water source became critically important.

On October 7, as Buell and his Union forces reached the vicinity of Perryville, skirmishes flared up with Wheeler's Confederate rearguard. Learning of the Confederate halt at Perryville, Buell planned an assault. His primary goal was to overcome the enemy forces, but securing control of the town for its water resources was also a key objective. Buell ordered a coordinated attack for the early hours of October 8, but logistical challenges, particularly the desperate search for water, delayed the movements of his I and II Corps.

Buell, having to postpone his attack to October 9 to allow for full deployment, faced further setbacks. A horse-riding accident rendered him unable to ride and oversee troop movements personally, forcing him to establish his headquarters at a distance from the front lines.

Meanwhile, Hardee was busy establishing a defensive line across the key roads leading into Perryville. Limited by available forces, he positioned Brig. Gen. Sterling A. M. Wood to the north of the town, with Brig. Gen. Bushrod Johnson near the Chaplin River, and Brig. Gen. St. John R. Liddell's Arkansas Brigade on the crest of Bottom Hill. The evening of October 7 saw the arrival of additional Confederate brigades, bolstering Hardee's position in anticipation of the impending Union attack.

The battle commenced in the early hours of October 8, with the first skirmishes sparked by the Union's desperate need for water. Troops from the 10th Indiana, upon discovering algae-covered pools in Doctor's Creek's dry bed, moved to secure this precious resource. This led to an initial confrontation with the 7th Arkansas, marking the beginning of hostilities.

In a decisive move, Buell and Gilbert, commander of the III Corps, instructed the newly promoted Brig. Gen. Phil Sheridan to capture Peters Hill. Sheridan, leading Col. Daniel McCook's brigade, swiftly took the hill, forcing the Arkansans to retreat to their main line. Despite this success, Sheridan's advance across the creek was halted due to Polk's cautious strategy. Polk, fearing a full-scale engagement and assuming a numerical disadvantage, instructed Buckner to withdraw Liddell's brigade rather than reinforce it. Concurrently, a concerned Gilbert ordered Sheridan to pull back to Peters Hill.

Meanwhile, Braxton Bragg, misled by Sills' diversion towards Frankfort, assumed Buell's main force was elsewhere and expected Polk to quickly overpower the Union forces at Perryville before rejoining with Kirby Smith. Polk initially planned an aggressive attack but opted for a defensive stance, frustrating Bragg. By mid-morning, Bragg, impatient for action and dissatisfied with Polk's inaction, arrived at Perryville to personally oversee the battle.

Upon arrival, Bragg critically assessed Polk's battle line, finding it disjointed and vulnerable. Unaware of Crittenden's II Corps' approach, Bragg mistakenly focused on the threat from McCook's I Corps north of town. He ordered a reorganization of his forces into a north-south line, intending to initiate an en echelon attack. Cheatham's division was to lead the assault on the Union's left, followed by a coordinated strike from Patton Anderson's and Buckner's divisions.

As the Confederate forces mobilized, their movement raised dust clouds, misleading some Union soldiers into believing a retreat was underway. This miscalculation heightened the impact of the Confederate attack later in the day.

By the afternoon, Buell's army was fully assembled, with McCook's I Corps on the left, Gilbert's III Corps in the center, and Crittenden's II Corps on the right. The battle primarily unfolded against McCook's corps. An unusual acoustic phenomenon prevented the sounds of battle from reaching Buell's headquarters, just 2 miles away, limiting his effective command and delaying the deployment of reserves until the battle's latter stages.

The battle intensified around midday, with Cheatham's artillery opening fire at 12:30 p.m. Despite this, Cheatham held back his infantry initially, allowing Union forces time to strengthen their position. They extended their flank northward, beyond the Confederates' planned point of attack. In response, Bragg repositioned Cheatham's division to Walker's Bend, targeting what he presumed to be the Union's vulnerable flank. However, this plan hit a snag when Confederate cavalry, tasked with reconnaissance, withdrew prematurely. This retreat occurred before McCook could fortify the position with Lt. Charles Parsons' artillery battery and Brig. Gen. William R. Terrill's brigade on the strategically significant Open Knob.

Brig. Gen. Daniel S. Donelson's brigade was the first to engage, crossing the Chaplin River and ascending the western bluffs for an attack around 2 p.m. With two regiments detached, the brigade's strength was diminished, leaving only three regiments for the assault. Cheatham's rousing call to action, "Give 'em hell, boys!" was famously echoed by Gen. Polk, an Episcopal bishop, who urged the troops to follow Cheatham's lead.

Donelson's brigade, however, faced an unexpected challenge. Instead of encountering a vulnerable flank, they found themselves executing a direct frontal assault on the Union's center. The 16th Tennessee Infantry, led by Col. John H. Savage and acting independently of Donelson's command, pushed ahead, aiming for Capt. Samuel J. Harris' artillery battery. Savage's disdain for Donelson's leadership and skepticism about the order's prudence led to this bold but risky move. As the regiment advanced into a depression, it was caught in a deadly crossfire from the 33rd Ohio Infantry and Parsons' artillery on Open Knob.

Recognizing the threat posed by the Union artillery on Open Knob, Cheatham ordered Brig. Gen. George E. Maney's brigade to engage them. However, Donelson's brigade, unable to withstand the intense Union fire, was forced to retreat by 2:30 p.m., suffering heavy casualties. Savage's regiment bore the brunt of this retreat, losing 219 of its 370 men.

The battle escalated as the inexperienced Union soldiers manning Parsons' eight guns on the Open Knob, largely drawn from the 105th Ohio Infantry, faced a severe test. Positioned to protect these guns, Terrill's 33rd Brigade braced for action. Amidst this, Confederate Brig. Gen. George Maney's brigade managed a stealthy approach through the woods, taking advantage of the Union's distraction by Donelson's assault. As Maney's forces neared, the Union artillery realigned, leading to an intense exchange of fire.

During the fierce combat, Brig. Gen. Jackson, the commander of the 10th Division, was killed, and command was swiftly passed to Terrill.

Terrill's fixation on safeguarding his artillery led him to make a critical error: he ordered the 123rd Illinois to execute a bayonet charge downhill. The inexperienced Union troops, numbering 770, suffered heavily against Maney's 1,800 battle-hardened Confederates. Reinforcements from the 80th Illinois and a contingent led by Col. Theophilus T. Garrard temporarily balanced the confrontation. However, the Union defenders, pounded by Confederate artillery under Lt. William Turner, eventually succumbed to Maney's uphill charge, leading to the capture of most of Parsons' artillery. Parsons himself was forcibly removed from the battlefield by his retreating men.

Maney's offensive didn't stop there. He pressed forward, descending the back of the Open Knob, traversing a cornfield, and crossing the Benton Road towards a ridge held by the Union's 28th Brigade, commanded by Col. John C. Starkweather, which was supported by twelve guns. Starkweather's well-placed artillery rendered the Open Knob indefensible.

In the midst of this, the 21st Wisconsin, newly formed and inexperienced, was positioned in the cornfield. As Maney attacked Parsons' guns, the 21st, obscured by towering cornstalks and unversed in combat, found themselves suddenly overrun by retreating forces from Terrill's brigade. Terrill's panicked retreat and command for another bayonet charge led to a hasty and ill-fated advance by 200 of the 21st Wisconsin soldiers, who were quickly overwhelmed by the advancing Confederates.

Caught in a precarious position, the 21st Wisconsin hesitated to fire, fearing friendly fire incidents, even as Starkweather's artillery inadvertently inflicted casualties on their own men. When the 21st finally did open fire, it was met with a massive Confederate volley that devastated their ranks, forcing the survivors to flee towards the Benton Road.

In an effort to plug a gap in their line left by Donelson's brigade, Confederate General Cheatham deployed Brig. Gen. Alexander P. Stewart's Tennessee brigade to support Maney's brigade in their offensive against Starkweather's Union forces. The 1st Tennessee regiment launched an attack on the northern end of the hill, while the rest of Maney's brigade charged directly up the slope. Despite Starkweather's fortified position, bolstered by strong infantry and artillery, the Confederates initially faced repulsion.

A subsequent charge led to intense hand-to-hand combat, pushing the Confederates to the crest of the hill, right among Starkweather's batteries. During this fierce struggle, Brig. Gen. Terrill re-engaged in the battle, leading his troops up the reverse side of the hill, only to be fatally wounded by shrapnel from an exploding artillery shell. He succumbed to his injuries the next day.

Starkweather, in the meantime, managed to retreat with half of his artillery, repositioning them 100 yards westward on another ridge. The day's tumultuous events propelled Col. Albert S. Hall from his initial role as the commander of the 105th Ohio to eventually assuming command of the 10th Division by day's end, following the deaths of several senior officers.

The Federals, once again entrenched in a strong defensive stance with the advantage of artillery and a stone wall atop a steep slope, resisted further assaults. Maney's and Stewart's brigades made three valiant attempts to breach this line, but each was rebuffed. Eventually, around 5:30 p.m., they withdrew to the vicinity of the Open Knob.

This prolonged and bloody engagement, led by Maney's brigade over three hours, marked a critical and perhaps the most decisive moment of the battle. Historian Kenneth W. Noe likened Maney's final repulse to the "high-water mark of the Confederacy in the western theater," comparing its significance to the pivotal moment at the Angle at Gettysburg.

The battle continued with an en echelon attack led by Anderson's division at the center. Around 2:45 p.m., coinciding with Maney's initial repulse at the

Open Knob, Col. Thomas M. Jones's brigade initiated an independent attack. Without direct orders from Anderson or Hardee, Jones was compelled to act by the sounds of combat nearby. His brigade advanced across a valley, but as they approached a large sinkhole, they faced a withering combination of musket and artillery fire from the Union 9th Brigade, commanded by Col. Leonard A. Harris. Despite efforts by Confederate artillery, notably Capt. Charles Lumsden's Alabama Light Artillery, to counter, they were stymied by an optical illusion that rendered their targeting ineffective.

As Jones's brigade retreated around 3:30 p.m., Brig. Gen. John C. Brown's brigade moved up to take their place. By then, the Union artillery had depleted their ammunition and withdrawn, sparing Brown's men the intense artillery barrage that Jones's brigade had faced. Brown's brigade faced stiff resistance from Union infantry, making little progress until coordinated Confederate successes on the left flank began to pressure the Union position.

The I Corps of McCook, primarily positioned on land owned by Henry P. Bottom, found its right flank under significant stress. Around 2:30 p.m., an engagement initiated by Major John E. Austin's 14th Battalion of Louisiana Sharpshooters against the 42nd Indiana, who were gathering water, escalated into a larger Confederate assault. Brig. Gen. Bushrod R. Johnson's brigade launched a disorganized attack from Chatham House Hill, hampered by last-minute order changes and friendly artillery fire that disrupted their lines. The ensuing infantry assault was marked by fierce combat, with Confederate artillery inadvertently setting fire to Squire Bottom's barn, tragically claiming the lives of Union soldiers seeking shelter there.

The 3rd Ohio, overwhelmed, withdrew and was replaced by the 15th Kentucky. As Johnson's brigade exhausted their ammunition, Brig. Gen. Patrick R. Cleburne's brigade entered the fray around 3:40 p.m. Despite being wounded and losing his horse to artillery fire, Cleburne pressed the attack. His brigade's advance was hindered by Confederate artillery fire, possibly due to his men wearing captured Union blue trousers, leading to a case of mistaken identity.

On Cleburne's left, Brig. Gen. Daniel W. Adams's brigade intensified the attack on the 15th Kentucky, reinforced by elements of the 3rd Ohio. The Union forces, facing mounting pressure, retreated towards the Russell House, McCook's headquarters. In the chaos, Col. William H. Lytle of the 17th Brigade was severely wounded and left for dead on the battlefield, resulting in his capture.

While Lytle's brigade was being forced back, Phil Sheridan's division was positioned a mere few hundred yards south on Peters Hill. A notable point of debate regarding the battle concerns why Sheridan chose not to engage more fully at this juncture. Earlier, he had been instructed by Gilbert not to initiate a general engagement. Around 2 p.m., as the sound of artillery fire reached the army headquarters where Buell and Gilbert were dining, they mistakenly thought it was Union artillery conducting drills and instructed Sheridan to conserve ammunition. Though Sheridan did engage in some artillery fire against the Confederate assault, Gilbert, upon arriving later, worried about a potential attack on Sheridan and ordered him back to his defensive positions.

Sheridan's division eventually became more actively involved towards the battle's end. The Confederate brigade led by Col. Samuel Powel, part of Anderson's division, was directed to move in coordination with Adams's brigade on Cleburne's left. However, Powel's brigade was significantly separated from the rest, positioned near Edwards House Hill, west of Perryville. Around 4 p.m., under Bragg's orders, Powel advanced along the Springfield Pike to target Capt. Henry Hescock's battery, which Bragg mistakenly believed to be an isolated unit rather than part of the entire III Corps. Powel's brigade encountered Sheridan's division, and despite initial concerns from Sheridan about the Confederate aggression, Powel's forces were quickly driven back.

Sheridan, who in later battles would be known for his aggressiveness, chose not to chase the retreating force and also declined Daniel McCook's request to assist his brother's corps to the north. Meanwhile, reinforcements requested earlier by Sheridan arrived; Col. William P. Carlin's 31st Brigade (Mitchell's division) supported Sheridan on the right. Carlin's troops vigorously pursued Powel's retreating brigade towards Perryville. Reaching the town's cemetery, intense artillery exchanges ensued.

Carlin, joined by Col. George D. Wagner's 21st Brigade (Wood's division, II Corps), advanced with the potential to seize Perryville and its crucial cross-roads, which were key to Bragg's retreat route. However, this aggressive push was halted by an order from Gilbert to Mitchell, much to Mitchell's frustration.

Bragg's offensive at Perryville evolved into a significant pincer movement, effectively squeezing both flanks of McCook's corps into a concentrated formation at the Dixville Crossroads. This strategic location, where the Benton Road intersected the Mackville Road, became a focal point. The Confederates, recognizing an opportunity, aimed to seize this intersection and potentially encircle the right wing of McCook's corps, isolating them from the rest of the Union army. The southern part of the pincer, however, began to lose momentum near the temporary Union line established at the Russell House, where Harris's and Lytle's brigades staunchly resisted Cleburne's and Adams's advances. The northern part of the pincer was effectively halted by Starkweather's resilient defense. Fresh brigades from Buckner's division, led by Brig. Gens. St. John R. Liddell and Sterling A. M. Wood, then joined the fray.

The primary target of this renewed assault was Col. George Webster's 34th Brigade. Webster, tragically, was mortally wounded, a significant loss for the 10th Division which had already lost Jackson and Terrill, the other senior commanders. In a poignant twist, these officers had previously discussed the improbability of all being killed in battle. Webster's infantry, alongside Capt.

Harris's artillery, initially repelled Wood's attackers. However, depleted ammunition forced Harris's battery to withdraw, and the Confederate attack drove Webster's men back towards the crossroads. Col. Michael Gooding's 13th Brigade then engaged, forcing Wood's men to retreat and paving the way for Liddell's brigade.

McCook's attempts to solicit support for his beleaguered corps began to bear fruit. At 2:30 p.m., he requested Sheridan, stationed at Peters Hill, to secure the right flank of the I Corps. A subsequent request for aid from the nearest III Corps unit eventually reached Buell, who, despite being initially skeptical of the severity of the Confederate attack due to the limited battle noise, ordered two brigades from Schoepf's division to assist the I Corps.

In a dramatic moment, Liddell's men mistakenly fired upon a unit they presumed to be friendly. Amidst calls to cease fire, Leonidas Polk, the wing commander, ventured forward to investigate, only to find himself amidst the 22nd Indiana. In a daring move, Polk bluffed his way through the Union lines, posing as a Union officer. Once clear, a volley from Liddell's men inflicted severe casualties on the 22nd Indiana, marking the highest percentage loss of any Federal regiment at Perryville. Despite Liddell's readiness to continue the assault, Polk, shaken by his close encounter, called off the attack, citing the approaching darkness.

As the Union units moved their supplies and consolidated their lines on a nearby chain of hills, McCook's corps, though heavily battered, remained intact. This sequence of events underscored the chaotic nature of the battle, the narrow margins between victory and defeat, and the role of individual decisions in shaping the outcomes of war.

Battle of Fredericksburg

In the tense autumn of 1862, President Abraham Lincoln was at a critical juncture. With the Confederate forces showing formidable strength in Kentucky and Maryland, the Northern public's faith in his leadership wavered. Despite repelling these invasions, the Confederate armies remained a potent threat. In a decisive move, Lincoln urged Major General Ulysses S. Grant to target Vicksburg, Mississippi, a key Confederate bastion. He shook up the Union leadership, replacing Maj. Gen. Don Carlos Buell with the more aggressive Maj. Gen. William S. Rosecrans in Tennessee. Frustrated by Maj. Gen. George B. McClellan's lack of initiative, despite halting General Robert E. Lee at Antietam, Lincoln replaced him with Maj. Gen. Ambrose Burnside, a commander known for his independence and earlier successes in North Carolina.

Burnside, though reluctant and self-doubting about leading an army-level command, took charge on November 7. Pressured by Lincoln and General-in-Chief Henry W. Halleck, he hatched a daring plan for a late fall offensive. His strategy was based on deception and rapid movement, intending to mislead Lee and strike swiftly towards Richmond. Concerned about a flank attack from "Stonewall" Jackson and doubting the adequacy of the Orange and Alexandria Railroad, Burnside chose a route through Fredericksburg. This plan, which deviated from Lincoln's preference for a more direct confrontation with Lee, was met with skepticism in Washington. Yet, Lincoln, understanding the urgency, gave a reluctant nod on November 14, emphasizing the need for swift action, albeit doubtful of Lee's reaction as Burnside anticipated.

On November 15, 1862, the Union Army embarked on a crucial march, arriving in Falmouth by November 17. However, Major General Ambrose Burnside's strategy soon encountered a major hiccup. He had planned a swift Rappahannock River crossing using pontoon bridges, but due to a mix-up in orders, the bridges frustratingly didn't arrive in time. This delay originated on November 7, when Burnside requested the pontoons and other supplies. Despite the 50th New York Engineers' readiness to move the pontoons by November 14, a shortage of 270 horses hindered their progress. Worse yet, Burnside was unaware that most of the bridging equipment was still far upstream.

As Major General Edwin V. Sumner reached Falmouth, he proposed an immediate river crossing to disperse the modest Confederate force in Fredericksburg and seize the strategic heights nearby. But Burnside, anxious about the rising autumn rains and fearing for Sumner's safety, ordered him to hold position.

General Robert E. Lee initially thought Burnside would outpace him across the Rappahannock. However, noticing Burnside's slow progress, Lee gathered his forces in Fredericksburg. By November 23, Lieutenant General James Longstreet had positioned his corps on Marye's Heights, with other divisions strategically placed around the town. Anticipating the need, Lieutenant General Stonewall Jackson had already started moving his troops towards the area on November 22.

The first pontoon bridge reached Falmouth on November 25, but it was too late for an unopposed crossing. Burnside, facing only half of Lee's army and before they were fully entrenched, missed a critical chance for a swift offensive. By the end of November, Jackson had arrived, bolstering Lee's defenses.

Burnside initially planned a crossing at Skinker's Neck, but Confederate defenses there, spotted by Union balloon observers, foiled this move. Switching tactics, he decided to cross directly at Fredericksburg. On December 9, he informed General Henry W. Halleck of his new plan, believing it would catch the Confederates off guard. Moreover, with 220 artillery pieces on Stafford Heights across the Rappahannock, Burnside's army was in a position to prevent any significant counterattacks from Lee's forces.

As dawn broke on December 11, Union engineers embarked on a critical mission to construct six pontoon bridges across the Rappahannock River near Fredericksburg. Two were set north of the town center, one at the southern end, and three near Deep Run's confluence with the river. The bridge facing the city became a perilous zone, as Confederate sharpshooters, led by Brig. Gen. William Barksdale, unleashed a torrent of fire from their concealed positions in house cellars. Despite the Union artillery's efforts with 150 guns, the sharpshooters' fortified positions proved impervious.

In a pivotal decision, Brig. Gen. Henry J. Hunt persuaded Burnside to deploy infantry across the river in boats to establish a foothold and dislodge the sharpshooters. Col. Norman J. Hall stepped up for the task, though Burnside initially hesitated, fearing heavy casualties. Inspired by their cheers, Burnside finally agreed. At 3:00 p.m., a massive artillery barrage covered the crossing of 135 soldiers from the 7th Michigan and the 19th Massachusetts, soon joined by the 20th Massachusetts. They succeeded in clearing the sharpshooters, leading to intense urban combat throughout Fredericksburg.

This operation marked the first significant instance of urban warfare in American history, with Union forces bombarding the town and its surrounding ridges with over 5,000 shells. By evening, Union troops occupied the town, indulging in looting that reached unprecedented levels, infuriating both Lee and the Confederates, particularly Virginians, and shocking many in the Union.

Meanwhile, south of the city, crossings by Franklin's Left Grand Division encountered less resistance, aided by Union artillery suppressing sniper fire. Despite initial delays, the crossings were completed by December 12 afternoon.

Burnside's strategy for December 12 involved Franklin leading a main attack on the southern flank, supported by Hooker, while Sumner launched a secondary attack in the north. However, Burnside's directives were vague and confusing. On the evening of December 12, despite pressure for clear orders for a morning assault, Burnside's instructions, delivered late the next morning, were unexpectedly conservative. He instructed Franklin to seize Prospect Hill with at least a division, while Sumner was to send a division through the city. His orders, perceived as an attempt to intimidate Lee into withdrawal, were met with conservative interpretation and confusion, exacerbated by map inaccuracies and ambiguous phrasing.

On the chilly, fog-shrouded morning of December 13, the Union and Confederate armies were veiled from each other's sight. Major General John F. Reynolds of the Union's I Corps was tasked by Franklin to choose a division for the attack. He selected Major General George G. Meade's smaller division of about 4,500 men, with Brig. Gen. John Gibbon's division in support. Meade's troops began their maneuver at 8:30 a.m., shadowed by Gibbon.

As the fog lifted around 10:30 a.m., Meade's men, moving parallel to the river and then turning towards the Richmond Road, faced unexpected enfilading fire from Major John Pelham's Virginia Horse Artillery. Despite Pelham's limited artillery resources, his steadfast defense drew admiration from General Lee and delayed the Union advance. The Iron Brigade, led by Brig. Gen. Solomon Meredith, was dispatched to counter Pelham's position, leading to a fierce exchange that eventually forced Pelham to retreat as his ammunition dwindled.

During this skirmish, Brig. Gen. George D. Bayard, a Union cavalry general, was mortally wounded. Meanwhile, Jackson's artillery, silent in the fog, now began bombarding the Union troops, hindering Meade's advance.

By 1:00 p.m., as Union artillery ceased to allow for infantry advancement, Jackson's concealed force of 35,000 waited on the wooded ridge. However, an oversight in the Confederate defenses—a 600-yard gap in A.P. Hill's line—became a critical vulnerability. Meade's brigades exploited this gap, catching Confederate Brig. Gens. James H. Lane and James J. Archer off guard and striking their flanks. The Confederates, unprepared and some unarmed, suffered heavy losses. In the chaos, Brig. Gen. Maxcy Gregg, mistakenly identifying Union soldiers as retreating Confederates, was fatally wounded.

The battle intensified as Archer called for reinforcements, unaware of Gregg's brigade's collapse. With ammunition dwindling, brutal hand-to-hand combat ensued. Many regimental officers on both sides fell in the melee, and though Meade emerged unscathed, his regiments suffered substantial officer casualties.

On the battlefield, Confederate reinforcements led by Brig. Gens. Jubal A. Early and William B. Taliaferro swiftly engaged, bolstering the wavering lines of Lane's and Archer's brigades. These fresh forces rallied and formed a new defensive line, encircling Meade's troops and subjecting them to intense fire from three directions. Amidst the chaos, Feger Jackson's bid to outflank a Confederate battery ended tragically when he was shot in the head, leaving his brigade leaderless until Col. Joseph W. Fisher assumed command.

Simultaneously, to Meade's right, Gibbon's division was poised for action. Brig. Gen. Nelson Taylor suggested a bayonet charge to support Meade, but Gibbon, citing his orders, delayed the advance. When Taylor's brigade finally advanced at 1:30 p.m., they faced daunting fire from Lane's brigade and Confederate artillery, lacking both cover and a strategic gap to exploit. Following Taylor, Col. Peter Lyle's brigade also struggled to advance. Gibbon then committed his reserve, led by Col. Adrian R. Root, but they too were stalled. Some Union soldiers briefly engaged in fierce hand-to-hand combat at the ridge crest, but eventually had to retreat. Gibbon himself was wounded, and command passed to Brig. Gen. Nelson Taylor.

In the aftermath, Meade criticized some of Gibbon's officers for their hesitancy, but his main frustration was with Brig. Gen. David B. Birney of the III Corps. Birney had been designated to support the attack but claimed confusion over the attack's significance and lack of explicit orders from Reynolds. Meade, infuriated by this perceived failure, confronted Birney with a vehement outburst, eventually ordering him forward.

In a pivotal moment, Early's division launched a vigorous counterattack, spearheaded by Col. Edmund N. Atkinson's Georgia brigade. This bold move galvanized the troops of Col. Robert Hoke, Brig. Gen. Archer, and Col. John M. Brockenbrough, who surged out of their railroad ditch positions. They forcefully drove Meade's and subsequently Gibbon's men back, turning a disciplined retreat into a disordered one. Although Early had instructed his brigades to halt at the railroad, the momentum of battle propelled many Confederates across the open fields to the old Richmond Road.

The Union artillery, positioned strategically, unleashed a ferocious barrage of canister shot at close range, decimating the advancing Confederates. Adding to the Confederate woes, the delayed but now advancing brigade of Brig. Gen. J. H. Hobart Ward, part of Birney's division, struck them hard. Brig. Gens. Hiram G. Berry and John C. Robinson's brigades followed suit, staunchly repelling the Confederate thrust that had threatened to overrun the Union lines. During this tumult, Col. Atkinson suffered a shoulder injury and was captured by Union forces.

As the Confederate advance waned, Brig. Gen. Daniel E. Sickles' III Corps division further bolstered the Union's right flank, stalling any further Confederate progression. Meanwhile, General Burnside, engrossed in the unfolding drama at Marye's Heights, was disheartened to learn that his left flank attack hadn't yielded the anticipated breakthrough. He ordered Franklin to intensify the assault, but Franklin, citing total engagement of his forces, refused. Contrarily, significant elements of his command, including the entire VI Corps and Brig. Gen. Doubleday's division, remained largely unscathed and idle.

Eventually, Confederate forces retreated to the safety of the hills. Despite considering a renewed counterattack, Stonewall Jackson was dissuaded by the potent Union artillery and the encroaching darkness. A critical opportunity for the Union had slipped away due to Franklin's failure to capitalize on Meade's initial success and leverage his substantial reserves.

The battle's intensity was reflected in the staggering casualty numbers: approximately 5,000 for Franklin and 3,400 for Jackson. As the confrontation shifted towards Marye's Heights, the Southern sector witnessed a grim aftermath. The air was heavy with the cries of wounded soldiers and horses, and tragically, fires ignited in the dry sage grass, leading to the horrifying fate of many injured men being burned alive.

At the northern end of the Fredericksburg battlefield, the tension was palpable as Brig. Gen. William H. French's division of the II Corps prepared for action amidst the fog and Confederate artillery fire raining down on the city. General Burnside had instructed Maj. Gen. Edwin V. Sumner, leading the Right Grand Division, to seize the high ground west of Fredericksburg, banking on the belief that the southern assault would be the pivotal moment of the battle.

The terrain for the Union advance was challenging, marked by open fields interspersed with houses, fences, and gardens, complicating the movement of troops. Near the town, a canal, crossed by only three narrow bridges, presented a significant bottleneck, forcing Union soldiers into tight columns.

The target of their advance, Marye's Heights, a ridge consisting of several hills including Taylor's Hill, Stansbury Hill, Marye's Hill, and Willis Hill, loomed about 600 yards west of Fredericksburg. The ridge, particularly the Marye's Hill and Willis Hill section, featured the Telegraph Road, a sunken lane fortified with a 4-foot stone wall and additional defensive structures, creating an ideal position for Confederate defenders. Maj. Gen. Lafayette McLaws' forces, approximately 2,000 strong, held the frontline, with another 7,000 in reserve. Supported by a formidable array of artillery, Confederate Lt. Col. Edward Porter Alexander confidently asserted that their firepower could decimate any advancing force.

As the fog cleared around 10 a.m., Sumner ordered the advance. Around noon, French's brigade, under Brig. Gen. Nathan Kimball, began its slow, treacherous approach. Facing intense artillery bombardment, the troops managed to cross the canal and formed a battle line behind a low bluff. Advancing with fixed bayonets up the muddy slope, they were met with a hailstorm of rifle fire from the stone wall. Despite some soldiers reaching within 40 yards of the wall, the devastating combination of artillery and rifle volleys forced the survivors to take cover. Kimball, severely wounded in the assault, saw his brigade suffer a staggering 25% casualty rate. The subsequent brigades led by Col. John W. Andrews and Col. Oliver H. Palmer fared even worse, enduring casualty rates nearing 50%.

At Marye's Heights, Major General Edwin V. Sumner's strategy continued to unravel. He had initially ordered Brig. Gen. Winfield S. Hancock's division to support French's troops. Hancock sent Col. Samuel K. Zook's brigade to follow Palmer's, but they encountered the same deadly resistance. The situation worsened with the advance of Hancock's Irish Brigade, led by Brig. Gen. Thomas F. Meagher. Armed with outdated Springfield Muskets, the brigade, comprising 1,200 men, faced severe casualties, with 545 not returning from their valiant but doomed charge.

Hancock's final brigade, commanded by Brig. Gen. John C. Caldwell, encountered a similar fate. Col. Nelson A. Miles, leading Caldwell's left regiments, suggested abandoning the conventional tactic of marching, firing, and reloading for a direct bayonet charge. However, Caldwell denied this proposal. Miles was subsequently shot in the throat during their advance, and Caldwell himself was soon incapacitated by gunfire.

Maj. Gen. Darius N. Couch, commanding the II Corps, was appalled by the destruction inflicted on his divisions. He briefly considered a large-scale bayonet charge but realized the diminished state of French's and Hancock's divisions made this impossible. Couch then planned for Maj. Gen. Oliver O. Howard's division to flank the Confederate left but had to redirect them to support the beleaguered troops instead. This decision led to further heavy losses: Col. Joshua Owen's brigade, Col. Norman J. Hall's brigade, and two regiments from Brig. Gen. Alfred Sully's brigade all entered the fray, along with Brig. Gen. Samuel Sturgis's division from the IX Corps. Despite these reinforcements, the Union forces could not break through, suffering 4,114 casualties in the II Corps and 1,011 in Sturgis's division alone.

On the Confederate side, General Lee, concerned about the massed Union troops potentially breaking his line, received assurance from Longstreet. With the Confederate ranks reinforced to four deep behind the stone wall and Brig. Gen. Joseph B. Kershaw replacing the mortally wounded Brig. Gen. Thomas R. R. Cobb, Longstreet confidently declared that with ample ammunition, he could repel any number of attackers crossing the same ground.

By mid-afternoon on that fateful day, General Burnside faced a grim reality: his attacks on both flanks had stalled, with the Union forces suffering heavy losses. Instead of reassessing his strategy, Burnside stubbornly ordered a continuation of the assaults. He instructed Franklin to renew the assault on the left (an order Franklin chose to ignore) and directed Maj. Gen. Hooker's Center Grand Division to join the fray across the Rappahannock and attack Marye's Heights. Hooker, unlike Burnside and Sumner, personally scouted the battlefield and returned to advise against the attack, but Burnside persisted.

In the meantime, Brig. Gen. Daniel Butterfield's V Corps, led by Brig. Gen. Charles Griffin, relieved Sturgis's exhausted men. However, Griffin's brigades, charging one after the other, were repelled by the reinforced Confederate position, now bolstered by Maj. Gen. George Pickett and a brigade from Maj. Gen. John Bell Hood.

A misinterpretation of enemy movements led to the belief that the Confederates might be retreating, prompting an attack by Brig. Gen. Andrew A. Humphreys's division. Despite being disorganized by the emotional pleas of their fallen comrades, Humphreys's brigade pushed forward, only to be decimated by Confederate rifle fire within 50 yards of their goal. Brig. Gen. George Sykes's division, sent to support the retreat, also found themselves trapped in a deadly crossfire.

Despite Hooker's objections, Burnside persisted. He ordered Brig. Gen. George W. Getty's IX Corps division to target Willis Hill, the leftmost portion of Marye's Heights. The brigades of Col. Rush Hawkins and Col. Edward Harland made a twilight approach along an unfinished railroad line but were eventually detected and repulsed.

In a series of fourteen disjointed charges by seven Union divisions, the Union army suffered between 6,000 to 8,000 casualties, with 918 soldiers confirmed dead on the battlefield. Confederate losses at Marye's Heights were around 1,200. As darkness fell and Burnside's subordinates implored for an end to the bloodshed, the attacks ceased. Longstreet later reflected on these futile charges as "desperate and bloody, but utterly hopeless."

The Union soldiers, many wounded or trapped, endured a frigid night on the battlefield, unable to aid their comrades due to ongoing Confederate sniper fire. Amidst this tragedy, Burnside initially attempted to shift blame to his subordinates, but they resolutely countered that the catastrophic outcome rested solely on his decisions.

On the evening of December 13, in the aftermath of the devastating battle, General Burnside, in a dramatic gesture, proposed to personally lead his former IX Corps in another attack on Marye's Heights. However, his generals dissuaded him from this perilous plan the next morning. The armies remained in their positions throughout December 14. In a somber gesture that afternoon, Burnside requested a truce from General Lee to care for the numerous wounded, which Lee graciously granted. The following day witnessed the Federal forces retreating across the river, bringing the harrowing Fredericksburg campaign to its conclusion.

A poignant episode amidst the battle's brutality involved Sergeant Richard Rowland Kirkland of the 2nd South Carolina Volunteer Infantry, known as the "Angel of Marye's Heights." Stationed at the stone wall along the sunken road, Kirkland was deeply moved by the agonizing cries of wounded Union soldiers during the frigid night of December 13, 1862. Without any formal ceasefire or truce, and upon receiving permission from Brig. Gen. Joseph B. Kershaw, Kirkland bravely ventured out with canteens to provide water to the injured Union soldiers lying on the battlefield. His selfless act, carried out under the clear risk of being targeted, prompted Union soldiers to refrain from shooting. Kirkland's humanity in the face of war is commemorated with a statue in the Fredericksburg and Spotsylvania National Military Park, although the exact details of this story, first recorded in 1880, have been subject to historical scrutiny and may have been romanticized.

Adding to the surreal atmosphere following the battle, the night of December 14 was marked by a rare appearance of the Aurora Borealis, an unusual phenomenon for that latitude, likely triggered by a significant solar flare. The sky lit up with a ruddy glow, adorned with the distinctive rays of the Northern Lights. This extraordinary natural display was noted in the diaries and letters of many soldiers at Fredericksburg, including John W. Thompson,

Jr., who witnessed the ethereal spectacle, adding a bizarre and memorable backdrop to the grim aftermath of the battle.

Battle of Stones River

In the wake of the pivotal Battle of Perryville in Kentucky during October of 1862, a significant shift occurred in the strategies and leadership of both the Confederate and Union forces. Confederate General Braxton Bragg, in a strategic retreat, moved his troops back into Tennessee. This maneuver led him to establish his headquarters in the town of Murfreesboro, just south of Nashville. This retreat, however, was not just a mere repositioning of troops; it had profound implications. It resulted in the loss of much of Tennessee for the Confederates and stirred up a storm of dissension and discord within Bragg's command. This internal strife reached a peak when Major General Leonidas Polk, representing Bragg's senior commanders, personally lobbied Confederate President Jefferson Davis in Richmond, advocating for Bragg's removal. Despite the growing clamor for change, Davis, holding firm in his support for his friend Bragg, refused to replace him, even in the face of his escalating unpopularity among all levels of his army.

Simultaneously, on the Union side, Major General Don Carlos Buell, despite his recent victory, faced his own challenges. His failure to capitalize on the success at Perryville led to his removal from command before the month's end. Seeking a more dynamic and assertive leader, U.S. President Abraham Lincoln appointed Major General William Starke Rosecrans, affectionately known as "Old Rosy" by his troops, to take command of the main Union Army in Tennessee, now dubbed the Army of the Cumberland. Rosecrans, fresh from two modest yet significant victories in Mississippi at Iuka and Corinth in September and October, brought a new vigor to the position. Although his immediate superior, Major General Ulysses S. Grant, criticized Rosecrans for his lackluster pursuit after both battles, Rosecrans was nonetheless recognized as a victor with a less conciliatory approach towards rebels and slaveholders compared to his predecessor Buell. Adding to this, Rosecrans, bolstered by his friendship with Secretary of the Treasury Salmon Portland Chase, a fellow Ohioan, received encouragement to wholeheartedly endorse the Emancipation Proclamation. Chase urged Rosecrans to mobilize his men with utmost speed.

In the latter part of October, upon taking command of his forces in Kentucky, General William Starke Rosecrans initiated a strategic advance towards Nashville. This movement, however, was hindered by a combination of factors, leading to a slow and arduous journey. The army eventually established its camp, where it stayed for the majority of November and December. The army's sluggish progress can be attributed to several key reasons: firstly, the challenging terrain presented significant obstacles; secondly, the army was grappling with disorganization in the aftermath of the Battle of Perryville and the departure of General Don Carlos Buell; and thirdly, Rosecrans harbored hopes that General Braxton Bragg's Confederate forces would venture closer to Nashville, potentially allowing him to engage in a more favorable battle without the added strain of navigating through mountainous regions. Bragg, on his end, seemed content to wait for Rosecrans to initiate action.

Meanwhile, the pressure on Rosecrans to push forward intensified, particularly as the Union faced setbacks on other fronts. The Union's defeat in the bloody battle of Fredericksburg under Major General Ambrose Everett Burnside, coupled with Ulysses S. Grant's failure to seize Vicksburg, Mississippi by the year's end, left the North in dire need of a military triumph. These losses cast a shadow over the Union's war efforts, and many looked to Rosecrans to provide a much-needed victory. General Henry Wager Halleck, conveying the urgency of the situation, warned Rosecrans of President Lincoln's growing impatience, even stating that he had been asked twice to replace Rosecrans as the army's commander. Despite these pressures, Rosecrans remained steadfast, refusing to advance until he deemed his army fully prepared.

Finally, on December 26th, with a significant portion of Bragg's cavalry engaged in raids behind Union lines, Rosecrans judged the circumstances favorable for advancement. His troops embarked on a demanding 40-mile march from Nashville towards the Confederate forces near Murfreesboro.

General William Starke Rosecrans devised a tactical plan for his forces to engage Confederate General Braxton Bragg at Stones River. His strategy involved using his right flank to engage Bragg, while his left flank would maneuver across Stones River towards Murfreesboro. Coincidentally, Bragg had formulated a similar plan, intending to hold with his right while attacking with his left. The battle commenced on December 31, 1862, with the Confederates striking first. Their attack quickly overwhelmed the Union right flank, posing a severe threat to Rosecrans's supply and retreat lines to Nashville. The situation was critical, and only the staunch resistance of General Phillip Henry Sheridan's troops, combined with the exhaustion of the Confederate forces, prevented a catastrophic defeat for Rosecrans.

The battle raged with intense ferocity. Rosecrans, along with his staff, risked their lives moving across the battlefield to stabilize their lines, constantly exposed to enemy fire. In a tragic incident, Rosecrans's aide-de-camp, Lieutenant Colonel Julius Peter Garesché, was killed by a cannonball, a fate narrowly avoided by Rosecrans himself. The day saw numerous casualties among his staff, yet Rosecrans succeeded in steadying both his flanks, averting an imminent disaster. Journalist Whitelaw Reid later recounted how Rosecrans turned the tide of retreat, rallying his forces with his fearless spirit and forging victory from the jaws of defeat.

That night, with the Army of the Cumberland having endured a grueling day, General Bragg anticipated a Union retreat. However, Rosecrans convened with his staff to deliberate their next move. Opinions were divided, with some advocating a retreat to Nashville, while others deferred to Rosecrans's judgment. After surveying the situation with Major General David Sloane Stanley, Rosecrans resolved to stand his ground and fight the following day, urging his generals to prepare for battle.

On January 2, 1863, Bragg launched an assault on the Union left flank, which proved to be a futile effort. Rosecrans had reinforced the position, and his troops easily repelled the Confederate attack, inflicting heavy casualties with their artillery. In a counteroffensive, Rosecrans's men pushed the Confederates off the field by nightfall. Bragg, recognizing the futility of his position and aided by rising river levels due to heavy rains, opted to retreat. Rosecrans, a devout Catholic, expressed his gratitude for the victory in a letter to his wife, crediting divine intervention.

This victory at Stones River was a much-needed boost for the Union, being the first significant triumph since the battles of Antietam and Perryville. It not only bolstered Union morale but also positioned Rosecrans as a pivotal figure in the Northern war effort.

The triumph at Stones River could have been even more resounding had General William Starke Rosecrans pursued General Braxton Bragg's disheartened forces more aggressively. Several factors, such as adverse weather conditions, unfamiliar terrain, heavy casualties, and a relative weakness in cavalry capabilities, contributed to Rosecrans's restraint in pursuing Bragg following the battle. In his official report, Rosecrans cited a lack of supplies and the loss of numerous artillery horses as key reasons for not pursuing Bragg beyond a short distance, concluding that further pursuit was unwise.

Despite this, the victory at Stones River was a beacon of hope for the North, especially in the shadow of previous setbacks at Fredericksburg and Vicksburg. The win not only boosted morale domestically but also bolstered the United States' international standing, particularly in England, where there had been discussions about intervening in the conflict. President Abraham Lincoln expressed his heartfelt thanks to Rosecrans and the Army of the Cumberland, acknowledging their contributions to the nation's cause. Secretary of War Edwin McMasters Stanton and Treasury Secretary Salmon P. Chase also extended their gratitude, with Chase hoping for further successes under Rosecrans's leadership.

The accolades for Rosecrans extended beyond political circles. Publications like Harper's Weekly lauded him as a top strategist, while the New York Times likened him to Napoleon Bonaparte in terms of his military prowess. The Catholic Telegraph, edited by Rosecrans's friend Reverend Edward Purcell and his brother Bishop Sylvester Horton Rosecrans, celebrated his victory, and others credited his religious faith as a contributing factor to his success. The soldiers in the Army of the Cumberland rallied around Rosecrans, with one general expressing utmost confidence in his leadership.

In the meantime, Bragg retreated approximately thirty miles south of Murfreesboro, establishing a position along the Duck River. Bragg attempted to present the first day's success and the heavy casualties inflicted on the Union as a positive outcome to his superiors, despite facing criticism from the Confederate press and calls for his removal by his subordinates. President Jefferson Davis, however, remained loyal to Bragg, allowing him to retain command for an upcoming confrontation with Rosecrans.

The subsequent period saw a lull in major campaigns until June, when Rosecrans, capitalizing on the strategic victory at Stones River, successfully forced Bragg to retreat in the Tullahoma Campaign. This maneuvering by Rosecrans kept the goodwill he had earned from his superiors intact. However, the stage was being set for a future confrontation, with Bragg's forces seeking retribution at the Battle of Chickamauga in September.

Bibliography

Bailey, Ronald H. The Bloodiest Day: The Battle of Antietam. Alexandria, VA: Time-Life Books, 1984.

Barrett, John G. The Civil War in North Carolina. The University of North Carolina Press, 1995.

Bearss, Edwin C. "The Battle of Pea Ridge." Arkansas Historical Quarterly 20.1 (1961).

Breiner, Thomas L. "The Battle of Perryville: Bragg's Kentucky Invasion." Accessed January 1, 2023.

Brown, Kent Masterson. The Civil War in Kentucky: Battle for the Bluegrass State. Campbell, CA: Savas Publishing Company, 2000.

Browning, Robert M. Jr. From Cape Charles to Cape Fear: the North Atlantic Blockading Squadron during the Civil War. University of Alabama, 1993.

Burton, Brian K. Extraordinary Circumstances: The Seven Days Battles. Bloomington: Indiana University Press, 2001.

Connelly, Thomas L. Autumn of Glory: The Army of Tennessee 1862–1865. Baton Rouge: Louisiana State University Press, 1971.

Cooling, Benjamin Franklin. The Campaign for Fort Donelson. National Park Service Civil War series. Fort Washington, PA: U.S. National Park Service and Eastern National, 1999.

Cozzens, Peter. Shenandoah 1862: Stonewall Jackson's Valley Campaign. Chapel Hill: University of North Carolina Press, 2008.

Cunningham, O. Edward. Shiloh and the Western Campaign of 1862. Ed. Gary D. Joiner and Timothy L. Smith. New York, New York: Savas Beatie, 2009.

Daniel, Larry J., and Lynn N. Bock. Island No. 10: Struggle for the Mississippi Valley. University of Alabama Press, 1996.

Davis, William C. Duel Between the First Ironclads. Doubleday, 1975.

Downs, Alan C. "Fair Oaks/Seven Pines." In Encyclopedia of the American Civil War: A Political, Social, and Military History, edited by David S. Heidler and Jeanne T. Heidler. New York: W. W. Norton & Company, 2000.

Editors of Time-Life Books. Lee Takes Command: From Seven Days to Second Bull Run. Alexandria, VA: Time-Life Books, 1984.

Eicher, David J. The Longest Night: A Military History of the Civil War. New York: Simon & Schuster, 2001.

Foote, Shelby. The Civil War: A Narrative. Vol. 1: Fort Sumter to Perryville. New York: Vintage Books, 1986 [1958].

Gallagher, Gary W., ed. The Fredericksburg Campaign: Decision on the Rappahannock. Chapel Hill: University of North Carolina Press, 1995.

Hattaway, Herman, and Archer Jones. How the North Won: A Military History of the Civil War. Urbana: University of Illinois Press, 1983.

Josephy, Alvin M. The Civil War in the American West. New York: Alfred A. Knopf, 1991.

Smih, Timothy B. Corinth 1862: Siege, Battle, Occupation. 2012.

Burnside, Ambrose E. "The Burnside Expedition." In Battles and Leaders of the Civil War, eds. Robert Underwood Johnson and Clarence Clough Buell. New York: Century, 1887–1888; reprint, Castle, n.d.

www.ingramcontent.com/pod-product-compliance
Lightning Source LLC
Chambersburg PA
CBHW072210150726
48002CB00005B/1740